The BATTLE of SARATOGA

GREAT BATTLES OF THE MODERN WORLD

Section from a painting by John Trumbull (1756–1843) now in the Yale University
Art Gallery.

The BATTLE of SARATOGA

RUPERT FURNEAUX

STEIN AND DAY/*Publishers*/New York

First published in 1971
Copyright © 1971 by Rupert Furneaux
Library of Congress Catalog Card No. 69-17940
Printed in the United States of America
Stein and Day/Publishers/7 East 48 Street, New York, N.Y. 10017
SBN 8128-1305-7

Acknowledgments

I acknowledge with many thanks the assistance of the staff at Saratoga National Park, who conducted me over the battlefield, which they are endeavouring to recreate fully in conformity with the battles fought on September 19th and October 7th, 1777. During my visit, at the time of year of these battles, I toured the area, visiting also the battlefields at Bennington, Hubbardton, and Fort Ticonderoga.

Contents

Illustrations

The BATTLE of SARATOGA

1 *London*

Leaving his army in Canada on the pretext that he needed to deal with his private affairs and to take his seat in Parliament, Lieutenant-General Sir John Burgoyne came to London in mid-December 1776 to advocate a plan whereby the rebellious American colonists might be dealt a decisive blow, and his own ambition furthered. His ability to talk well made his plan sound easy of accomplishment, especially to the ears of men who were eager to grasp a solution to an annoying difficulty: Sir William Howe, the Commander-in-Chief in America had unexpectedly changed his plan of campaign. Howe's letters, which by the slow communications of the period took two months to cross the Atlantic, placed Lord George Germain, the Secretary of State for the Colonies, in a quandary to which Burgoyne supplied the answer. He did far more than that, for he offered Germain the best of both possible worlds.

The correspondence shows how the Grand Strategy, the imaginative plan to end the war by one decisive blow, was allowed to deteriorate into an ineffective sideshow, which culminated in one of Britain's greatest military disasters.

The question 'Who blundered?' is not easy of solution, for it requires the somewhat tedious examination (without which the campaign is incomprehensible) of the letters that passed between the three men: the secretive and taciturn Howe; the ebullient and ambitious Burgoyne; and the allegedly indolent and maladroit minister who is supposed to have stranded Burgoyne alone and unaided in the American wilderness, the long-discredited Germain. The last of these became the victim of the malice of his political enemy, Lord Shelburne, who concocted the ludicrous story of the 'pigeon-holed despatch', which made him the laughing-stock of several generations.

The war for American independence (which Germain proverbially lost) was two years old.

The rebellion of Britain's American colonists began in 1775. Their desire for independence dated back to 1763, when, relieved from fear of French aggression by Britain's great victory in the Seven Years War—the decisive campaigns of which had been fought at their back door and in which they had played a conspicuous part—they sought freedom to run their lives without interference from the mother country.

Today, we find the colonists' attitude is understandable, and the coercive policy pursued by the government of King George III indefensible. Some Americans wanted what we would now call 'dominion status', the device by which a Commonwealth of independent nations is held together by common allegiance to the Crown. But, in 1774, there was no constitutional means by which such a desire could be satisfied, and no inclination to adopt it. The English had won a great empire—which they had not yet learned to administer—at enormous cost, to which they asked the Americans, the chief beneficiaries of the war, to contribute. The colonists recognized their indebtedness but, on good constitutional grounds, refused to be 'taxed without representation'. When Parliament imposed duties, the angry Bostonians tossed a cargo of tea into the sea.

The war began in 1775 with skirmishes at Lexington and Concord, in Massachusetts; and the British won a Pyrrhic victory at Bunker Hill, Boston, where Sir William Howe, acting as second-in-command to General Gage, lost half his force. The Continental Congress—the representatives of the Thirteen Colonies, meeting at Philadelphia—formed the Army of the United Colonies, and appointed as its Commander-in-Chief the Virginian gentleman, George Washington. He was an experienced soldier, who had fought with the British in the French and Indian war, as the Americans called the earlier conflict. While Washington was occupied in raising an army, a volunteer force, led by Ethan Allen and Benedict Arnold, marched to Lake Champlain and captured by surprise Fort Ticonderoga. Then, joined by General Montgomery, this force invaded Canada and siezed Montreal, but failed to take Quebec. Montgomery was killed, Allen was captured, and Arnold was wounded. In 1776 the rebels were forced to withdraw, after an audacious operation which, had it been successful, might have united Canada to the Thirteen Colonies and thereby have deprived the British of one handle of the fulcrum which Burgoyne planned to use.

The British failed to realize the magnitude of the task they had undertaken. In their usual over-confident way, they despised the military capabilities of the colonists, just as they had failed to understand their natural aspirations. At first they waged the war in a leisurely, desultory fashion, relying upon the doubtful support of the loyalists, and hoping that the rebels' resistance would collapse. Somehow the colonists survived. More mobile than the British, they slipped away to fight another day, and the British failed to bring their elusive enemy to a battle in which their superior discipline could win a decisive victory. Geography and terrain favoured the Americans, for the British needed to ferry their troops and all their supplies across the Atlantic by voyages of unpredictable duration. Moreover, their soldiers, trained for European warfare and encumbered by unwieldy baggage trains, were forced to campaign over a vast area thick with forests and lacking roads, and to fight in rough, broken country where American 'frontier' tactics, loose order, marksmanship, and individual enterprise, proved superior to close-ranked formation, volley-firing, and unthinking obedience.

The British evacuated Boston, and Gage was succeeded as Commander-in-Chief by Sir William Howe who, with his brother Admiral Lord Howe, was appointed a commissioner with authority to discuss peace with the colonists.

In 1759 Howe had led Wolfe's do-or-die assault on Quebec, and his sympathy for the colonists' aspirations made him the ideal choice for command, if they were to be chastised and conciliated rather than crushed, with the minimum of bitterness. Howe saw the war as a police operation designed to break up organized rioters and he set out, cautiously, to achieve limited objectives and slowly to enlarge the areas of British re-occupation. His detractors claim that he campaigned half-heartedly and missed opportunities to crush the revolt. He had grown fat and indolent and he owed his appointment, not to his military skill, but rather to his left-handed cousinship to George III. Scandalous gossip alleged that his mother was the illegitimate daughter of George I's mistress, the Baroness Kielmansegge. Howe was a competent soldier, a man of his times. He scandalized the puritanical Americans by flaunting his mistress the notorious Mrs Loring, the 'Sultana', wife of a complaisant commissary officer, and by his heavy drinking and general self-indulgence. He was an uncommunicative man, and an unsatisfactory correspondent. In June 1777, Lord George Germain complained that Howe was so fond of concealing his operations that he could not guess 'where he will begin his operations or where he proposes to carry them'. The fault may, however, have been Germain's, who could not bring himself to believe that Howe could misunderstand or would ignore his wishes.

The colonists, too, were beset by difficulties, some of their own making. Racked by internal jealousies, short of everything necessary with which to conduct a war, and faced with the ever-present threat of the Loyalist fifth column, they could mobilize only an improvised army formed partly of 'Continentals', who disbanded at the end of a year's service, and partly of militia, the part-time amateur soldiers of each state who served for short periods and usually only in protection of their own region. But they could be mobilized quickly and hurried to the threatened district. The mass of people were apathetic; there were few true patriots. Ragged, hungry, ill-equipped, dangerously dispirited and torn by jealousies, several times defeated, they fought on stubbornly, hoping for a saving miracle. The colonists eventually despaired of acquiring home rule and declared their Independence on July 4, 1776. They called themselves the United States of America and sought friends and allies in Europe amongst Britain's jealous rivals.

Without foreign aid the colonists could not win a decisive military victory, and foreign intervention would not be forthcoming until they showed themselves capable of winning. They needed a resounding victory, though to stave off defeat was the most they could hope for. Benjamin Franklin was sent to Paris to plead the rebel cause.

Yet final American victory—the satisfaction of the colonists' desire for independence—was inevitable, for Britain dared not ruthlessly crush the revolt of her colonists. Such a step would have robbed her of the fruits of victory, the reconciliation of the colonists and the restoration of British control. Furthermore, to achieve their aims, the British would have needed to destroy the revolutionary organization and to conquer geography, a colossal undertaking, far beyond Britain's limited capabilities. Moreover, Britain's counsels were divided; Howe wished to subdue and Germain to crush the rebels who had flouted the rule of law.

On the British side, as well as two different war aims, there were two distinct sources of initiative: the decisions of the Commander-in-Chief on the spot and, 3000 miles away, the authority of the Secretary of State in London. Their responsibilities were ill-defined, and the two office-holders, Howe and Germain, nurtured a grudge against each other dating back to the military and naval expedition against St Malo in 1758. Natural antipathy, and Howe's distaste for the one-time officer who had been cashiered, forced a 'gentlemanly' correspondence couched in stilted and fulsome language; a laboured politeness that led to ambiguity when the situation in America and the plans contemplated demanded precise and exact definition.

The war in America did not get going until September 1776, when General Clinton occupied Rhode Island and Howe wrested New York City from Washington. Washington's army, badly mauled and shrunken by sickness and desertion to 3153 officers and men, withdrew beyond the Delaware, pursued by Lord Cornwallis. Howe failed to follow up his advantage and, on December 25th, Washington won a small victory at Trenton, and another at Princeton, which put new life into the colonists and blasted British hopes for the speedy termination of the war. Philadelphia, the rebel capital, was temporarily saved; Washington stood on the defensive, and Howe retired to New York for the winter.

Meanwhile, Sir Guy Carleton, the Governor-General of Canada, who had saved the province from Arnold's invasion and had recovered Montreal, and to whom Burgoyne served as second in command, failed to recapture Ticonderoga from the rebels in the autumn of 1776. Pursuing the retreating Americans, Carleton hesitated and delayed building a fleet on Lake Champlain, where he was impeded by Arnold's spirited action (whereby he lost the American fleet which he had been ordered to preserve) at Valcour Island. By the time the British reached Ticonderoga it was too late in the season to lay siege to the fort, an omission for which Germain, who failed to understand the severity of the Canadian winter, unjustly blamed Carleton. He accused Carleton of conducting the campaign 'without sense or vigour'. Burgoyne took a ship to England; Carleton evacuated Crown Point, the fort on Lake Champlain above Ticonderoga, and returned to Montreal, unaware that he had been superseded in his military command, for the ship carrying Germain's despatch of August 22nd had been delayed by storms and forced to return to England.

In America the British retained the advantage. They held New York City and Montreal, the fulcrum they could use to subjugate the colonists by one decisive blow, as apparently they intended to do.

The Grand Strategy, which is believed to have been the design approved for 1777, was too obvious to have been the brain-child of any one soldier, and it had several fathers. It was based on the adoption of the classic invasion route, north and south: the Richelieu River, Lakes Champlain and George, and the Hudson River. Except for the twenty-mile portage between the lakes and the Hudson, this provided a water route from Montreal to New York City. Because the route bisected the colonies, it has been assumed that the British intended, by advancing from north and south, to create a barrier that would separate New England, the stronghold of the rebellion, from the other colonies. As originally conceived, the plan called for the advance of the two armies from Montreal and New York City to effect a junction at Albany. Such a move would have established a chain of strong posts from the St Lawrence to the Atlantic isolating New England. This was a bold, imaginative design which was feared by the colonists who foresaw the dangers of such a conquest. In 1775 the Provincial Congress of New York wrote to the Continental Congress at Philadelphia:

'If the enemy persist in their plan of subjugating these states to the yoke of Great Britain, they must, in proportion to their knowledge of the country, be more and more convinced of the necessity of their becoming masters of the Hudson River, which will give them entire command of the water communication with the Indian nations, effectually prevent all intercourse between the eastern and southern confederates, divide our strength, and enfeeble every effort for our common preservation and security.'

Nor were the British lacking in strategic preception; they were simply and characteristically inept at putting their thoughts into action.

As early as 1767, Carleton had suggested the setting up of a 'place of arms' at New York City, a citadel at Quebec, and a chain of forts on the Champlain–Hudson line, as a means of crushing a possible revolt. He repeated his advice in 1775, and it was endorsed by Lord Dartmouth, the Colonial Secretary. In his *Reflections upon the War in America*, which he presented to the government in 1775, Burgoyne had advocated the double invasion of New York State; and, early in 1776, Howe had urged the capture of New York City, because it would make possible the junction of the northern and southern armies along the Hudson. But he told his brother, Admiral Lord Howe, that he felt himself unequal to co-ordinating the several operations. Germain, in his undelivered letter to Carleton in August 1776, ordered that Burgoyne be directed to advance southwards from Montreal 'to put himself under the command of Sir William Howe'.

Everyone concerned with the conduct of the war, Carleton and Burgoyne, Howe and Germain, appeared to be agreed on the excellence of the plan and the desirability of putting it into operation. They lacked the foresight to understand how such a complicated undertaking could become bogged down by slow and imprecise correspondence, and they failed to perceive its essential ingredient—the necessity to look into each other's minds.

Burgoyne was a dangerously ambitious soldier, and he hoped to win all the glory. Like his contemporaries of the English governing class, Burgoyne lacked sensitivity, and he shared their overweening confidence in their ability to overcome any difficulty, which had been induced by England's sudden and unexpected emergence, only seventeen years earlier, as a world power. Flushed with success, Englishmen believed themselves to be supermen.

Burgoyne had made an inauspicious start, for as a penniless captain of Dragoons he had eloped with the Earl of Derby's sister. This love match forced him to resign his commission and lost him nine years' seniority before being reinstated by the Stanley influence. He served briefly in the war against France which began in 1765, rising to the rank of Lieutenant-Colonel and finding favour with both George II and his grandson, George III. He bought a seat in Parliament, an important stepping-stone to military advancement, and during the twelve years of peace that followed he toured Europe and sent home reports about foreign armies without, however, making any profound comments. Then, as now, weapons dictated tactics, and Burgoyne learned to fight European battles. None the less, when he campaigned in America he showed some glimmering of a realization that the different conditions required imaginative changes in established routine.

He was tall, handsome and talented (he wrote several plays, one of which was attributed to Sheridan), debonair, witty, genial with his equals and condescending to his inferiors. A keen gambler, Burgoyne became popular with the bucolic George III who bestowed upon him the lucrative sinecure of the governorship of Fort William, a post which was rarely given to an officer below the rank of full general.

He was promoted Major-General in 1772, and three years later he was one of the three officers holding that rank who were selected to serve in America. Howe and Clinton were the other two. He wished to decline the appointment because of distaste for uncongenial service in that continent rather than disinclination to punish the rebels whom he thought had 'already been spoilt by too much indulgence'. He reached Boston in 1775, hoping that the colonists would be 'convinced by persuasion and not by the sword', and he witnessed Howe's costly attempt to dislodge the rebels from Bunker and Breed's hills on June 17th. He described the rebels as a 'rabble in arms', swept by success into insolence. But their defence was 'well conceived and obstinately maintained; the retreat was no flight; it was even covered with bravery and military skill'. Although they had these qualities, Burgoyne continued to despise the military capabilities of the colonists, and he doubted their resolution. The battle for Bunker Hill convinced him that cannon were necessary to dislodge the Americans from the fortifications they were 'so adept in constructing and behind which they fought with tenacity'.

In 1776, during a visit home in the dead period of the winter, Burgoyne was appointed second-in-command to Carleton in Canada, and, along with Howe and Clinton, was upgraded in rank to Lieutenant-General. Acting under Carleton's orders, he was forced to abandon the assault at Fort Ticonderoga, and he returned to England in the fall of 1776. In his military career Burgoyne had shown himself to be a capable and energetic soldier, a man likely to succeed in the face of difficulties.

Lord George Sackville was the third son of the Duke of Dorset, and had adopted the name of Germain in order to benefit from a bequest. During the Seven Years War he commanded the British contingent which fought in 1759 at the battle of Minden under Ferdinand of Brunswick, who accused him of repeatedly disobeying orders to bring his cavalry into action, and thereby prevented the full exploitation of victory. A court martial convicted Sackville of disobedience and he was sentenced to be degraded and dismissed from the army. He was lucky, perhaps, not to have been shot like the unfortunate Admiral Byng, who lacked the influential support which Lord George gained from his family connections. Germain's dereliction of duty may not have been as serious as his political enemies alleged. None the less, his fall was 'prodigious', as Horace Walpole declared. Surprisingly, even in those lax days, he survived his disgrace, attaching himself to Lord North who, as Prime Minister, appointed him to conduct the war against the rebellious colonists.

Germain has been charged both with trying to direct the war from London by hampering the generals on the spot by over-precise orders, and with leaving them too much to their own devices. Howe, it is claimed, lacked military insight; he failed to perceive the importance of the part he was expected to play in the Grand Strategy designed for 1777. Burgoyne escaped blame, and history has dealt kindly with him. Yet he was the 'man on the spot' in both senses of the term. He stood at Germain's side when the Secretary of State was dealing with Howe's correspondence and replying to his letters.

Late in December, King George received Burgoyne in audience, and, in the servile language of the period, he laid himself at His Majesty's feet 'for such active employment as he might think me worthy of'. He was observed riding in Hyde Park with the King, a mark of the royal esteem he had enjoyed previously and had not apparently lost. Confident of his future, Burgoyne called at Brooks's Club on December 25th. There he met Charles James Fox, the opposition leader. 'Within the year I shall return from America victorious,' Burgoyne boasted. The two men agreed to a wager of a 'pony' (fifty guineas, or about 150 dollars), and the bet was duly recorded in the club's book. On January 1, 1777, Burgoyne went to Bath to take the waters, promising Germain that he was available to return to Canada at a day's notice.

Neither the plan for the year, nor the part Burgoyne might play, had yet been decided. Howe's letters placed Germain in a dilemma.

Howe wrote on October 9, 1776, stating his intention, which he said was his 'principle object', of beginning the campaign in 1777 by 'opening up a communication with Canada', by occupying the line of the Hudson so as to launch an attack upon 'the heart of the rebellion' in New England. In a further letter, written on November 30th, in which he asked for reinforcements which would bring the troops at his command up to 36,000 men, he allocated 15,000 soldiers, nearly half the total, to hold New York City and 'to attack Albany from New York'. Twelve thousand more would hold Rhode Island and attack Boston, and another 10,000 would 'cover New Jersey and threaten Philadelphia', which he proposed to attack in the autumn 'provided the other operations succeed'.

If the required reinforcements were sent, he predicted that his troops would strike such terror through the country that 'little resistance would be made to the forces of His Majesty in the provinces of New England, New York, the Jerseys and Pennsylvania, after the junction of the northern and southern armies'.

Three points need to be noted. Howe allocated 10,000 troops for the purpose of taking Albany by an advance from New York; he implied that the junction of the northern and southern armies would precede the attack on Philadelphia, which was contingent upon the success of the other operations; and he asked for reinforcements, an additional 15,000 soldiers, to accomplish these designs.

Germain received Howe's letter of November 30th on December 30th, and he replied on January 14th. 'When I first read your requisition for a reinforcement of 15,000 rank and file,' he told Howe, 'I must own to you that I was really greatly alarmed, because I could not see the least chance of my being able to supply you with the Hanoverians or even the Russians in time.' (In the previous year Britain had hired 17,000 German mercenaries and had failed to obtain a number of Russians.)

Germain indulged in specious arithmetic. By checking Howe's army returns, which showed a theoretical strength of 27,000 officers and men, he interpreted Howe's request as for 7800 men, the number needed to bring his total strength up to 35,000 men. He achieved this figure by including the sick, the prisoners, and the deserters as part of the effective strength of the army, a manoeuvre that infuriated Howe. Germain did not comment upon Howe's plans, other than to say that they would be laid before the King.

By December 20th, when he wrote again, Howe had changed his mind, possibly because he foresaw that his plans were too expensive for the government and that the reinforcements he had requested would not be forthcoming, or perhaps for other reasons. He may have realized that, because the northern army could not reach Albany before September, he would be forced to remain inactive for several months while its commander gained the glory. He may have felt it necessary to do something himself to justify his position.

Howe announced a radical change of plan which was necessitated, he implied, by the inability of the government to fulfil his demands for reinforcements, which would restrict his operations. He was also influenced by his desire to capture the rebel capital, which was a stronghold of loyalism and could be taken easily. He was persuaded, he told Germain, that his principal army should act offensively against Philadelphia: 'By this change, the offensive plan towards Boston must be deferred until the proposed reinforcements arrive from Europe, that there may be a corps to act defensively upon the lower part of the Hudson River, to cover Jersey on that side, as well as to facilitate, in some degree, the approach of the army from Canada.' Howe did not expect the northern army to reach Albany before the middle of September, and its subsequent operations would 'depend upon the state of things at that time'.

The northern army, as far as Howe was now concerned, would act on its own, supported from New York only by a defensive movement on the lower Hudson. The principal impetus of the campaign would be against the rebel capital. Thus, as Howe conceived it, the advance from the north would be a sideshow, and would not be actively supported. There would be no junction of armies at Albany.

The advance up the Hudson must await further reinforcements, unless Howe completed his campaign at Pennsylvania in time to turn north; and he implied that the move against Philadelphia was not incompatible with support of or co-operation with the army from Canada. He made no mention of going to Philadelphia by sea, implying that his land march through Pennsylvania would place his army between General

Washington and the Hudson River. The new plan called for little more than half the troops he had requested on November 30th.

Germain received Howe's letter of December 20th on February 23rd, and another written on January 20th, in which he reiterated his intention to go to Philadelphia, on March 3rd. He replied to both on March 9th, endorsing Howe's changes of plan and saying that 'the King entirely approves of your proposed deviation from the plan you formerly suggested, being of the opinion that the reasons which have induced you to recommend this change in your operations are solid and decisive'. He added that he could send only 2900 reinforcements, less than one-fifth of the number Howe had requested, and he recommended a 'warm diversion' on the coast of New England. Of Burgoyne and his plan there was no mention.

According to the usual interpretation, Germain simultaneously approved two incompatible plans—Burgoyne's for the junction of the two armies on the Hudson, and Howe's for the invasion of Pennsylvania—and failed to warn Burgoyne of Howe's changed intentions, or to order Howe to subordinate his plan to the strategical necessities. This explanation is too simple. Burgoyne, who was in an out of Germain's office in Cleveland Row at the vital time, must have learned of Howe's proposed change of plan, although he may have believed that Howe would be ordered to support him. Germain failed to send Howe a direct order; he relied upon Howe's military judgment, and he misunderstood Howe's timing and the direction of his offensive.

On February 28th, Burgoyne submitted his *Thoughts for Conducting the War from the Side of Canada*. His reasoning seemed clear and compelling. Yet his plan may not have been the brilliant conception it has been assumed, despite his seemingly emphatic statement that 'these ideas are formed upon the supposition that it be the sole purpose of the Canadian army to effect a junction with General Howe, or after co-operating so far as to get possession of Albany and open communications to New York, to remain upon the Hudson River, and thereby enable the General to act with his whole force to the southward'.

Alternatively, he suggested, the Canadian army, having reached Albany, could threaten Connecticut, or it could be shipped from Quebec to New York to assist Howe. Neither of alternative designs was approved.

What exactly did Burgoyne propose? His intentions have puzzled many historians. Did he expect Howe to join him at Albany, or did he intend to gain possession of that town and maintain himself there while Howe did something to the southward? Or, knowing that Howe proposed first to go to Philadelphia, did Burgoyne hope to play his part in the grand design unaided, and gain all the glory for himself?

There is another question. What did Howe and Burgoyne mean by the term 'junction'? Did they—either or both—expect that the two armies would actually join at Albany, or would Howe's army merely complete the span after Burgoyne had built the arch? Owing to the imprecision of their phraseology, it is difficult to surmise either Burgoyne's intentions or Germain's and Howe's understanding of the situation.

Burgoyne, it may be assumed, was told by Germain of Howe's change of plan which proposed the junction of armies on the Hudson. He may have learned, too, that on February 24th Prime Minister Lord North had written to the King: 'Lord Germain will tomorrow propose Clinton for Canada and Burgoyne to join Howe. I thoroughly approve of this.'

Burgoyne was not going to get the job he coveted. Four days later he submitted his own proposals, which were accepted, and he was nominated to command the army destined for Clinton, who outranked him. What caused the Government to change its mind? And why did Germain, on March 9th, approve Howe's plan without mentioning Burgoyne's plan? Germain approved Burgoyne's plan because it solved the difficulty created by

Howe's change of plan. It did far more than that, for it offered Germain the best of both possible worlds, control of the Hudson valley and the capture of the rebel capital, in the same year.

However much Burgoyne may have paid lip-service to the designs of the Grand Strategy (the junction of two armies on the Hudson), he believed he could reach Albany on his own, and he persuaded Germain, who was easily persuaded, that there was no need to await Howe's active co-operation from New York. Eventually, when Howe had finished his business in Philadelphia, he could complete the movement. Confident that he could overcome any difficulty, Burgoyne made his plan sound easy of accomplishment. If he succeeded, a coveted peerage would be his least reward. Ennobled and richly rewarded, John Burgoyne, the one-time penniless captain of dragoons, the Westminster schoolboy who had eloped with his rich classmate's sister, the man whom gossip hinted had been illegitimately born, would take his place beside Clive and Wolfe, the heroes of the empire. He would ascend from the Commons to the Lords, then the 'best club in the world'.

Burgoyne, Germain, and Howe did not expect that the northern army would experience any great difficulty in reaching Albany; it would be a matter merely of transporting sufficient supplies. Colonial opposition would be negligible, for Howe would keep Washington occupied in Pennsylvania. Neither general reckoned on a *levée en masse* by the militia of New York and New England, and neither expected that Burgoyne would find his way barred, and his retreat cut off, by an army of farmers and shopkeepers, and that he would need to be rescued.

Burgoyne over-confidently assumed he could achieve his objective on his own. Germain lacked the perception to see that the various plans conflicted with the Grand Strategy, and he failed in his duty to make abundantly clear the part that each general was expected to play. He believed that Howe could both execute his plan to capture Philadelphia, and return in time to support Burgoyne, after he had reached Albany. By drawing Washington from the Hudson, Howe thought that he would remove the major, and probably the only, threat to Burgoyne's progress. That finally he went to Philadelphia by sea, rather than by land, did not change the situation, for Washington made no move to bar Burgoyne's path. Like Howe, Washington was obsessed by the threat to Philadelphia, a town of no strategic importance.

In his *Thoughts*, Burgoyne asked for 8000 regulars, a powerful train of artillery, a corps of watermen, 2000 Canadians and 1000 Indians. These should be ready by May 20th, and he predicted the capture of Fort Ticonderoga by early summer. 'The next measures must depend upon those taken by the enemy and upon the general plan of campaign concerted at home.'

On Burgoyne's *Thoughts*, George III commented, writing in his own hand, 'As Sir William Howe does not think of acting from Rhode Island into Massachusetts, the force from Canada must join him at Albany,' words which seem to indicate that the British Government still expected the junction of the two armies. It approved Burgoyne's plan for an advance to Albany, and for a diversion on the Mowhawk River, in the belief that Howe would return to New York in time to co-operate. Germain may have thought (and Howe's talk of easy victory gave him reason) that the capture of Philadelphia would be little more than a week-end jaunt, enabling Howe to return to New York in plenty of time to give priority to the nothern campaign. Germain assumed that Howe would not go to Pennsylvania if such a move would jeopardize the success of Burgoyne's invasion. He trusted Howe's military judgment and his evaluation of the strategic situation, and be believed that, in his invasion of Pennsylvania, Howe would be placing his army between General Washington and Burgoyne, thus securing the latter from molestation by the colonists' main army.

Howe, if he fathomed the government's intentions, was indifferent to them: deliberately he postponed the 'junction' plan, the chief arch of the Grand Strategy, in order to gain limited objectives at Philadelphia. His excuse for his failure to support Burgoyne? The government had denied him the reinforcements he requested for achieving all his objectives for the year, and, had he gone to join Burgoyne after Ticonderoga fell, his enemies would have accused him of enviously grasping a share of the merit.

Upon the King's approval of Burgoyne's plan, Germain drew up the orders for the northern part of the campaign, which he conveyed in a letter, dated March 26th, to Sir Guy Carleton, the Governor-General of Canada. Burgoyne was directed to proceed with all possible expedition to join Howe and to put himself under his command. Germain went on: 'With a view of quelling the rebellion as soon as possible, it is become highly necessary that the most speedy junction of the two armies should be effected.' Carleton was instructed, after providing sufficient troops to protect Canada, to employ the remainder of the army upon two expeditions, the one under the command of Lieutenant-General Burgoyne 'who is to force his way to Albany', and the other under the command of Lieutenant-Colonel Barry St Leger, who was to make the diversion on the Mowhawk River. Carleton was superseded in military command, as he had been already without his knowledge in August 1776, since when he had shown lack of vigour by failing to take Ticonderoga and by evacuating Crown Point.

Concluding his instructions, Germain told Carleton, 'I shall write to Sir William Howe from hence by the first packet; but you will nevertheless endeavour to give him the earliest intelligence of this measure, and also direct Lieutenant-General Burgoyne and Lieutenant-Colonel St Leger to neglect no opportunity of doing the same, that they may receive instructions from Sir William Howe. You will at the same time inform them, that, until they have received orders from Sir William Howe, it is His Majesty's pleasure that they act as exigencies may require, and in such manner as they may judge most proper for making an impression on the rebels and bringing them to obedience; but that in doing so they must never lose sight of their intended junctions with Sir William Howe as their principal objects.'

This final sentence in the instructions after the event was called by Germain the 'Saving Clause', by which Burgoyne was authorized to modify the plan should exigencies require. Following his surrender at Saratoga, Burgoyne refused to accept that he had been given any discretionary powers; his orders were mandatory, to force his way to Albany. He complained, not that his orders were ambiguous, but that they were over-precise.

Germain did not write to Howe as he had promised. William Knox, the Under-Secretary of State for the Colonies, disclosed in 1782 what happened (*Report on the Knox Papers, Historical Manuscripts Commission,* 1909):

'When all was prepared, and I had them to compare and make up; [meaning the documents necessary for Burgoyne's campaign] Lord Sackville [i.e. Germain] came down to the office to sign the letters on his way to Stoneland, when I observed to him that there was no letter to Howe to acquaint him with the plan or what was expected of him in consequence of it. His Lordship started, and D'Oyley [the Deputy-Secretary] stared, but he said he would in a moment write a few lines. "So", says Lord Sackville, "my poor horses must stand in the street all the time, and I shan't be to my time anywhere." D'Oyley then said he had better go, and he would write from himself to Howe and enclose copies of Burgoyne's Instructions, which would tell him all that he would want to know; and with this his Lordship was satisfied, as it enabled him to keep his time, for he could never bear delay or disappointment; and D'Oyley sat down and writ a letter to Howe but he neither shew'd it to me or gave a copy of it for the office, and if Howe had not acknowledged the receipt of it, with the copy of the Instructions to Burgoyne, we could not have proved that he ever saw them. I applied upon this occasion to D'Oyley for a copy of his letter, but he said he kept none. I then desired he would get one from Howe who had the original, but he would not ask for it, and Lord Sackville did not call upon Howe for it. Thurlow [the Lord Chancellor] would, however, have called for it if the inquiry had gone on, as I had told him all the circumstances'.

Not content with this explanation, Lord Shelburne (Lord Fitzmaurice, *Life of William, Earl of Shelburne*, 1912) enlarged upon Knox's story, basing his version on information he claimed to have derived from Germain's own secretary and 'the most respected persons in office', who assured him that Germain had arranged to call at his office on his way to the country in order to sign the despatches; but those addressed to Howe had not been 'fair copied', and as he was not disposed to be baulked on his projected visit to Kent, they were not signed and were forgotten on his return to London.

By what has been called 'a truly formidable misinterpretation of history', Edward de Fontblanque, in his *Life of Sir John Burgoyne* (1876) carried the story further, alleging that 'by one of these shameful acts of neglect, of which our history unfortunately affords but too many examples, this document [the explicit instructions to Howe as to his co-operation with Burgoyne] was suffered to be pigeon-holed, where it was found (after the culmination of the campaign) carefully docketed and only wanting the signature of the minister'. No such document has ever been found and the story of the 'pigeon-holed despatch' is now completely discredited.

Burgoyne was appointed to command the northern army of invasion and he left England on March 20th, carrying a copy of the orders to Carleton—whom protocol demanded should be instructed—and professing to believe that Howe had been ordered to join him at Albany, or at least to support him actively.

II *Montreal*

Burgoyne reached Canada and disembarked at Quebec on May 6th, fourteen days earlier than he had said in his *Thoughts* was the earliest date by which the melting snows and the break-up of the river ice would make campaigning possible. The winter had been unusually mild and the St Lawrence had freed itself from floating ice, which had broken up two weeks before, by the end of April. But the roads were a quagmire, and the streams were overflowing, thus hindering the concentration of troops and supplies.

With Burgoyne came most of the reinforcements and supplies he had requested, though several transports did not arrive until June 12th. He travelled to Montreal where, on May 12th, he met Sir Guy Carleton, who was ignorant of any event to the southward since the previous September, although he had heard rumours from captured Americans of Washington's success in December at Trenton. For this reverse, he now learned, Germain partly blamed him. If Burgoyne had had any doubts as to the co-operation he would receive from the disgruntled governor, they were quickly dispelled. Sir Guy Carleton could not have done more had he been acting for himself or his own brother, as Burgoyne testified later, when he was accused in Parliament of having intrigued to obtain the commission that belonged rightly to his superior officer who, without his knowledge, had been superseded in active command in the previous August.

The attainment of his objective, the town of Albany, did not appear to present insuperable difficulties, for once Fort Ticonderoga had been reduced and its garrison captured, opposition should be negligible. Success depended upon

33

transport and, except for the twenty-mile portage between the lakes and the Hudson River, water supplied the means, and Carleton had built the boats in the previous summer. Whichever route the expedition took from Lake George to the Hudson (there were two alternatives), many horses would be required to carry the supplies and to drag the boats and artillery overland. Burgoyne soon learned that horses were scarce in Canada.

In the preparations for his campaign Burgoyne encountered difficulties which, from his previous experience in Canada, he might have foreseen. He seems, too, to have been strangely lackadaisical in the matter of obtaining transport, for he failed to make the necessary requisitions until June 12th. After his arrival in Montreal, two weeks elapsed before he wrote to Carleton: 'It also appears to me that seven or eight hundred horses may become indispensibly necessary to my purposes' (a number he deemed inadequate after he had discussed the matter with Nathaniel Day, the commissary-general at Montreal, whom he had asked to furnish an estimate of the number of horses and carts necessary to convey thirty days' provisions for 10,000 men, 'together with about 1000 gallons of rum').

Four hundred horses were required to drag the artillery overland, stated Major-General Phillips, Burgoyne's second-in-command. Another 1000 were required to pull the 500 light carts, in which it had been decided the provisions and camp equipment would be carried. The construction of these carts seems to have been an afterthought and they were hastily built from unseasoned wood. The exact number of horses procured is unascertainable, but they fell far short of the estimate, despite the decision to hire them by the day, which was the lucrative method preferred by the contractors to outright purchase, and which, by the Treasury officials, was deemed a better bargain than purchase at the cost of £20,000 to £30,000. For each horse lost the contractors were to be recompensed by £15.

In the matter of transport Burgoyne may have been a victim of the procrastination, and possibly the venery, of the civilian department of the Treasury which, until 1799 when the Royal Wagon Train was established, supplied transport by a complicated system of vouchers and requisitions, together with civilian drivers who were not amenable to military discipline. Wherever the fault lay, only 637 horses were available when they were needed most, at the portage, and of these 237 were required to drag the guns with which Burgoyne encumbered his expedition, following the reduction of Ticonderoga, the last fort he was likely to encounter *en route* to Albany. He added further to his difficulties by loading twenty carts with his own camp furnishings and supplies, at a time when he ordered his officers to dispense with unnecessary gear. Burgoyne's self-indulgence and hypocrisy were typical of the age, for they were the perquisites of rank.

Burgoyne suffered other disappointments. Canadians were loath to volunteer to join the expedition in which they had no interest, and of the 2000 'hatchet men' and workmen, for whom Burgoyne had asked, less than 300 were available. To secure even these few Sir Guy Carleton was forced to invoke the 'corvée', the relic of French rule whereby forced labour might be commanded. Even so, the ranks of the 300 were decimated by desertion, and the contingent, which finally numbered 150 men, was officered by Captains Boucherville, Monin and MacKay.

Though naturally more enthusiastic than the Canadians, the American Loyalists—those who were already in Canada, and those Burgoyne had hoped to recruit *en route*—failed to come up to his expectations, despite the optimistic promises of the three Loyalist leaders, Colonel Philip Skene, John Peters, and Ebenezer Jessup. During the campaign the Loyalists fought, in Burgoyne's words, 'with spirit', and they performed useful services, but the promised numbers failed to materialize, probably due to their fear to commit themselves until the outcome of the campaign could be foreseen.

35

More serious was the failure to recruit the '1000 or more savages', whom Burgoyne had listed in his *Thoughts*, and without whose assistance, Germain told Carleton, the plan could not be advantageously executed. Only 400 Indians assembled under the command of the Chevalier La Corne St Luc, a member of Carleton's Council, and Charles de Langlade, a veteran of the French and Indian war who had fought against Braddock and Washington in 1755. These Indians, who were expected to act as the eyes of the army, proved a disappointment, for, as Burgoyne wrote in July, they were no better than 'spoiled children', and grew more unreasonable and importunate 'upon every new favour'. Burgoyne's employment of Indians was vehemently criticized by the Americans, who would have used them for the same purpose had they had the opportunity. They also complained equally bitterly against the British use of German mercenaries.

Leaving the army to assemble at St John's on the Richelieu River, and its composition to the next chapter, we may return to consider the overall situation. Burgoyne was 'surprised and mortified', he informed his friend Lord Harvey the adjutant-general, following his arrival in Montreal, at finding a paper circulating, giving such accurate information of the campaign as might have been copied from Germain's orders, while his caution had been 'such that not a man in my own family [meaning his staff] had been let into the secret'. Yet, despite this leak of information, as we shall learn, the Americans were ignorant of Burgoyne's intention to invade New York State.

Still Sir William Howe did not understand the part he was expected to play. On April 2nd he wrote to Carleton, sending Germain a copy of his letter:

'Having but little expectation that I shall be able from a want of sufficient strength in the army to detach a corps in the beginning of the campaign to act up Hudson's River consistent with the operations already determined upon, the force your Excellency may deem expedient to advance beyond your frontiers, after taking Ticonderoga, will, I fear, have little assistance from hence to facilitate their approach, and, as I shall probably be in Pennsylvania when the corps is ready to advance into this country, it will not be in my power to communicate with the officer commanding it so soon as I could wish; he must therefore pursue such measures as may, from circumstances, be judged most conducive to the advancement of His Majesty's service constantly with your Excellency's orders for his conduct.'

This letter did not worry Carleton or Burgoyne, who believed that Howe would shortly receive the copy of the instructions which would indicate the course Howe was expected to follow. Howe received the copy on June 5th.

Before sailing from Plymouth, Burgoyne had sent Howe a copy of his instructions, and on his arrival at Quebec he wrote a second letter to Howe, repeating his statement that he had been entrusted with the command of the army destined to march from Canada, and that his orders were to force a junction with Howe. He expressed also his wish that latitude had been left him 'for a diversion towards Connecticut'. Such an idea was, however, out of the question, by his orders 'being precise to force the junction', and he mentioned it only to introduce the idea 'still resting upon my mind' to induce the suspicion in the minds of the enemy that 'I still pointed towards Connecticut'. But, 'under the present precision of my orders', he told Howe, 'I should really have no view but that of joining him, nor think myself justified by any temptation to delay the most expeditious means I could find to effect that purpose.'

Burgoyne wrote to Howe again from St John's, before the expedition started, in order to give him 'intelligence of my situation at the time, and my expectation of being before Ticonderoga between the 20th and 21st June'. He repeated his 'perseverance in the idea of giving jealousy' (i.e. making a feint) to the side of Connecticut, and he gave his assurance that 'I should make no manoeuvre that could procrastinate the great object of a junction.'

The correspondence between Germain and Howe continued after Burgoyne had sailed for Canada, and it should have been obvious to both men that they were at cross-purposes and that someone had blundered. Burgoyne's letters made clear that he expected to join Howe.

On April 2nd Howe wrote a letter which Germain received on May 18th, stating that his main objective would be Philadelphia, where he proposed to go by sea. New York would be held by 4700 regular troops, and 3000 Loyalists would act on the Hudson or in Connecticut 'as circumstances may point out'. Due to lack of reinforcements, his hopes of terminating the war within the year had vanished; by the end of 1777 he hoped to be in possession of the provinces of New York, the Jerseys, and Pennsylvania, 'though this in some degree must depend upon the success of the northern army'.

The letter contained no hint of co-operation with Burgoyne, and even more disastrous was Howe's statement that he proposed to invade Pennsylvania *by sea*, which meant that 'from this arrangement we must probably abandon the Jerseys which by the former plan would not have been the case'. Thus, there would be no army to stand between General Washington and the Hudson, and Howe would not be able to hold out a helping hand to Burgoyne. And, remarking upon the long delays which would occur in the evacuation of the Jerseys, Howe stated: 'It is probable that the campaign will not commence as soon as your Lordship may expect.' With this letter, Howe enclosed a copy of his letter to Carleton in which he said that Burgoyne could expect no co-operation from him.

On April 19th, Germain wrote Howe a letter that contained two clear hints that the latter was expected to act on the Hudson, for Germain told him that the Hanau *chasseurs*, which were intended as reinforcements for New York, would form part of St Leger's force, and he stated that the 'brigadiers' of the northern army would hold that rank only until that army joined his.

Two fresh factors had been introduced into the deteriorating situation; the late invasion of Pennsylvania, and its invasion by sea rather than land. Germain lacked the capacity to foresee that Howe's decisions jeopardized Burgoyne's invasion of New York State from the north. Despite Howe's emphatic statement that the start of his campaign would be delayed, and that he could not return to New York in time to co-operate with Burgoyne, Germain replied on May 18th, making it clear that, while he left the decision to Howe, he was expected to support Burgoyne. Germain wrote:

'As you must from your situation and military skill, be a competent judge of the propriety of every plan, His majesty does not hesitate to approve the alterations which you propose; trusting however that, whatever you may meditate, it will be executed in time for you to co-operate with the army ordered to proceed from Canada and put itself under your command.'

To this letter Howe replied simply on August 30th that he could not obey. By that date the fate of the northern expedition was sealed.

Unaware that he would not be supported, or refusing to accept that possibility, or more probably hoping that he would not, Burgoyne assembled his army at St John's on the Richelieu River.

III *St John's*

Defective as was his army in irregular soldiers, Burgoyne had no cause to complain about his regular troops, British and German. They were professionals and veterans, and numbered 8300 rank and file which, with officers, sergeants and musicians, brought the total strength to 9500 men. The non-combatants, the commissariat and transport men, and the women camp-followers, numbered another 1000. How many women accompanied the expedition is unknown; according to eighteenth-century military practice, many officers and soldiers were allowed to bring their 'wives', who acted as laundry-women and nurses, and normally forty women per thousand men were permitted. True to the custom of the age, Burgoyne quickly acquired a mistress, the wife of an unnamed commissariat officer, who shared his tent throughout the campaign

The British troops came from the 9th, 20th, 21st, 24th, 47th, 53rd, and 62nd Regiments, each of which was composed of ten companies, all 'crack' regiments, with long traditions of military honours. They were grouped in three brigades, the First, Second, and the Advance Corps, the members of which were drawn from the Grenadier companies, composed of the tallest and strongest men in each regiment (who no longer carried 'grenades') and the light-infantry, or 'sharpshooters' as they were called. This *élite* corps was commanded, until his death, by Brigadier-General Simon Fraser, who had fought with Wolfe at Louisburg and Quebec. He was succeeded by the Earl of Balcarres who, with the other two Brigadiers, Henry Watson Powell and James Hamilton, rose subsequently to the rank of full general, as did Burgoyne's quartermaster, Captain John Money, and his engineer-officer Lieutenant Twiss.

40

Burgoyne's chief officers were men of proven worth and ability. Several were distinguished in British social and political life, or were younger sons of great families, and three, like their commander, were Members of Parliament. Major-General William Phillips was an artilleryman of thirty years' experience, who had distinguished himself at Minden and Warburg during the Seven Years War by bringing up his guns at the gallop, an unheard of feat. He was a man of energy, resource and courage and, it is said, of furious temper. Thomas Jefferson, who entertained him at Monticello, Virginia, during his captivity, called Phillips 'the proudest man of the proudest nation on earth'. As an officer of artillery, which with the engineers shared a secondary status within the British army, Phillips was not normally permitted to command troops, a difficulty which Burgoyne overcame by an emergency order; and Phillips acted as second-in-command of the expedition and as commander of the right wing. He had campaigned with Burgoyne and Carleton in 1776, as had the two Brigadiers. The adjutant-general, Major Robert Kingston, had fought under Burgoyne in Portugal, and Simon Fraser and the young Earl of Balcarres were Burgoyne's intimate friends. The latter shared his commander's love of cards; and of Simon Fraser, Burgoyne observed 'he grudged a danger or care in other hands than his own'.

Other notable British officers included Major John Dyke Acland, an able and active soldier who was accompanied by his thirty-year-old wife, Lady Harriet, the daughter of the Earl of Ilchester, of indomitable spirit, as we shall learn; as was also the chaplain of the expedition, the Reverend Edward Brudenell who shared her exploit. Captain Alexander Fraser, who is reputed to have been a nephew of Simon Fraser, commanded the sharpshooters and superintended the Indians. Captain Viscount Petersham, the future Earl of Harrington, shared membership of the House of Commons with Burgoyne, Phillips and Acland. The youthfulness of Lords Torphichen and

Napier was offset by the experience of such officers as Colonel Fitzroy, Colonel Viscount Ligonier and Captain Edward Gay, who had all fought at Minden, as had Phillips and the German von Riedesel. Edward Pellew, a young midshipman of the naval contingent which navigated the boats, rose subsequently to the rank of Admiral, and to the peerage as Viscount Exmouth.

The American Loyalists, or Tories as they were called, included Lieutenant-Colonel John Peters who came from Connecticut and had been educated at Yale University, and who, disliking independence, had fled to Canada; also the Jessup brothers from Glen Falls in upper New York State; and Philip Skene, a former British army major who, following thirty years' service in Europe and America, had settled at Skenesborough, the house he had built and by which the expedition was destined to pass. Skene had espoused the royal cause from the start of the rebellion, and he acted as Burgoyne's political officer. He had been wounded in 1758 during General Abercrombie's attempt to take Fort Ticonderoga and, a year later, he had been present at General Amherst's capture of the fort. Another Loyalist, the young David Jones, who came from the country around Fort Edward which lay on the intended line of march, expected that the expedition would reunite him with his betrothed, Jane McCrea.

With the expedition marched the four 'diarists': Captain Thomas Anburey, a grenadier officer; Lieutenant William Digby of the Shropshire Regiment; Lieutenant James Hadden, an artillery officer; and the famous Sergeant Lamb, a surgeon's mate in the 9th Regment, who between them supply some of those intimate details which in those days were rare and which have now become the custom of military adventure. Another diarist, still anonymous despite the researches of his 'editor', provided some information.

Despite the rigours and uncertainties of their life, the British soldiers were keen and spirited, and they proved themselves excellent troops when they were well led. Burgoyne was highly popular with his men and consequently received the best from them. Lieutenant Digby says that he was 'idealized' by them, and that 'on every occasion he was the soldier's friend'. They did not resent the fact that their general campaigned in comfort while they toiled and sweated, burdened by a load that weighed sixty pounds and clothed in traditional uniform unsuited to the rough country and humid heat in which they were forced to campaign. The long service of some in Canada, wherein they had become acclimatized, had resulted in some amelioration of their lot; their scarlet tail-cotas had become so tattered that, in order to provide patching material, they were cut into short jackets, and their cocked hats had been made into caps, adorned with tufts of coloured hair to denote the different regiments. The necessity for this distinction led to strife with the inhabitants, for the soldiers cut off cows' tails to obtain the white hair which was found most suitable to take the brightly coloured dyes.

The smooth-bore Brown Bess musket, with which the British army was armed, had a barrel three feet eight inches long, and a bayonet fourteen inches in length, and it fired a leaden bullet weighing one ounce. To fire this flint-lock the soldier was required to tear off the end of the paper cartridge with his teeth, sprinkle a few grains of powder in the priming-pan and ram ball and cartridge down the muzzle with the ramrod, an operation that required twelve separate motions. The procedure permitted fire at the rate, on the average, of two to three shots per minute, depending upon the soldier's skill and the weather conditions. High wind might blow the powder from the pan, and rain might damp it. To counter these dangers, Burgoyne urged 'use of the bayonet'. Discharge was controlled by volleys which, due to the maximum range of the weapon, were delayed until the enemy were within one hundred yards. In European warfare it had become the accepted practice to hold fire as long as possible as the opposing lines converged, a

43

technique of brinkmanship that proved ineffective against an elusive foe trained in Indian-frontier tactics, and 'aimed' fire.

Brave though they were (as brave on a battlefield as any soldiers that could be found in the world, according to the Duke of Brunswick-Lüneburg), the British soldiers were ill-trained to fight men who fired from cover and who refused to stand up and be mown down by volley firing, the tactic in which British soldiers excelled. Burgoyne was familiar with the Americans' capabilities for skirmishing and in defence of prepared positions. To combat the former, he had formed the corps of sharpshooters; and to batter down fortifications he encumbered his army with an artillery train comprising, at the start of the campaign, 138 brass pieces. That he dragged forty-two of these guns with him following the reduction of Fort Ticonderoga, the last 'fort' he could expect to encounter on his way to Albany, was one of the principal criticisms levelled against Burgoyne, for they slowed his progress at the time when, if he was to reach his goal, speed was essential. Sir Guy Carleton, on the other hand, stated that he would have carried a similar artillery train had he been commanded to lead the expedition.

Burgoyne started out with these pieces:

16 twenty-four-pounders.
2 light twenty-four-pounders.
10 heavy twelve-pounders.
8 medium twelve-pounders.
1 light twelve-pounder.
26 light six-pounders.
6 eight-inch howitzers.
6 five-and-a-half-inch howitzers.
46 mortars of various calibres.

The movement and operation of these guns required the services of 600 men, of whom 250 were regular gunners, 100 German gunners, and 150 recruits drawn from the infantry.

By standard practice four horses were required to drag each six-pounder gun, three each three-pounder, and three each howitzer. The light six-pounders were mounted on carriages, called Congreve carriages, or could be carried on the backs of horses or mules. The heavy 'siege' guns, the twleve- and twenty-four-pounders, the howitzers and the thirteen-inch-bore mortars, were organized in a 'park', and were employed for the reduction of earthworks and fortifications. The smaller guns were grouped in three batteries, one at the left of the line, another at the centre, and the third on the right—a recent development, as 'the effect of fire becomes much more formidable than when scattered along the whole front of the line'.

The seven German regiments of infantry—one regiment of light-infantry and one company of Jagers (the former royal huntsmen), who were equipped with short, heavy rifles—other than one regiment from Hesse-Hanau, had been hired from the Duke of Brunswick, and the whole contingent was commanded by Friedrich Adolf, Freiherr von Riedesel, aged thirty-nine, a cavalry man and experienced soldier who in his youth had served as the Duke's favourite staff-officer. Von Riedesel had distinguished himself at Minden and, by 1776, had risen to the rank of major-general. He was noted for his courage, daring, coolness and charm, and he had instituted a system of light-infantry training, in which soldiers were encouraged to take advantage of cover and to move and fire rapidly. He was a more experienced and versatile soldier than Burgoyne, with whom he had campaigned in 1776. His two brigadiers were named Johann Friedrich von Specht and W. B. von Gall. Von Riedesel spoke little English and he and Burgoyne conversed in French. He was accompanid through the latter part of the campaign by his little, blue-eyed wife Frederika, the daughter of a general, who carried with her their three tiny daughters, and three maids. It is to her that we are indebted for the most lively descriptions and comments on the campaign.

Although von Riedesel attempted to make their dress more

suitable by the addition of 'Canadian-type' summer-weight trousers of blue and white striped material, the Germans and particularly the dragoons, though dismounted from lack of horses, were forced to wear their cumbersome, long cavalry boots, complete with spurs, leather breeches and long leather gauntlets, and enormous hats with trailing plumes, and to carry heavy swords which trailed upon the ground. They were further impeded in their movements by their dark-blue, heavy-weight uniforms, and by the poor quality of their shoes. Shipped to England, they were hurried overseas, the contractors supplying them with cheap cloth and boxes of ladies slippers. The attempt in Canada to refit them had been only partly successful, due to lack of supplies. The mobility of these German troops suffered further from pedantic military tradition which made drill and alignment almost a religion.

Without the aid of these 'foreign hirelings', England could not have waged war in America; for the population of Great Britain, almost 8,000,000 people, could muster a standing army of only 50,000 men, half of whom were required to garrison other colonies and to safeguard the homeland from the threat of foreign invasion. In 1776, the government of George III hired 17,000 soldiers from the petty principalities of Hesse-Cassel, Hesse-Hanau, Brunswick, Anhalt, Ansbach and Waldeck, whose rulers made hard bargains, selling their subjects as so many cattle to fight in 'foreign shambles', as Lord Chatham (William Pitt the Elder) remarked with scorn. These serfs of princely and ducal states were shipped, unprotesting, to North America to fight in a war they little understood.

On June 3rd the army moved from its winter quarters at Chamby, close to Montreal, the soldiers leaving behind, at their general's orders, their blanket-coats and leggings, which were not considered to be necessary in the climate in which they were expected to campaign. The officers, Burgoyne ordered, were not to encumber the wagons with more baggage than was absolutely necessary for the campaign 'where movements may be expected to be sudden and alert'—an admonition he repeated frequently and to which he himself paid no heed.

According to the 'returns' made when the army assembled at the Boquet River on July 1st, the British regulars numbered 3724, the Germans 3016, the artillerymen 473, the Canadians and Tories 250, and the Indians 400; a total of 7863 fighting men.

The rough roads between Chamby and St John's played havoc with the hastily built carts, wagons and gun-carriages, and there were many breakdowns and consequent delays, an occurrence that boded ill for the later stages of the journey when there would be no roads at all.

The fleet lay ready on the banks of the Richelieu River at St John's. Most of these ships, including the *Inflexible* armed with eighteen twelve-pounder guns, had been constructed in the previous summer, and they were made serviceable for another campaign through the exertions of Lieutenant Twiss and Naval-Lieutenant John Schanck, a mechanical and engineering genius who, amongst other achievements, had invented sliding keels, or 'the centre-board' as it became called, which enabled the flat-bottomed boats to sail on the lake both in high winds and close to the shore—he rose eventually to the rank of admiral. During the winter months a new frigate, the *Royal George*, had been built, and, following the melting of the ice on the river and lake, soldiers had been trained to row the 200 *bateaux*. The naval contingent numbered 700 officers and seamen.

The flotilla set sail on June 21st from the assembly point at Cumberland Head, north of Valcour Island. Lieutenant Anburey found the sight so novel and pleasing that it could not fail to fix the admiration of everyone present:

'When we were in the widest part of the lake, it was remarkably fine and clear, not a breeze was stirring, when the whole army appeared at one view in such perfect regularity as to form the most complete and splendid regatta you can possibly conceive.

47

In front the Indians went with their birch-bark canoes, containing twenty or thirty men each; then the advanced corps in regular line with the gun-boats, then followed the *Royal George* and *Inflexible,* towing large booms—which are to be thrown across two points of land—with the two brigs and sloops following; after them Generals Burgoyne, Phillips and von Riedesel in their pinnaces; next to them the 2nd Battalion followed by the German Battalion; and the rear was brought up with the sutlers and followers of the army.'

While the main army from Canada advanced towards Crown Point and Ticonderoga, Colonel Barry St Leger with a thousand men—regulars and Canadians—and Sir John Johnson with the Royal Greens, the Loyalist regiment, moved up the St Lawrence and through the Great Lakes on their journey to take the Americans in the rear.

The flotilla reached the Boquet River on the first night, and Burgoyne took the opportunity of the halt to express his high opinion of the troops and to make two proclamations. The first, addressed to the rebel-colonists and couched in pompous and extravagant language, threatened the vengeance of the savages if resistance was prolonged, and the second warned his Indian allies. He advised the civilian population to avoid obstructing his advance, and the Indians he warned to spare, from knife and hatchet, 'even in the time of conflict, aged men, women, children and prisoners' who 'must be held sacred'. To take the scalps of the dead, 'when killed in fair opposition' was permissible, but 'on no account were they to be taken from the wounded or dying'.

When they learned of Burgoyne's proclamation, the Americans jeered, and Francis Hopkinson, a member of the Continental Congress and one of the signers of the Declaration of Independence, lampooned it in a similar proclamation which was circulated throughout the colonies.

Burgoyne's injunction to the Indians drew from Edmund

GENERAL BURGOYNE.

1. General John Burgoyne (*Mansell Collection*)

2. Daniel Morgan. By Chappel (*New York Public Library*)

Burke, in Parliament, a sarcastic simile from the royal menagerie at the Tower of London: 'Suppose there was a riot on Tower Hill. What would the keeper of His Majesty's lions do? Would he not fling open the dens of the wild beasts and then address them thus—"My dear lions, my humane bears, my sentimental wolves, my tender-hearted hyenas, go forth; but I exhort you as you are Christians and members of a civilized society, to take care not to hurt any man, woman or child." ' Prime Minister Lord North, states Horace Walpole, was reduced to tears of mirth by Burke's sarcasm at the policy of Indian recruitment, which he himself had sanctioned against Carleton's advice.

The Indians, who proved themselves treacherous and brutal, promised constant obedience to the general's order, whereupon liquor was served and a war-dance performed. General Burgoyne was pleased to find the Indians to tractable, Anburey was informed by a staff-officer.

The horses sent through the woods arrived safely on June 25th at Crown Point, where two scalps were brought in by the Indian scouts. Two inhabitants who surrendered to the picket reported that the rebel lines at Ticonderoga were very strong and that the garrison comprised between five and six thousand men, a piece of misinformation which appears to have been confirmed next day by an officer from Ticonderoga, one of nine prisoners taken by Captain Fraser's light troops. Before leaving Canada, Burgoyne had been told by Carleton's spies, correctly as we shall learn, that the fort's garrison was ill-supplied, and weak. He does not seem to have passed this information to his officers, for we find Lieutenant Anburey remarking, 'By all accounts that can be collected, the Americans are in force at Ticonderoga, nearly to the number of 12,000 men, and a considerable number occupy Lake George, sustained by a naval power.'

When the army reached Crown Point on June 30th, Burgoyne issued a general order to the army:

49

'The army embarks tomorrow, to approach the enemy. We are to contend for the King, and the Constitution of Great Britain, to vindicate Law, and to relieve the oppressed—a cause in which His Majesty's Troops and those of the Prince's his Allies, will feel equal excitement. The services required of this particular expedition are critical and conspicuous. During our progress occasions may occur, in which, nor difficulty, nor labour, nor life are to be regarded. This Army must not Retreat.'

Burgoyne did not expect to retreat. Whether or not he believed that he would be supported from the south, he had no doubt that he would achieve his goal. He had reached Crown Point in the previous summer and had been forced to abandon the attack on Fort Ticonderoga. Now the great American bastion, 'the Gibraltar of the north' as they called it, lay eight miles ahead.

Anburey reached Crown Point on June 30th, noting in his diary, 'We are now within sight of the enemy, and their watch-boats are continually rowing about, but beyond reach of cannon shot.' But, the strong American naval force which had been expected to bar the flotilla's progress did not materialize. It had been lost, we know, in the previous summer by General Arnold. Lieutenant Digby, who advanced to Three Mile Point, came in sight of Ticonderoga, observing the 'Flag of Liberty' floating above the fort, every detail of which he discerned through his glasses. He found it 'entertaining enough, being a scene of life I had not been accustomed to before, and its novelty made it amusing.'

July 1st dawned fine and clear. The army re-embarked; the mile-wide lake was quickly covered with *bateaux*; with drums beating and pipes playing, the army moved to its first encounter with the enemy. The advance guard was already engaged.

IV *Fort Ticonderoga*

What were the British up to? This question perplexed the
colonists as the campaigning season drew near. Their spies
had briefly reported Burgoyne's return to Canada but, despite
the most diligent efforts and the leak of his orders of which
Burgoyne had complained, the British security screen proved
effective, and nothing could be learned of his strength or intentions. When, on June 15th, the garrison at Ticonderoga
were told by a prisoner of Burgoyne's preparations for an advance southward with 10,000 men, with a diversion on the
Mohawk, the colonists refused to take the threat seriously.

Wintering in Pennsylvania after his remarkable success on the
Delaware at Christmas, General Washington sought an answer
to the problem that could decide the fate of the colonies; Sir
William Howe lay in New York with an army composed of
25,000 regulars and 5000 American Tories, a powerful force
nearly four times the strength of his own ill-equipped, ragged,
starving, and dispirited army of colonials and militia; the
long- and short-service men, many of whom were eager to go
home on the expiration of their term of service.

Howe might ascend the Hudson to take Albany, or march
southwards to capture Philadelphia. Washington discounted
the threat to divide the colonies by a junction of armies on the
Hudson. Such a plan, involving 'the penetration of the country
by way of the lakes', was, he believed beyond the capability
of the British, and Fort Ticonderoga constituted a bastion to
daunt and repel an invasion from the north.

Washington had not visited Ticonderoga and he shared the
American illusion of its impregnability. In March 1777,
General Philip Schuyler, the commander of the strategically

important Northern Department, requested 10,000 additional troops to garrison the fort and another 2000 to guard the Mohawk valley. In reply, Washington expressed the opinion that 'much too large a part of your force is directed to Ticonderoga'. It was probable, he wrote, that the British would transport their troops from Canada to New York by sea, in order to reinforce Howe, a danger that made it unnecessary to maintain a 'useless' body of troops at Ticonderoga when 'the service here [New Jersey] might suffer an irreparable loss for want of it'.

Washington believed that the chief threat would be directed against Albany (the supply base for the Northern Department), the loss of which would force the evacuation of Ticonderoga ninety-five miles to the north. In the summer of 1776, in order to prevent Howe from sailing up the Hudson to within forty miles of Albany, he had built two forts, named Washington and Lee, to close the lower Hudson. By November the British had captured both forts, and the colonists built two more, higher up on the Highlands, which commanded the river, named Montgomery and Clinton, and work was started on a third, Fort Constitution, across the river from West Point. The British raid in late March, on Peekskill, on the Hudson, increased Washington's fears that Howe planned to ascend the river, and to counter that danger he sent four regiments to the threatened area, with orders to move quickly to the relief of Ticonderoga should that prove necessary. 'If I can keep Howe below the Highlands, I think their schemes will be entirely baffled,' Washington told Schuyler.

Washington's inability to divine the enemy's plans, which, as we know, were as confused as he was, and his unwarranted belief in the impregnability of Ticonderoga, lulled the commanders on the spot into an attitude of false complacency. They underestimated British audacity, and overestimated the capability of the fort to repel attack. They therefore did nothing to improve its defences, but frittered away their energies in

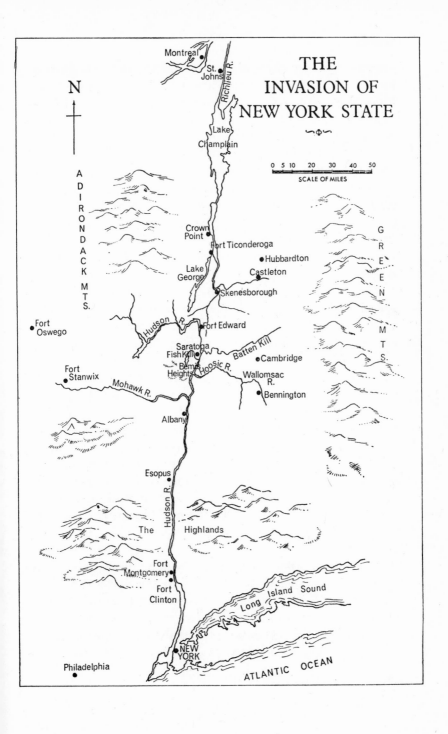

N

THE
INVASION OF
NEW YORK STATE

SCALE OF MILES
0 5 10   20   30   40   50

Montreal
St. Johns
Richlieu R.

Lake Champlain

A
D
I
R
O
N
D
A
C
K

M
T
S.

G
R
E
E
N

M
T
S.

Crown Point
Fort Ticonderoga
Hubbardton
Castleton
Lake George
Skenesborough

Fort Oswego

Hudson R.
Fort Edward
Saratoga
Fish Kill
Bemis Heights
Batten Kill
Cambridge

Fort Stanwix
Mohawk R.
Hoosic R.
Wallomsac R.
Bennington

Albany

Esopus
Hudson R.

The
Highlands

Fort Montgomery
Fort Clinton

Long Island Sound

NEW YORK

Philadelphia

ATLANTIC OCEAN

increasing the perimeter of defence although sufficient force to man the works did not exist. They remained blind to the fort's major defect even when, in the summer of 1776, Colonel John Trumbull, the twenty-year-old artist son of the Governor of Connecticut, called attention to it.

In 1690, the first crude earthworks had been built on the tapering tongue of land which slopes gradually down to Lake Champlain at the point nearest to the jutting promontory on the Vermont shore. These commanded the narrows, a quarter of of a mile wide, where Lakes Champlain and George converge, thereby forming a junction of the two water routes to the south. The Indians called the spot 'Ticonderoga', the place 'where the lake shuts itself'. On the New York side, a creek and a short portage gave access to Lake George. In 1750, the French built a square bastion on the tongue of land, and later added an earthwork shaped like a horseshoe to protect the fort on the north-west. These fortifications came to be known as the 'Old French Lines'. By 1775 the ramparts and ditches had fallen into ruins, and the Americans, when they captured the fort, made an attempt to improve and extend the defences. They built an outwork, which they named Mount Hope, to protect the saw-mills and command the outlet to Lake George, and further extended the perimeter of defence by the fortification of Mount Independence, the promontory on the Vermont shore. A force of 12,000 men was required to man these defences fully; but even had that number been available, it is doubtful whether the fort could have lived up to its reputation as an impregnable bastion, the 'Gibraltar of the North'.

As Trumbull noticed, the fortifications were overlooked and dominated across the narrows to the north-west by a sugar-loaf hill, 800 feet high and subsequently named Mount Defiance. He expressed his conviction that the defences lay within cannon shot of the mount, and although he was laughed at for his fears, he obtained permission from General Gates to experiment in reverse. A double twelve-pounder fired from Mount Independence struck halfway up Mount Defiance, one and a half miles away, and a six-pounder from Ticonderoga nearly reached the summit. To counter the argument that Mount Defiance was inaccessible to artillery, Trumbull, accompanied by Anthony Wayne and the lame Benedict Arnold, scrambled up the precipitous eastern face of the mount, an ascent that convinced him that a loaded gun-carriage could be dragged up the far easier northern face. Nevertheless Gates remained unconvinced, although in June 1777 he did order a further reconnaissance of the hill. No defences were constructed on Mount Defiance.

The appointment, in 1776, of Horatio Gates to command the army in Canada, which had been led by Allen and Arnold, and to withdraw their troops to Ticonderoga, created an ambiguous situation which further weakened the defence of the fort. Gates interpreted his appointment as an independent command within the Northern Department, to the supreme command of which Philip Schuyler had been appointed by Congress, with authority second only to Washington. The two officers appealed to Congress for clarification and, to Gates's mortification, that body reaffirmed Schuyler's authority. Gates refused to serve under him and, in mid-November, hurried to Baltimore, where Congress was meeting temporarily, to plead his cause and to undermine Schuyler's standing. He was assisted in his design by the arrival of a sharp letter from Schuyler which gave great offence to the powerful representatives of New England, who had no love for the New Yorker. They succeeded in persuading Congress to appoint Gates to the overall command at Ticonderoga, with such authority as, virtually if not officially, made him Chief of the Northern Department. Upon hearing of his supersession, Schuyler threw up his command, journeyed to Philadelphia where Congress had returned, and demanded ratification of his authority. On May 22nd Congress withdrew its censure and reaffirmed

Schuyler as supreme commander of the North, including Ticonderoga. By then the damage had been done: while Congress vacillated and the generals wrangled, the threat to Ticonderoga became forgotten.

The dispute stemmed from the mutual antipathy of two men of different backgrounds, which was exacerbated by Gates's intriguing nature and Schuyler's overbearing and haughty manner. The New Englanders favoured Gates and resented the discipline imposed on their free and easy soldiers by Schuyler, a New York landowner and a patrician of ancient Dutch lineage. They accused Schuyler of being a secret Tory, an unwarranted libel which derived from his encouragement of the claims of his state for the 'Hampshire Grants', the tract of land which later became Vermont and was coveted by the New Englanders. Gates, on the other hand, being the son of upper-class English servants, resented Schuyler's aristocratic birth and his military superiority. As a British commissioned officer who had served in the French and Indian War, and had married and settled in America at its close, Gates considered himself entitled to the high command which the amateur soldier Schuyler had attained. At the outbreak of the revolutionary war, Gates had been appointed adjutant-general of the Colonist army and commissioned major-general. He proved an excellent administrator, as also did Schuyler. In time, Gates reaped where Schuyler had sown.

Before he departed from Ticonderoga, to plead his cause to Congress, a journey from which he returned temporarily triumphant, Gates appointed 'mad' Anthony Wayne, the Colonel of the 4th Pennsylvania Militia, to command the fort because, as he explained to Congress, Wayne had the 'health and strength fit to encounter the inclemency of that cold, inhospitable region'. These attributes seem to have been called for by Wayne's own description of the place as one which 'appears to be the last part of the world that God made, and I have some ground to believe it was finished in the dark'. Wayne believed Ticonderoga to be the 'ancient Golgotha or Place of Skulls—they are so plentiful here that our people for want of other vessels drink out of them, whilst the soldiers make tent pins of the shin and thigh bones of Abercrombie's men.' (Wayne was recalling General Abercrombie's fatal assault on the old French lines in 1758.)

By December the garrison of the fort numbered a bare 1700 men, one-third of whom lacked shoes. Food was short and conditions were deplorable. Wayne reported: 'I paid a visit to the sick yesterday, in a small house called a hospital. The first object presented to my eyes, one man lying dead at the door, the inside two more lying dead, two living lying between them: the living with the dead had so lain for four and twenty hours.' Writing later in the month to the Pennsylvania Committee of Safety, he said: 'We have neither beds nor bedding for our sick to lay on or under, other than their own clothing; no medicine or regimen suitable for them; the dead and dying lying mingled together in our hospital, or rather our house of carnage, is no uncommon sight.'

The cobbler son of Colonel Asa Whitcomb of Massachusetts made a praiseworthy attempt to remedy the shortage of shoes, but this led to a bloody fracas; the exercise of his trade by an officer caused offence to the officers of Pennsylvania. Their Colonel Craig burst into Whitcomb's quarters, smashed the cobbler's bench, and struck the elderly Colonel Whitcomb, injuring him seriously. The noise attracted a crowd and a fight developed in which the men of Pennsylvania fired a number of shots, severely wounding several men of Massachusetts. Despite Craig's inexcusable conduct, the affair ended in farce when his men presented Colonel Whitcomb with a fat deer and joined him in a feast of venison.

At the end of January 1700 reinforcements reached the fort, thus releasing some of the undisciplined Pennsylvania Militia whose time had expired. In mid-February, however, when a further company decided that their time was up, and announced that they were going home 'come hell or high water', Wayne prevented them from leaving at pistol point. At the suggestion of the newly arrived engineer-officer, Colonel Jeduthan Baldwin, who found 'no sense of urgency or haste' at the fort, Wayne put the effectives to work building an abattis and two new block houses, and collecting lumber for the new bridge which was destined to replace the existing footbridge to the Vermont shore. Work on the new twelve-foot bridge was started when the ice began to break up at the end of March.

On his promotion to the rank of Major-General, Wayne, left Ticonderoga in April to join Washington. He informed his chief that 'all was well' at the fort and that 'it can never be carried, without much loss of blood', an inaccurate statement which further increased Washington's belief in the fort's impregnability and its consequent safety from attack. Gates, on the other hand, argued that the British would advance on Ticonderoga, and he hoped that 'Providence would conceal from Howe his true interest', which lay, Gates believed, in forming a junction of two armies on the line of the Hudson. Schuyler based *his* plans on the belief that the British in Canada would advance on Albany by the western route, via the Great Lakes and the Mohawk valley, rather than by the southern route through Ticonderoga. To counter both possibilities he ordered the construction on Lake George of two schooners, to replace those lost by Arnold in the previous summer, and he warned Nicholas Herkimer, in the Mohawk valley, to mobilize the Tyron County Militia. The schooners were built and manned, but there were no spare cannon with which to arm them.

An attempt early in May, by Major Benjamin Whitcomb, the chief scout at Ticonderoga, to learn the enemy's plans was frustrated when his scouts were driven away by the Indians who formed a screen around the British posts south of Montreal. The garrison at the fort remained in ignorance of Burgoyne's arrival until the end of the month, when a prisoner named

William Amsbury, who had been captured on the Onion River, revealed that the British had 10,000 troops in Canada, and that Burgoyne intended to advance on Albany, by way of Ticonderoga, with a diversion on the Mohawk. Was Amsbury's story true, or had he been sent to spread false information? He carried a British pass and a large sum of money, and letters to colonists from people in Montreal. St Clair, the new commander of the fort, concluded that Amsbury was a spy and sent him to Schuyler who passed on St Clair's opinion to Washington. On June 13th, Washington replied that, even if Amsbury's information was true, 'I cannot conceive it will be within the power of the enemy to execute it'.

Amsbury's true but suspect information increased the doubts and hesitations at Ticonderoga, where Gates, who was still in overall command, was advised by the recently arrived young Polish volunteer engineer-officer, Thaddeus Kosciuszko, that the ascent of Mount Defiance by large guns was practicable, once the steep sides had been graded by fatigue parties. But neither Gates nor anyone else commanded sufficient men to garrison the Mount in addition to the fort. When he was forced to relinquish his command, Schuyler, who complained that Gates had 'done nothing, comparatively speaking' to strengthen Ticonderoga, appointed the ex-British officer, Colonel Arthur St Clair, to command the fort. St Clair, who had served under Howe at the taking of Quebec, had settled in America at the end of the French war, marrying the heiress granddaughter of Governor James Bowdoin of Massachusetts. He reached the fort on June 12th, and there Schuyler followed him on June 19th.

Schuyler came to Ticonderoga to attend a council of officers, which was composed of Major-General St Clair and Brigadiers Roche de Fermoy, Poor, and Patterson. They agreed that, in the case of attack, the defence of both banks of Lake Champlain should be attempted; that if one or the other needed to be abandoned, the New York side should be evacuated first;

that the defences of Mount Independence should be improved; and that six weeks' work was required to strengthen them. Should the attack prove serious, more than a mere threat, it was decided that the garrison should retire before its retreat was cut off. With the recently arrived reinforcements, 3000 men—2000 of them Colonials and the rest militia—were available to man the frontage of 2000 yards. Many were barefoot, all were ragged, and the supplies were insufficient to hold the fort against a prolonged siege. Following his visit, Schuyler reported that the condition of the troops was beyond his worst apprehension, and there was little to encourage expectation of an adequate defence. Besides the garrison at Ticonderoga, only 700 men were under arms in the Northern Department.

Ticonderoga was a trap. The enormous prestige of the fort made evacuation without a fight unthinkable; a retreat, except in the face of a serious assault, would make impossible the position of the officer who ordered it. To evacuate the garrison in order to save it to fight another day would require a brave decision.

After the council had dispersed, scouts brought news that Indians had been seen on the lake; on June 25th they were observed at Crown Point, fifteen miles to the north. And Colonel James Wilkinson, the fort's adjutant, told his friend Horatio Gates, to whom he wrote to lament the fort's shortcomings, that the sails of a number of large vessels had been sighted.

What should be done? asked Wilkinson. He believed that the garrison should fall back on Fort George, at the end of the lake; for to attempt the defence of the fort could lead the garrison to 'lose all', and leave the country defenceless. Fortitude, enterprise, perseverance and temerity could do naught when a naked, ill-disciplined and badly-armed body of men were opposed by a vastly superior body of seasoned British troops.

Wilkinson, who was only twenty-one years of age, wrote his *Memoirs* of the campaign in which he served throughout as deputy adjutant-general to Gates, and in which, in his own opinion, he played an important part. He showed himself to be a zealous, if at times too eager officer, and earned for himself the dislike of his contemporaries. Whatever his failings may have been, we should, without his narrative, know little of the American side of the campaign against Burgoyne.

On June 30th, the British troops were within three miles of Ticonderoga, and in full view. Preceded by the gunboats, and the two frigates, the 200 *bateaux* and a host of lesser craft sailed majestically down the lake, undisguisable proof of British power and intention. Still St Clair refused to believe that the British advance constituted more than a feint. Before he left Philadelphia, Congress had assured him that the British would ship their army from Canada to New York by sea. No wonder St Clair was assailed by doubts.

v *Mount Defiance*

Noting in his diary, 'We are now within sight of the enemy', it pleased Anburey to think, 'We are now arrived before a place that is more talked of in this war than the last'.

Advancing from Crown Point, Burgoyne disembarked his troops, on both sides of the lake, the British on the west bank and the Germans on the eastern shore, three miles short of Ticonderoga. The two frigates, the *Inflexible* and the *Royal George*, with Burgoyne on board the latter, sailed to just beyond gunshot of the fort, which stood on the western bank of the lake, across the narrows from the recently fortified Mount Independence. The lofty summit of the Mount was now surmounted by a star-shaped fort, well supplied with artillery and containing a square barrack. The side of the hill that projected into the lake was well entrenched, and fortified with heavy artillery, some halfway down and some at water level, and all pointed down the lake, in the direction from which the attack was expected. The twelve-foot bridge to Ticonderoga was protected by a heavy barrier of logs chained together. On the west bank, Fort Ticonderoga itself was enclosed by the Old French lines, and guarded a mile to the west by the fortifications on Mount Hope. These consisted of one blockhouse on the summit and another by the 'carrying-place' to Lake George, where the rapidity of the creek running between the two lakes necessitated a portage. All three forts were dominated and overlooked by the unoccupied Mount Defiance. Examining the position, Anburey concluded, 'Fortified as the enemy are, nothing but a regular siege can dispossess them.'

To batter the fort into submission, Burgoyne had brought up a prodigious train of artillery. To prevent the garrison's escape, he needed to block three routes: the creek to Lake George, the waterway down Lake Champlain, and the wagon-track that ran south-eastwards from the rear of Mount Independence to Hubbardton and Castleton. Burgoyne sent Simon Fraser's brigade ahead to seize Mount Hope and he ordered von Riedesel and his Germans to circle round the isthmus upon which stood Mount Independence, a task in which he was impeded by the impassable marches, and by the East Creek on that shore, which forced him to make a wide detour.

Realizing that his men on Mount Hope were too exposed for safety, St Clair ordered its garrison to withdraw, a movement he sought to protect by a sortie. This, however, was driven back by Burgoyne's Indians, whose impetuosity allowed the Americans to retire with small loss, an incident which James Wilkinson, who stood in the Old French Lines, saw in detail. St Clair, he says, had ordered his troops to sit down with their backs to the parapet to prevent them from throwing away their fire, while the officers kept an eye on the enemy. A light infantryman crept up to within forty paces, taking refuge behind a stump whence he fired on the American lines. Wilkinson ordered a sergeant to rise and shoot him. The order was obeyed, and at the discharge of the musket every man arose, mounted the banquette, and without command fired a volley; the artillery followed the example, as did many of the officers, from the colonels down to the subalterns. Notwithstanding the exertions of the general, his aides, and several other officers, three rounds were discharged before they could stop the firing. When the smoke dispersed, the enemy were observed at three hundred yards distance, retreating helter-skelter.

Casting my eyes on the stump where I had perceived the infantryman whom I directed to be shot, I discovered him lying prostrate on his back, and mentioned the circumstance to General St Clair, who though exceedingly heated by the conduct of the troops, which he reprehended in the strongest language, replied to me with that mild philanthropy which distinguished his character, *"Send out a corporal and a file of men, and let the poor fellow be brought in and buried."* But as the corporal approached the supposed dead man, he jumped up, clubbed his musket, and exclaimed, "By Jasus, I killed the man at the sallyport; a fair shot". The fellow was brought in; he belonged to the 47th Light Infantry, and was intoxicated and insolent, refusing to give a word of information'.

The prisoner proved a valuable acquisition, as Wilkinson relates:

'To acquire such information as the prisoner might possess, a Captain Johnson of the artillery (a son of Hibernia) was metamorphosed into a Tory, and thrust into the guard-room with him: he soon became acquainted with his countryman, and with the aid of a bottle of rum which Johnson had concealed among his tattered apparel, he before midnight procured from his companion, who happened to be an intelligent old soldier, the number and name of every corps under General Burgoyne, with an estimate of their strength, afterwards found to be pretty accurate. This information removed all doubts relative to the force of the enemy, and their movements indicated an "investissement". Still General St Clair lacked resolution to give up the place, or in other words to sacrifice his character to the public good: for by several manoeuvres of his adversary on the 3rd and 4th, he was cheered with the hope that General Burgoyne intended to hazard an assault, which he was determined to await at all events'.

St Clair now knew the danger in which Ticonderoga stood. Still he hesitated; the British made up his mind for him.

The dramatic moment of the siege is unrecorded. On July 4th, someone, presumably engineer-officer Lieutenant Twiss for he has been given the credit, spotted Ticonderoga's glaring weakness—that both forts were dominated and overlooked by the sugar-loaf hill, named Fort Defiance, which rose to the south of the creek between the two lakes.

'Where a goat can go, a man can go, and where a man can go, he can drag a gun,' declared Phillips, who next day hauled two guns up the northern face of the Mount, after a path had been cleared by a fatigue party.

The British feat was disclosed by two blunders. First, the Indians committed the folly of lighting fires on the summit, and an even greater indiscretion has perpetrated, according to Wilkinson, by the gunners who fired at a vessel in the narrows, thus disclosing that they had succeeded in dragging up cannon, a statement which disposes of the allegation that St Clair ordered the evacuation of the forts before a gun had been fired from Mount Defiance. Hearing the firing he turned to Wilkinson, observing: 'We must away from this, for our situation has become desperate.' The council of officers which was immediately convened supported their general, each officer agreeing that the garrison should retreat at once. There was no alternative, for once the British had established artillery on the Mount, the fate of both forts was sealed.

The British were not ready to close the trap, for von Riedesel and his Germans were still labouring through the marshes on the eastern shore and the escape route remained open. At nightfall, Burgoyne retired to the *Royal George*. The full moon brilliantly illuminated the landscape.

As darkness fell, the evacuation of Fort Ticonderoga began. The secrecy with which the operation was conducted led to confusion: James Thacher, a doctor serving with the Continental army, was not aroused from sleep until midnight, when he was informed that the army was in motion. 'I could scarcely believe that my informant was in earnest, but the confusion and bustle soon convinced me.' He was ordered to collect the sick and wounded and to assist their embarkation on board the boats and *bateaux* lying at the landing-place. Escorted by armed ships and galleys, in which a number of women had also been loaded, and guarded by 600 soldiers commanded by Colonel Long, the heavily laden *bateaux* got away safely and sailed leisurely down the lake, their destination Skenesborough. Their passengers and crews laughed and exulted over their quiet and expeditious escape, believing that the boom and bridge across the narrows would delay pursuit.

The majority of the garrison, about 2500 men, having attempted ineffectually to destroy the bridge behind them, assembled on Mount Independence. Not, however, before three deserters had slipped away to the British lines, which they reached just before daylight, by which time the retirement had been disclosed by the Mount's slothful commander, the French adventurer Roche de Fermoy. He was found asleep in his tent, his men unprepared for evacuation. While they stumbled about, striking tents and loading packs, he gave the game away by setting fire to his tent, causing a conflagration that illuminated the scene and a dense column of smoke that was spotted at dawn by von Riedesel. Realizing that something was afoot, he advanced to the neck of the isthmus, but in time only to harrass the rear-guard of the garrison with a few parting shots.

The deserters brought the news of the retreat to the British just as dawn was breaking. Without waiting for General Burgoyne, to whom he sent an officer, Simon Fraser advanced his men to pursue the retreating garrison. So quickly did the pickets move that by daybreak the British flag had been hoisted on the ramparts of Fort Ticonderoga.

Simon Fraser's advance brigade hurried to seize the bridge of communication—to guard which four men had been posted on the eastern shore with a loaded cannon, trained on the bridge. Had these men obeyed their orders, says Anburey, 'they would, situated as our brigade was, have done great mischief'. But, 'allured by the sweets of plunder and liquor', instead of obeying, they were found lying dead drunk beside their cannon, with their matches lighted in readiness to fire it.

Even so, their purpose was nearly effected. At the time when the 9th Regiment was passing the bridge, an Indian of the advance bridge, which had repaired and crossed the bridge, came upon the cannon and, in Anburey's words, 'As he was very curious in examining everything that came his way, he took up the match that lay on the ground, with some fire remaining in it, when a spark dropping upon the pinning of the cannon, it went off, loaded with all manner of combustibles, but it fortunately happened that the gun was so elevated that no mischief was done.'

The advance brigade, followed by the Germans, hurried in pursuit of the retreating Americans who, Anburey learned, had gone to Hubbardton. The day was hot and sultry and the British marched very expeditiously, picking up stragglers, until 4 p.m., when we shall hear of them again.

Knowing, as he related in his despatch, 'how safely' he could leave the land pursuit to Simon Fraser, Burgoyne stationed one British and one German regiment to garrison the abandoned forts and ordered the fleet to break the boom across the narrows and pursue the American flotilla. This bridge, stated Burgoyne, was raised on twenty-two sunken piers, in between which were separate floats, each fifty feet long and twelve feet wide, strongly fastened together by chains and rivets. The bridge was further protected on the north by the boom made of large pieces of wood riveted and chained together. The retiring garrison believed that this formidable obstacle would delay pursuit in time for the boats to reach Skenesborough. Aided by the following wind, the British gunboats smashed through boom and bridge within half an hour. By 9 a.m. the water route to the south had been reopened.

The deeply laden American boats and *bateaux*, into which a number of cannon had been loaded, sailed in leisurely fashion down Lake Champlain which, within six miles of Ticonderoga, narrows to less than a quarter of a mile between the steep cliffs. The sun burst forth in the morning with uncommon lustre, the day was fine, the water's surface serene and unruffled,' recorded Dr Thacher:

'The shore on each side exhibited a variegated view of huge rocks, caverns and cliffs, and the whole was bounded by a thick, impenetrable wilderness. My pen would fail in the attempt to describe a scene so enchantingly sublime. The occasion was peculiarly interesting, and we could but look back with regret, and forward with apprehension. We availed ourselves, however, of the means of enlivening our spirits. The drum and fife afforded us a favourite music; among the hospital stores we found many dozens of choice wines, and we cheered our hearts with the nectareous contents.'

So convinced were the fugitives that they had left their pursuers far behind struggling to break through the boom and bridge, that they neglected to utilize the narrowness of the lake—'so narrow in some places that the Ships' Yards almost touched the Precipies which over-hung them', according to Hadden—to post guns on the cliffs to delay the British. Hadden says, they 'might have done great execution by leaving a Detachment on shore to harass them, and this Party would have retired and concealed themselves from any force landed against them'.

Confident that they had outstripped their pursuers, the Americans reached Skenesborough (the modern Whitehall) at 1 p.m., anchoring and drawing their vessels ashore in South Bay and Wood Creek, the sluggish stream that led to Fort Anne, sixteen miles to the south.

'Here', says Dr Thacher, 'we were unsuspicious of danger, but behold! Burgoyne himself was at our heels. In less than two hours we were struck with surprise and consternation by a discharge of cannon from the enemy's fleet on our gallies and bateaux lying at the wharf. By uncommon efforts and industry they had broken through the bridge, boom and chain, which cost our people such immense labour, and had almost overtaken us on the lake, and horridly disastrous indeed would have been our fate. It was not long before it was perceived that a number of their troops and savages had landed and were rapidly advancing towards our little party.'

Preceeded by gunboats, the *Royal George* and *Inflexible*, followed by numerous *bateaux* carrying three regiments, swept into the bay, firing upon the American vessels, setting fire to three and causing the crews to abandon two. Burgoyne landed his troops between South Bay and Wood Creek with the intention of enveloping the log fort at Skenesborough, where the Americans had taken refuge. He underestimated the difficulties of the rough and wooded terrain, which delayed the British advance, giving the fugitives time to burn the stockaded fort, and the iron works belonging to Colonel Skene, and retreat. Dr Thacher continues his story:

'The officers of our guard now attempted to rally the men and form them in battle array, but this was found impossible, every effort proved unavailable and in the utmost panic they were seen to fly in every direction for personal safety. In this desperate condition, I perceived our officers scampering for their baggage; I ran to the bateau, seized my chest, carried it a short distance, took from it a few articles, and instantly followed in the train of our retreating party. We took the route to Fort Anne through a narrow defile in the woods, and were so closely pressed by the pursuing enemy that we frequently heard calls from the rear to "march on; the Indians are at our heels". Having marched all night, we reached Fort Anne at 5 o'clock in the morning, where we found provisions for our refreshment. A small rivulet called Wood Creek is navigable from Skenesborough to Fort Anne, by which means some of our invalids and baggage made their escape; but all our cannon [and] provisions and the bulk of our baggage, with several invalids, fell into the enemy's hands.'

Colonel John Hill, with a small detachment, 190 strong, was sent in pursuit. Bad roads, broken bridges, and burning trees— for the conflagration at Skenesborough had spread into the pine forest—delayed him, and it took the soldiers all day to march to within one mile of Fort Anne, capturing on Wood Creek several boats loaded with women and invalids. Hill's men halted and lay on their arms all night.

Sergeant Roger Lamb, the diarist who acted as surgeon's mate, takes up the story:

'Early next morning, 9th July, an American soldier came from the fort; he said that he had deserted, though it was afterwards discovered that he was a spy; he stated that there were one thousand men in the fort, and that they were in the greatest consternation, under an apprehension of the British attacking and storming them; upon this intelligence Colonel Hill dispatched a message to General Burgoyne stating his situation, and how far he had advanced, which was eight to ten miles from the main army.

Not many minutes after this message was sent off, the pretended deserter disappeared; he had viewed the situation and seen the strength of the British, which did not amount to above one hundred and ninety men including officers. It was soon found that he made a faithful report to his friends, for in less than half an hour they came out of the fort with great fury. The British outlining sentries received them with the great bravery and steadiness, and obliged them to retreat; they then returned again and came on with redoubled violence.'

The Americans, encouraged by the spy's report and the arrival of 400 New York Militia, led by Colonel Van Rensselaer, attacked the British in a narrow defile, which Dr Thacher calls a 'covert in the woods'.

'The two parties were soon engaged in a smart skirmish, which continued for several hours and resulted greatly to our honour and advantage; the enemy being almost surrounded, were on the point of surrendering, when our ammunition being expended, and a party of Indians arriving and setting up the war-whoop, this being followed by three cheers from their friends the English, the Americans were induced to give way and retreat. One surgeon, with a wounded captain (Captain Montgomery), and twelve or fifteen privates, were taken and brought into our fort. The surgeon informed me that he was in possession of books, etc., taken from my chest at Skenesborough, and, singular to relate, some of the British prisoners obtained in the same manner, and had in their pockets a number of *private letters* which I had received from a friend in Massachusetts, and which were now returned to me.'

Thacher, like his compatriots, was deceived by that war-whoop. Upon receiving the spy's intelligence that the Americans at Fort Anne had been reinforced, Colonel Hill had sent a message to Burgoyne, stating that he would hold his ground and await reinforcements. When he received this message, Burgoyne sent orders to Hill to retire and despatched the remainder of the first Brigade, under Brigadier-General Powell, to cover his retreat.

Meanwhile, Hill's position had become critical, for, by crossing the creek, the Americans had gained his rear. Fearing that his position might be turned, Hill abandoned his wounded men and retreated to the summit of the hill, where he stood off the American attack for two hours, until both sides ran out of ammunition. At that moment a war-whoop was heard from the woods to the north. Suspecting that this denoted the approach of British reinforcements, the Americans fled. In fact, the war-whoop came from a lone British officer who, deserted by his Indian scouts, had employed this stratagem to lead the enemy to believe that he headed a powerful force.

This minor skirmish a mile and a half from Fort Anne may have been the first occasion on which the 'Stars and Stripes' were flown in battle, for Hadden describes a captured American flag as having thirteen red and white stripes and a 'constellation'.

The Americans who, according to the anonymous diarist, had suffered 200 casualties, withdrew to Fort Anne which they set on fire, and retreated thirty miles southward to Fort Edward. The British also withdrew leaving behind in the defile the wounded men of whom Sergeant Lamb had charge, and who could not be moved. He describes his experience:

'It was a distressing sight to see the wounded men bleeding on the ground; and what made it more so, the rain came pouring down like a deluge upon us. And still, to add to the distress of the sufferers, there was nothing to dress their wounds, as the small medicine box, which was filled with salve, was left behind with Surgeon Shelly and Captain Montgomery at the time of our movement up the hill. The poor fellows earnestly entreated me to tie up their wounds. Immediately, I took off my shirt, tore it up, and, with the help of a soldier's wife (the only woman who was with us, and who kept closely by her husband's side during the engagement), made some bandages, stopped the bleeding of their wounds, and conveyed them in blankets to a small hut about two miles to our rear. Our regiment now marched back to Skenesborough, leaving me behind to attend the wounded, with a small guard for our protection. I was directed, that in case I should be either surrounded or overpowered by the Americans, to deliver a letter, which General Burgoyne gave me, to their Commanding Officer.

'Here I remained seven days with the wounded men, expecting every moment to be taken prisoner; but, although we heard the enemy cutting down trees every night during our stay, in order to block up the passages of the road and river, yet we were never molested. Every necessary which we wanted was sent us from the camp at Skenesborough, and all the wounded men (except three who died) were nearly fit for duty when we arrived at headquarters.'

Thus, within five days of the occupation of Mount Defiance, Burgoyne had captured forts Ticonderoga and Independence, and had pursued the Americans who had fled down Lake Champlain, destroyed their boats, captured their guns, and had forced them to retreat to Fort Edward, the post on the Hudson River. We can now return to the morning of July 6th, Generals Simon Fraser and von Riedesel are in pursuit of the bulk of the garrison who have taken the circuitous route to Hubbardton.

VI *Hubbardton*

Simon Fraser halted his men at 4 p.m. With General Burgoyne's approval he had marched at full speed from Mount Independence at 5 a.m. in pursuit of the retreating garrison, which had taken the rough wagon-track to Hubbardton, and Castleton. Allowing his 850 men, the *élite* of the British troops, no time to eat, collect rations, or even to fill their canteens, and rounding up a handful of Indians from those who were plundering the abandoned forts, Fraser plunged into the thickly wooded hilly country, which was intersected by streams and dotted with ponds and lakes. Behind, at Burgoyne's command, marched General von Riedesel, leading his advance corps and one regiment of the Brunswickers, about 1100 men, with orders to act on his own judgment. Halting frequently to align their ranks, the plodding Germans lagged behind the swifter British troops.

Burgoyne had achieved his ostensible objective—the capture of Fort Ticonderoga, but the garrison had escaped, and might combine with the party that had escaped by boat to bar his path to Albany.

Fraser, with von Riedesel in support, was sent to chase and push St Clair towards Skenesborough, where Burgoyne, with his main army, would be awaiting him. It was a good plan, but one which failed to take into consideration two important factors. The retreating Americans would be campaigning in rough, wooded country that favoured their mobile, frontier-trained troops; and St Clair, learning of Burgoyne's presence at Skenesborough, would make a wide detour, thereby drawing his pursuers deeper and deeper into the trackless wilderness.

How quickly could Simon Fraser catch St Clair? He needed

74

to bring him to battle before the lagging Germans fell too far behind to act in support. Hurrying ahead of his men, von Riedesel joined Fraser at 4 p.m., when he halted to give his troops a breather. The two officers conferred. The day had become intensely hot and the corpulent German sweated profusely, his wig hanging askew.

Von Riedesel's superior rank made the situation awkward; a clash of personalities could destroy the objective of the pursuit. It was a delicate interview, for Simon Fraser was a particular friend of Burgoyne's who, from the start of the expedition, had snubbed the German officer, excluding him from staff conferences. Fortunately Fraser and von Riedesel were both reasonable men.

Although, as he wrote later to a friend in England, 'he felt very much hurt to be embarrassed by a senior officer', Fraser explained that he acted on General Burgoyne's direct order to 'push on and at his discretion to attack any body of rebels that he might come up with', and that he was determined to do that. With von Riedesel's 'permission' he would march on for a further three miles, bivouac for the night, and attack the Americans next day. Von Riedesel deferred to Fraser, whom he respected as an active regimental commander and as an experienced soldier who had campaigned for most of his life in North America. When Fraser advanced, he would bring up his slow-moving Germans to the place where the British advance corps had halted, and would march to support them at 3 a.m. next day. If Fraser found the Americans too strong to attack, he would await von Riedesel's arrival.

The difficulty thus amicably settled and an understanding reached, Fraser marched his men on for three miles, reaching a place known as Lacey's Camp, which the Americans had left not an hour before. He settled his men down for the night, foodless except for the flesh of a cow which the marksmen had killed in the woods.

During the hours of darkness, the Indians prowling ahead

captured and brought to the British camp an American sentry. From this man, or from the several stragglers his men had picked up during the day, Fraser learned that the American rearguard was composed of picked men and was commanded by one of their best officers, Colonel Ebenezer Francis. The bulk of the retreating garrison were well ahead, the militia eager to increase their distance from their pursuers.

The capture of the sentry was to have startling repercussions for, apparently, the exhausted Americans had left only one man to watch for the enemy's approach. Denied timely warning, they were caught napping.

Pushing on vigorously all day, St Clair, with his main force, skirted the northern end of Lake Bomoseen. He reached the tiny hamlet of Hubbardton (now East Hubbardton), where the twenty-two-mile wagon track from Mount Independence joined the old road from the eastern shore of Lake Champlain opposite Crown Point, and ran southwards to Castleton. St Clair did not stop at Hubbardton. Spurred on by the rumour that 500 Tories and Indians had passed that way, a true though exaggerated report, he marched his troops for another six miles and halted for the night at Castleton.

Before leaving Hubbardton, St Clair ordered Colonel Seth Warner, with his regiment of 'Green Mountain Boys', and Colonel Nathan Hale and his 2nd New Hampshire Regiment, to await the arrival of the rearguard, with positive orders to Warner, the senior officer, to bring all three regiments at once to Castleton. Francis, with his 11th Massachusetts Regiment, caught up with Warner and Hale about 4 p.m., and all three officers retired to a cabin, built by a settler named Sellick, where they conferred.

It has been argued that Warner, by disobeying orders, failed to draw Fraser upon St Clair's superior force, thereby costing the Americans a notable victory, and that, by bringing the pursuers to precipitate action, he saved the American main body from annihilation. In a more realistic view, he risked disobeying orders and endangered his own force in order to safeguard the main body, the correct procedure in retreat. His decision to halt, however, may have been induced by the exhausted condition of Fraser's and Hale's regiments who, after their march in sweltering heat, were unable to go further. The three colonels, believing that they had outpaced the slow-moving regulars, may have decided to give their men a rest before catching up with the main body.

The New Hampshire Regiment, about 360 men, with a hundred or so stragglers bivouacked for the night on Sucker Brook, the little stream that crossed the road and drained the valley to the east of which rose the high ridge, surmounted by the wagon-track leading to its junction with the old road to Castleton. Francis, who commanded 420 Massachusetts Continentals, occupied the high ground around the Sellick cabin, some of which was cleared farm land. Warner, with his 173 Vermonters, took position in the woods along the ridge which enabled him both to guard the road from Crown Point, and, if necessary, to act in support of Francis and Hale. The American left was dominated by a towering, rocky hill 1200 feet high, with a precipitous face, which was later named Zion Hill.

Colonels Warner and Francis formed a plan: in the case of attack the Vermonters would provide the pivot upon which the Continentals could manoeuvre, with the object of turning the enemy's left, while, in case of need, either could support the other. It is not clear why Hale's regiment, the weakest of the three, was allowed to occupy the most advanced and vulnerable position. Maybe Hale and his men, having reached the brook, refused to budge. Nathan Hale (no relation to the Connecticut spy of that name), came in for as much criticism after the battle, as did his chief, Seth Warner. Hale and his men were accused of cowardice whereas, it seems, they were overcome by panic when they were unexpectedly surprised at their breakfast. The Americans did not expect to be caught that night or early next day; they underestimated the zeal of their pursuers.

Shortly before sunrise, or about 4.40 a.m., on July 7th, Fraser's advance corps, with the Tories, Jessup and Peters, in the van, found themselves, after a march of three miles, near the rebels. According to his promise, von Riedesel had set his troops in motion, forging ahead himself with 180 jagers and grenadiers.

Fraser, whose small force was made up of the 24th Regiment of Foot, led by Major Grant, the Light Infantry commanded by the Earl of Balcarres, and the Grenadiers by Major Acland, halted his men on the lip of the valley through which ran Sucker Brook, about 800 yards distant. From the floor of the valley came the twinkle of camp fires. Fraser ordered the 24th Regiment to flush out the breakfasters.

Deploying his men into extended order, Grant led them down the wooded slope. From the New Hampshire soldiers came the cry, 'The enemy is upon us'. The regiment, says young Ebenezer Fletcher, one of the stragglers who had been picked up the day before, was 'in a very unfit posture for battle'. Hale's men, led by their colonel, scattered into the woods. Warned by the popping of muskets that Hale's regiment had been caught, Warner launched his Vermonters. Taking cover behind fallen trees, they fired into the advancing British, killing twenty men, including Major Grant who had exposed himself by climbing on to a tree trunk to reconnoitre the position.

From their vantage point by the Sellick cabin, Warner and Francis watched the rout of the New Hampshire regiment, and saw the British surging across the creek and swarming up the slope, a scene from which their attention was diverted by the clatter of hoofs. The galloper from St Clair brought terrible news: the British had broken through the boom at Ticonderoga, sailed to Skenesborough and had captured the garrison's baggage, powder, and cannon. The escape route to the south had been cut, and St Clair would be forced to make a wide detour, via the town of Rutland, to reach the Hudson. He ordered

Warner to follow at once, but it was too late. The lagging rear-guard had been caught and the British were advancing to get astride the road to Castleton.

'In great haste', Colonel Francis hurried back to his Massachusetts Regiment, which he found had drawn up on the Crown Point–Castleton road, on the orders of his adjutant, Major Moses Greenleaf, who meticulously noted the time in his diary '7.¼', a two-hour discrepancy from the times recorded by the British diarists that cannot be accounted for. 'We must move with great expedition, or the enemy will be upon us', remarked Francis; a superfluous comment, it would seem, for the situation was developing with startling rapidity.

Along the half-mile front, the British, sweeping aside the few Vermonters who had gone to Hale's rescue, were swarming up the slope with the clear intention of cutting the Americans' retreat. Warner and Francis sought to counter this move by turning the British left which would drive them back across the wagon-track, and sever their line of communications. Which tactic would succeed would depend upon imponderable factors. On the one side, there was the ardour and zeal of the British, fired by their achievement in catching their prey; on the other, the steadfastness and discipline of the Americans. For they, although surprised while in full flight, gained by their higher position, greater mobility, capacity to take cover, and accurate rapid fire, which led the inexperienced Lieutenant Digby, whose first serious engagement this was, to overestimate their numbers. Less than one thousand British were attacking double that number, he thought.

Although he was outnumbered Simon Fraser did not hesitate. He sent Balcarres with the Light Infantry and the 24th Regiment to ascend the steep slopes ahead, with orders to fan out and roll up the enemy's right, thus pushing them away from the road to Castleton. Major Acland with his grenadiers was ordered to climb the precipitous height of Mount Zion, the summit of which commanded the road. To von Riedesel he sent word that he was committing his whole force to full battle, urging him to hurry.

Colonel Francis, 'that gallant and brave man', as Digby calls him, advanced his regiment to the crest of the ridge and swung it into line; below, the British were fast climbing the slopes of 'Monument Hill', as it was later called. Into the jumbled mass of climbers, the Massachusetts men poured their well-directed fire. The Light Infantry reeled back under the shower of ball and buckshot, stumbling and tumbling down the slope they had climbed with such zeal. Young Digby thought he would find himself suddenly projected into the presence of his Creator, an idea to which he reconciled himself by the pious thought that 'a proper resignation to the will of the Divine Being is the certain foundation of true bravery'. Shout as they might, the officers failed to halt the retreat until the soldiers had recrossed the brook. Twenty-one men of the leading platoon had been killed or wounded, and Balcarres had been shot through the arm. At the end of the action he counted thirty bullet holes in his jacket.

On the right, the British had achieved their objective. Slinging their muskets and scrambling up the incline, which Anburey calls 'almost inaccessible', clutching tree roots and sometimes resting their feet on pieces of rock, Acland's grenadiers, in imminent danger of falling ('had any been so unfortunate as to have missed his hold, he must inevitably have been dashed to pieces') or being fired upon, reached the summit of the unoccupied Mount Zion. Too late, Warner sent some of his men to forestall them. Spotting that threat, Acland detached two companies of grenadiers. Anburey describes the incident:

'During the battle the Americans were guilty of such a breach of all military rules as could not fail to exasperate our soldiers. The action was chiefly in woods, interspersed with a few open fields. Two companies of grenadiers, who were stationed in the skirts of the wood, close to one of these fields, to watch

3. Horatio Gates. By Chappel (*New York Public Library*)

4. Philip Schuyler. By Chappel (*New York Public Library*)

that the enemy did not outflank the 24th Regiment, observed a number of the Americans, to the amount of near sixty, coming across the field with their arms clubbed, which is always considered to be a surrender as prisoners of war. The grenadiers were restrained from firing, commanded to stand with their arms and shew no intention of hostility; when the Americans had got within ten yards, they in an instant turned round their muskets, fired upon the grenadiers, and ran as fast as they could into the woods; their fire killed and wounded a great number of men, and those who escaped immediately pursued them and gave no quarter.'

Acland, struck in the thigh by a musket-ball, urged his men on; a small guard stayed with him while the rest of the climbers, and the survivors of the American stratagem, ran down the hill and threw themselves across the Castleton road. Warner, his left flank exposed, pulled his men back to the road junction in the vicinity of the Sellick cabin, where they took cover behind the log and stone fence, protected in front by open fields which were exposed to fire.

The British repulse on the left had been compensated by the success on the right. The Americans' retreat to Castleton was barred, but their defence stood firm. Again the infantry pressed up Monument Hill. On the crest, the Massachusetts Regiment crouched behind fallen logs and the stone fence. Lapping his men round the American right, Balcarres pushed up the hill. Realizing the danger, Francis threw his regiment down the slope the men taking cover behind trees whence they poured a point-blank fire upon the crowded British infantry. The unexpected counterattack halted the assault, and again the British recoiled. A ball grazed Balcarres's shoulder and two officers were killed. Colonel Francis's right arm was shattered by a bullet. He pulled his men back to the crest of the ridge.

For the second time Simon Fraser's offensive had failed. Casting anxious glances to the rear, he sent a message to von

Riedesel that the enemy were in such force that he was unable to withstand 'unless he was speedily reinforced'.

Hearing 'brisk firing' ahead, von Riedesel urged on his 180 jagers and grenadiers. He had set forth at 3 a.m., as he had promised, followed by Lieutenant-Colonel Heinrich von Breymann's regiment of one thousand men. The jagers and grenadiers panted up the hill from where, earlier that morning, Fraser had spotted the New Hampshire men at breakfast. From the same knoll, von Riedesel swept the battleground with his gaze; his experienced eye noted the predominance of musketry on the left, on the slopes of Monument Hill. Sending back word to von Breymann to hurry, and cursing his slowness, he led the sweating advance guard to the British left, where the need was greatest. He ordered their little band to play them into battle in order to make the enemy believe that his whole regiment was engaged.

The crackle of musketry carried the seven miles to Castleton. Guessing its significance, St Clair despatched his aides, Colonel Brockholst Livingstone and Major Dunn, to turn back the two militia regiments, which had encamped four miles from Castleton, and hurry them to Warner's rescue. He ordered his own men to prepare for action, exhorting them, records Wilkinson, to courageous conduct. 'I perceived a manifest repugnance in the corps to turn about and march upon the enemy; even one of the Brigadiers was open in his opposition to the measure.' Livingstone and Dunn encountered a similar distaste for battle when they met the two militia regiments fleeing from the scene of action, and beyond the control of Colonel Bellows. Finding them deaf to entreaties, they hurried on towards Hubbardton, two miles away, taking solace from the swelling rattle of musketry.

Fraser had launched his third assault on Monument Hill, the crest of which was held by Francis's men who half encircled the summit. Unaware as yet of von Riedesel's approach, Fraser sent Balcarres and his infantry to carry the hill and dislodge the

Massachusetts men at bayonet point—a task that might have proved beyond them, but for the timely arrive of von Riedesel. From across the valley came the sound of music, the braying of hunting horns, the squeal of hautboy, and the singing of battle hymns. The strange noise made Anburey apprehensive that the American rearguard had received reinforcements from the main body.

Keeping up an incessant fire with their rifles, Captain Clark von Geyso's 100 jagers came up on Balcarres' left. Captain Maximilian Schottelius's 800 grenadiers encircled the hill, gained the crest on the American's right, and turned southward to envelop them. The Massachusetts men fell back in disorder across the road, where Francis rallied them behind the log fence, ordering his men to reload their muskets. With their front cleared, the British infantry surmounted the crest. Pausing only to catch their breath, they and the jagers dressed their ranks for a charge.

Francis seized the opportunity while the enemy were in disarray to leap over the breastwork and call upon his men for one good volley. A German rifle bullet crashed through his heart. Dispirited by their leader's death (the Monument marks the spot), the Massachusetts men melted into the woods, forestalling by their flight the British bayonet charge and the concentrated volleys of the advancing grenadiers. Realizing that the fight was lost, Warner coolly told his Vermonters to 'scatter, and meet me at Manchester'. They, too, drifted away through the woods.

The action which lasted for forty-five minutes was over. Saved in the nick of time by von Riedesel's arrival the British had won the hill and driven off the American rearguard. But once again they had failed to capture part of the retreating garrison.

Listening anxiously at Castleton, St Clair heard the crackle of musketry die away. The silence was broken by the clattering feet of Colonel Bellows' two regiments of militia, who had bolted rather than face the British. An hour later, Livingstone and Dunn returned to report the result of the action. 'All is over,' announced St Clair. He turned his men in the only direction left open, leading them, via Rutland and Manchester, and Bennington, to Fort Edward on the Hudson, where he linked up with General Schuyler on July 12th.

On the battlefield the exhausted British counted their losses fifty killed and one hundred wounded, which, with the German casualties (ten killed and fourteen wounded) brought the total to 174, and rounded up their prisoners. At the end of the action, soldiers who had been sent to scour the woods for wild cattle found Hale's men wandering about. They surrendered with their colonel, bringing the total number of prisoners to 228, including one colonel, seven captains, ten subalterns, and 210 men. The victors collected 200 muskets. Nathan Hale was released on parole on July 20th in order, at his request, to answer the allegations of cowardice and treason that had been made against him. No charges were made and, when he was not exchanged, he gave himself up. He died on September 23, 1780, while a prisoner of war on Long Island. His behaviour at Hubbardton was never investigated and it remains ambiguous.

Fraser did not know whether the enemy had fled or were, in his words, 'in force near me, and gathering strength hourly'. With 150 wounded men of both armies on his hands, he ordered a halt. His soldiers were exhausted by their long march in stifling heat, and the steep climb, and were in no state to continue the pursuit. Those wounded in the battle, irrespective of nationality, were treated with equal care. They were carried into the Sellick cabin and, when that was full, laid under cover of rough arbors which the able-bodied prisoners had been put to work to build. Ebenezer Fletcher, aged sixteen who had only just recovered from the measles, had been shot in the back. Feigning dead, he was spotted by looters, who were in the act of stripping off his boots when a British officer arrived on the scene and secured their return. Fletcher's wound was dressed and it healed gradually. Two weeks later, on July 23rd, he escaped into the woods, reaching his home after a series of adventures, including a chase by wolves. Fifty years later he wrote the story of his adventures that day, and of his miraculous escape from captivity.

Several Americans, apparently, had halted in their flight and remained in the woods, sniping at the victors on the ridge. A ball struck and mortally wounded Captain Shrimpton of the 62nd Regiment, as he was standing over the body of Colonel Francis, examining his pocket-book and papers. A drummer-boy secured Francis's watch before the body was buried, an incident to which Digby supplies an epilogue. In 1778 when he and other officers were prisoners at Cambridge in Massachusetts he says:

'A few days since walking out with some officers, we stopped at at a house to purchase vegetables. While the other officers were bargaining with the woman of the house, I observed an elderly woman sitting by the fire, who was continually eyeing us, and every now and then shedding a tear. Just as we were quitting the house she got up, and bursting into tears, said; "Gentlemen, would you let a poor distracted woman speak a word to you before you go?" We, as you must naturally imagine, were all astonished, and upon enquiring what she wanted, with the most poignant grief and sobbing as if her heart was on the point of breaking, she asked if any of us knew her son, who was killed at the battle of Hubbardton a Colonel Francis. Several of us informed her, that we had seen him after he was dead. She then enquired about his pocket-book and if any of his papers were safe as some related to his estates, and if any of the soldiers had got his watch; if she could but obtain that in remembrance of her dear-dear son, she should be happy. Captain Ferguson, of our regiment, who was of the party, told her, as to the Colonel's papers and pocket book, he was fearful that they were either lost or destroyed, but pulling a watch from his fob, said, "There, good woman, if that can make you happy, take it and God bless you.' We were all much surprised, as unacquainted, as he had made a purchase of it from a drum boy. On seeing it, it is impossible to describe the joy and grief that was depicted in her countenance; I never in all my life beheld such a strength of passion. She kissed it, looked unutterable gratitude at Captain Ferguson, then kissed it again; her feelings were inexpressible. She knew not how to express or show them. She would repay his kindness by kindness, but could only sob her thanks. Our feelings were lifted up to an inexpressible height. We promised to search after the papers, and I believe, at that moment, could have hazarded life itself to procure them.'

The long day ended in drenching rain and the British and Germans spent a miserable night under arms, 'not knowing', records Digby, 'but the enemy might be reinforced and come again to attack'. There was no need for alarm for, during the day, Colonel von Breymann had arrived with his fresh troops. Next day, von Riedesel marched his Germans to Skenesborough, where he was followed by Fraser, leaving the wounded to be evacuated to Ticonderoga, which they reached on July 22nd.

In his despatch describing the week's events, Burgoyne paid scant justice to the decisive intervention of von Riedesel in the battle, remarking only that 'the Germans pressed for a share in the glory and they arrived in time to obtain it'. Writing three weeks later, he unconsciously paid tribute to the American achievement in slipping away to fight another day, saying, 'The New Hampshire Grants [i.e. the unconquered area on his flank] now abounds in the most active and rebellious race of the Continent, and hangs like a gathering storm on my left.' When Burgoyne wrote those words he was already beginning to despair; but on July 12th, he was still full of confidence.

VII *Fort Edward*

Alarmed by reports of Burgoyne's progress down Lake Champlain, and disturbed by stories that the Indians were murdering and scalping along the border from Fort Stanwix to the Susquehanna River, General Schuyler left his home at old Saratoga on July 5th with the intention of travelling to Ticonderoga. On the 7th, *en route* to Fort Edward, he met Colonel Hay who reported that the fort had been evacuated, and that St Clair had disappeared into the wilderness. Schuyler sent reinforcements to Fort Edward and returned to his base at Albany, whence he wrote to General Washington;

'I have not been able to learn what is become of General St Clair and the enemy. And what adds to my distress is, that a report prevails that I had given orders for the evacuation of Ticonderoga, whereas not the most distant hint of such an intention can be drawn from any of my letters to General St Clair, or any other person whatever. What could induce General Officers to a step that has ruined our affairs in this quarter, God only knows'.

He himself (Schuyler told Washington) could muster no more than 1500 men; and his prospect of preventing the enemy from penetrating further was 'not much'. 'They have an army', he said 'flushed with victory, plentifully provided with provisions, cannon and every warlike store. Our army, if it should once more collect, is weak in numbers, dispirited, naked, in a manner destitute of provisions, without camp equipage, with little ammunition, and not a single cannon.' He did not know what had become of St Clair and feared he might have been overtaken and compelled to surrender. 'The country is in the deepest consternation,' Schuyler lamented.

Washington, in his reply, did not conceal his chagrin and surprise at an event 'not apprehended, nor within the compass of my reasoning'. To the commander-in-chief the whole affair was so mysterious that 'it even baffles conjecture'. The prospect was dark and gloomy, but 'our affairs are not desperate, and our exertions ought to be in proportion to our misfortunes and our exigencies'.

Throughout the Colonies, and especially in New York and New England, the abandonment without a fight of the 'Impregnable Bastion' occasioned, in the words of Dr Thacher who had reached Fort Edward, 'the greatest surprise and alarm'. 'No event,' he said, 'could be more unexpected, nor more severely felt throughout our army and country.'

Incredulity quickly gave way to wrath, and an explosion of charges and counter-charges. The New Englanders raised a clamour against Generals Schuyler and St Clair, who became the objects of furious denunciation. They were accused of treachery, it being said openly that they had been paid for their treason by silver balls, shot by Burgoyne's guns into the camp at Ticonderoga, which had been collected at their order and divided between them. In a letter to his wife, John Adams observed that 'we shall never be able to defend a post until we have shot a general'.

The truth, that the undermanned fort had become a trap, and that St Clair, as John Trumbull remarked, 'merited thanks for having saved part of the devoted garrison', was too unpalatable for general acceptance. He would have ordered the retreat, even if the council of officers had disagreed, stated St Clair on his arrival at Fort Edward, for 'the loss of the fort was infinitely preferable to the loss of the army'. In 1778 he was charged with 'neglect of duty' and honourably acquitted by a court martial.

Schuyler's vindication came too late to save him from the malice of the New Englanders. He was subjected to violent personal attacks, and the loss of the fort was attributed to his evil genius. Gates, it was implied, would have saved Ticonderoga.

The controversy surrounding Schuyler and Gates, and the loss of Ticonderoga, derived from inter-state rivalry. Neither general could have defended the fort with the means at their disposal. Even if Washington had correctly discerned Burgoyne's purpose, he could not have both reinforced the Northern Department and kept his own army in existence. He did not believe that the British were capable of dividing the colonies by advancing from Canada to Albany. That they could achieve that remained to be proved, and the garrison of Ticonderoga had been saved. The Americans had suffered a misfortune which might ultimately prove advantageous, as Dr Thacher observed in his journal, by drawing the British into the heart of the country, and thereby place them more immediately in our power'.

Alexander Hamilton put it more succinctly: 'I am in hope that Burgoyne's success will precipitate him into measures that will prove his ruin. The enterprising spirit he has credit for, I expect, may easily be fanned by vanity into rashness.'

Emerging from the obscurity of his roundabout march of 110 miles, St Clair reached Fort Edward seven days after he had left Ticonderoga, his men haggard and worn, but safe. Their escape increased the number of troops available to defend the Northern Department to 4000 men, 3000 of whom were Continentals. At Washington's order, Brigadier-General John Nixon hurried north from Peekskill with 600 men. But as General Schuyler lamented, 'Desertion prevails, and disease gains ground; nor is it to be wondered at, for we have neither tents, houses, barns, boards or any shelter except a little brush; every rain that falls, and we have it in great abundance almost every day, wets the men to the skin. We are besides in great want of every kind of necessaries, provision excepted. Camp kettles we have so few, that we cannot afford one to twenty men.' A third of his Contental troops were 'not fit for the field, and many of the officers would be a disgrace to the most contemptible troop that ever was collected'. He had only thirty cannon at Fort George, and no carts by which to move them. The British were only twenty miles away and 'a very great proportion of the inhabitants are taking protection from General Burgoyne, as most of those in this quarter are also willing to do'. Schuyler despaired of holding Burgoyne 'who is bending his course this way'. He begged Washington for reinforcements.

Washington had none to send. He debated which course to pursue; to hurry north to crush Burgoyne and return quickly to defend Philadelphia, or to watch and follow Howe whom, he believed, might either sail up the Hudson or go to Philadelphia. Washington's mind was made up for him; one-fifth of his soldiers had no shoes, and two forced marches over rough roads were impossible. He remained in New Jersey to watch Howe. In the north the road to Albany lay open. If Burgoyne could have pushed on at once he might have reached his objective unopposed. In fact, twenty days elapsed before he arrived on the Hudson, twenty-three miles distant from Skenesborough. The delay gave the Americans time to gather their forces.

Burgoyne had achieved his first objective, the reduction of Fort Ticonderoga by early summer, as he had forecast. When his messenger, Captain Henry Gardner, reached London on August 22nd, all England exulted. King George III rushed in unannounced on his Queen, who was dressed only in a chemise, waving Burgoyne's despatch before her scandalized ladies, and shouting, 'I have beat them, I have beat all the Americans.' Burgoyne became the toast of the hour. Only Horace Walpole struck a sour note: 'I suppose this silent, modest, humble, General Burgoyne has not yet finished his precise description of the victorious manner in which he took possession of it.' The King suggested to Lord Derby, through Germain, that the red ribbon of the Garter would be an appropriate award for his kinsman. Derby, however, scouted the idea, due probably to some hint dropped previously by Burgoyne, who may have preferred to await the conclusion of his successful campaign, when a peerage or an earldom would be his just reward.

Almost without firing a shot, Burgoyne had won the key position in the north. In England, everyone expected to hear of his final achievement which would end the war, and the Loyalist *émigrés* chartered ships to carry them back to America. Germain expected Burgoyne's further progress to be 'rapid', and that he would win through 'unaided'.

Ignoring the fact that Sir William Howe had washed his hands of the expedition from the north, Burgoyne informed him of his success, and of his intention to follow implicitly the ideas he had previously communicated to him. Burgoyne's letter had reached Howe in New York eight days before he sailed on his expedition against Philadelphia, and it had failed to deter him from his purpose. Before he left New York, Howe wrote to Burgoyne stating that his intention was 'for Pennsylvania where I expect to meet Washington, but if he goes to the northward contrary to my expectations, and you can keep him at bay, he assured that I shall soon be after him to relieve you'. Howe was confident that Burgoyne could reach his objective, and 'after your arrival at Albany, the movements of the enemy will guide yours'. Howe expressed his wish that 'the enemy be drove out of this province [New York] before any operation takes place in Connecticut', thereby denying Burgoyne his cherished alternative, which the exactness of his orders prevented him from adopting.

In ten days, Burgoyne had captured the border forts, a flotilla of 200 vessels, 100 cannon and a prodigious quantity of stores, powder, and shot. The rebels were in flight, disorganized, deprived of the means of waging war, and dismayed. He had dealt them a crushing blow and had reached within seventy-five miles of Albany. Yet, despite his success, and his propensity to optimism, a hint of anxiety crept into his correspondence. Twenty-three miles of rough, swampy country lay between Skenesborough and Fort Edward, the post on the Hudson River, where the waterway recommenced. For every mile advanced, the length of his supply line increased. The next stage would be crucial.

Thousands of words have been written, from hindsight, about 'Gentleman Johnny's mistake'. According to several modern commentators he took the wrong route to cover the next stage of the journey to the Hudson; and it is claimed that, if he had pushed ahead at once with a few regiments and some light guns, he would have taken Albany virtually unopposed. He could have achieved that, had he taken advantage of the panic caused by the fall of Ticonderoga, according to General Gates, whose military judgment may perhaps have been warped by his desire to employ the fall of the northern bastion to discredit his rival, Schuyler, whom he hoped to supersede.

If he had pushed forward ahead of his main body, it is possible that Burgoyne might have reached Albany in less time than it took his whole army to cover the twenty-three miles to the Hudson. But what then? He would have been besieged and forced to surrender from lack of supplies. His whole campaign turned on supplies, and their transportation along the ever-increasing distance from Canada. As he said, 'How zealously soever a General in such an undertaking as mine may be served by the chiefs of departments, for one hour he can find to contemplate how to fight his army, he must allot twenty to contrive how to feed them.'

Burgoyne had 180 light carts and thirty ox-carts, and one-third of the horses he had asked for, with which to transport his supplies, provisions, ammunition, cannon and boats overland, whichever route he adopted: that from Skenesborough to Fort Edward, or, having sailed down Lake George, from Fort George, at the extremity of the lake, to the Hudson.

In his *Thoughts*, in which he had outline his plan of campaign, Burgoyne had discussed the relative advantages of the two routes southward from Ticonderoga, calling the one via Lake George, which required only a ten-mile land journey, 'the most expeditious and most commodious route to Albany'. The route from Skenesborough was 'much less desirable' inasmuch as 'considerable difficulties' were to be expected. 'The narrow parts of the river [Wood Creek] may easily be choked up and rendered impassable, and at best there will be a necessity for a great deal of land carriage for the artillery, provisions, etc'. He foresaw that the Americans would unquestionably 'take measures to close the road from Ticonderoga to Albany by way of Skenesborough, and by felling trees, breaking bridges, and other obvious impediments', to delay his progress.

Despite these objections, Burgoyne chose the more difficult route by which to move his army, claiming that to return to Ticonderoga, which the adoption of the water route required, would have been a retrograde step, damaging to the army's morale. He adopted the longer and more difficult land route from Skenesborough to Fort Edward, comprising twenty-three miles of rough country which had, as he had predicted, been rendered impassable by the exertions of 1000 American axemen, and required the rebuilding of forty bridges, and the construction of a two-mile long causeway across a swamp. In the view of some modern critics, Burgoyne made a 'fatal decision'. By implication such critics claim that had he taken the water route via Lake George, all would have been well and he would have reached Albany triumphant.

Burgoyne used both routes. He did not possess sufficient boats by which to transport his army and his supplies from Ticonderoga to Fort George, and he employed the water route only to transport his heavy artillery and supplies southwards, leaving his soldiers to cut their way through the woods, swamps and lagoons from Skenesborough to Fort Edward. He failed, however, to throw forward a flying column to prevent or impede the destruction and obstruction of the road southward from Skenesborough, where, according to Lieutenant Digby, he dallied unnecessarily. Ulterior motives, it is claimed, conditioned Burgoyne's choice of route and his failure to advance quickly. Colonel Skene persuaded Burgoyne, for his own ends, to rebuild the road, which would enhance the value of his property, and Burgoyne was enjoying himself at that gentleman's commodious stone house. Burgoyne's high living at Skenesborough (which local tradition records) appears to lend substance to the second accusation, which is further supported by his gift of four dozen bottles of port and a similar number of bottles of Madeira—the quality of which he deplored—to General von Riedesel. He had remained at Castleton in order to overawe the Hampshire Grants, and to puzzle the enemy into thinking that he intended to advance eastwards into Connecticut rather than southwards to Albany.

Whether or not Skene pressed the advantages of the Skenesborough route, Burgoyne could not have chosen other than he did. To advance he needed to transport twelve heavy guns, nine tons of projectiles and powder, and the food and camp equipage required to feed and house his army. Each of his 180 carts carried 800 pounds of stores, the ration for 237 men for one day. There were insufficient horses and oxen both to drag the canon overland and to pull the carts, and also to transport the boats across the portage at Ticonderoga and overland from Fort George to the Hudson. Ten to fifteen animals were required to drag each boat.

The great expedition, which Burgoyne had confidently predicted would quickly achieve its objective, ground to a halt, for delay was inevitable while supplies were built up for the next forward step. The respite gave the Americans opportunity to mobilize their forces to bar his way, but they seemed loath to take it. The militiamen threatened to decamp *en masse*; they demanded to return home to gather the harvest, and Schuyler succeeded only in persuading them to adopt a rota system, whereby half the men went home, and the other half stayed until they returned.

In truth, as Washington had predicted, the advance from Canada, in conjunction with a northward move from New York, was beyond the capacity of the British to accomplish. Twice as many boats and three times as many carts and horses were required to carry the expedition forward from Ticonderoga, the easy capture of which had lulled Burgoyne into false complacency. With the contempt of the professional soldier for the amateur, he despised the fighting qualities of the Americans, whose capabilities in defence he nonetheless feared. That he dragged fifty-two cannon of varying calibre from Ticonderoga cannot be held against him for, as St Leger's failure at Fort Stanwix proved, they were required to batter down the fortifications and entrenchments which the Americans were so adept at building.

Furthermore, as Burgoyne progressed his army diminished in numbers, from the necessity to establish posts, and to garrison Fort Ticonderoga. He had hoped that Carleton would have occupied this fort, but the latter refused to send troops because he felt he was unauthorized to do so by the King's orders. The 400 and 950 regular soldiers Burgoyne was compelled to leave at Crown Point and Ticonderoga, the latter under the command of Brigadier-General Henry Watson Powell, were inadequately compensated for by the 600 professed Tories who came to Skenesborough to volunteer, following the fall of Ticonderoga. More useful were the 100 Indians, the Ottowans who came from distant parts of Canada and now caught up with the expedition. Braver and less poisoned by civilization than the original contingent who had been recruited from around Montreal, they were, in Burgoyne's words, 'more tractable', and less inclined to pillage and insubordination. The local inhabitants, whom Burgoyne found 'frightened and submissive', proved a disappointment. Those who pretended to be good subjects he allowed to carry arms and to walk without restraint about the camp, where they gathered intelligence which they communicated to the enemy.

Burgoyne took the opportunity of the delay occasioned by the slow build-up of supplies to reward his soldiers for their achievements at Ticonderoga and at Hubbardton by the holding of divine service, and the firing of a *feu de joye*. He also summoned a congress of Indians, and again admonished his officers against carrying excessive baggage, for which he continued to set a bad example. Those officers, says Anburey, who complied with the order and sent their baggage back to Ticonderoga never saw it again. Anburey himself reduced his camp equipment to a buffalo-skin which, with his horse, he had acquired on the field of Hubbardton.

By the time Burgoyne was ready to advance, Schuyler had (to use the word of a German officer) made the country into a 'desert'. Unmolested by Burgoyne's soldiers, his men felled immense trees, interlacing their branches, across the road, rolled rocks into endless little brooks, dug trenches to carry swamps across dry land, swept the country clean of cattle, and burned the crops, leaving 'neither a hoof or a blade of corn". The heavy July rains turned the country into a quagmire, from which rose millions of gnats and mosquitoes to plague the sweating fatigue parties that laboured to clear the way for the army.

The main body of the army advanced from Skenesborough on July 24th, taking two days to march the fourteen miles to Fort Anne, where it halted to allow Simon Fraser to push ahead with his advance guard to Pine Plains, two miles short of Fort Edward. The whole army came up on the 29th and marched to the Hudson. Schuyler did not wait to be surrounded and besieged in the ancient and dilapidated fort which he described as being 'utterly defenceless'. Ordering the evacuation of Fort George, the road from which would soon be cut, he transported his 700 Continentals, and those militiamen who had remained on duty, across the Hudson and retreated to Saratoga. Again the Americans had been forced to evacuate a fort. Dispirited and despairing of the fate of the Revolution, they fell back be-

5a. Fort Ticonderoga, with Lake Champlain in foreground and Lake George in distance. Mount Defiance between.

b. Fort Ticonderoga and Lake Champlain. (*Photos R. K. Dean*)

6a. Major-General Arthur St Clair (*New York Public Library*)

b. Major-General Benedict Arnold (*New York Public Library*)

fore the invader who had regained the water route to the south.

There seemed to be little chance of stopping Burgoyne's triumphal progress. The majority of the Colonists were apathetic. They needed a spark to galvanize their opposition to their former rulers, who had recruited Indians and German mercenaries to coerce them. That spark was supplied by one of Burgoyne's Indians, a man picturesquely named Wyandot Panther.

There are several versions of the Jane McCrea story. They agree only that she was aged about twenty-three years, tall and beautiful, and was noted for her long, lustrous hair, which reached to the ground. She lived at Moses Kill, on a tributary of the Hudson, with her brother John, a colonel of the local militia, who had joined General Schuyler. Unlike her brother Jane was a Tory, and before his departure from the district she had become engaged to David Jones, from Fort Edward, who marched with Burgoyne. On July 27th, Jane went to the cabin at Fort Edward owned by Mrs McNeil, a large, talkative widow who happened to be a cousin of Brigadier-General Simon Fraser, to await the arrival of her lover.

That morning, two days before the British surrounded Fort Edward, a party of the newly-joined Ottowan Indians surprised an American picket, killing its commander and making several prisoners. One of them, named Miles Standish, later declared that he saw the Indians enter Mrs McNeil's house and drag out the widow and Jane McCrea. Another version of the story relates that the Indians had been bribed by David Jones with the promise of a barrel of rum to rescue his betrothed from the Americans and bring her to the British camp. Yet another version records that Lieutenant Palmer and the soldiers whom he had been sent to protect Jane and Mrs McNeil, were forestalled by the Indians.

According to Standish, the Indians caught two horses, mounting Jane upon one and, being unable to hoist the fat Mrs McNeil upon the other, forced her to walk, stripping her

97

naked. She fell behind and did not see what then occurred.

According to the traditional story, Jane was killed on her way to the British camp by Wyandot Panther, in the course of an argument between her two captors who each claimed her as his prize. Wyandot then scalped her and smashed her skull, and stripped her body naked. He carried her scalp into the camp, where it was instantly recognized by David Jones, and also by Mrs McNeil, when she arrived greatly to the embarrassment of her cousin, who was forced to provide his overcoat to cover her nakedness.

Wyandot Panther stated that the girl had been killed by a shot fired by the survivors of the American picket who, because in the opinion of General Fraser 'they aimed too high when the mark was on elevated ground', hit the girl on the horse rather than the Indians at whom they had aimed.

General Burgoyne, who ordered an inquiry, did not accept this convenient explanation of the girl's death. He went to the Indian camp and demanded that the girl's murderer should be given up to justice, stating that he would be put to death. Their leader, the Frenchman, La Corne St Luc, intervened. If Wyandot Panther was executed, he said, the Indians would desert and return to Canada, massacring everybody and destroying everything in their path. His reply placed Burgoyne in a dilemma. He does not seem to have doubted that Jane Mc-Crea had been murdered by the Indians, who, he stated later in a letter to General Gates with whom he corresponded on the matter of alleged Indian atrocities, had been sent to guard and convey her to the British camp. According to Sergeant Lamb, he told La Corne St Luc that 'he would rather lose every Indian in his army than connive at their enormities', but that 'he determined to be a soldier, not the executioner of the State'. The murderer's life, states Lamb, was spared upon the Indians' agreeing to terms, 'which the General thought would be more efficacious than execution to prevent similar mischiefs'.

Burgoyne's clemency did not achieve the desired result for,

as Anburey records, the majority of the Indians deserted next day, leaving the camp loaded with plunder, 'till scarcely one of those that joined us at Skenesborough is left'. His failure to avenge the girl's death aroused the indignation of the colonists, who declared that even the betrothed wife of one of Burgoyne's Tory officers was unsafe from the fiendish atrocities committed by his Indian allies.

Yet, it seems possible that Jane may have been shot accidentally for, when her body was exhumed from its temporary resting-place for reburial in the Union Cemetery at Fort Edward, her skull was said to have been found unbroken, and three gun-shot wounds in her body were still discernible. According to her granddaughter who made the statement in 1848, Mrs McNeil, who did not witness the girl's death, believed that she had been shot accidentally. The expedition diarists accepted the murder explanation, as did Burgoyne who, in his reply to Gates, denied other alleged Indian atrocities—'upward of one hundred men, women and children', according to Gates.

Whatever is the truth, the girl's death created the 'Yankee Joan of Arc', the need for whom had been suggested by Thomas Paine. As the story spread, thousands of farmers and shopkeepers, and even sailors, in New England and New York, abandoned their callings to 'go agin' Burgoyne.

Burgoyne lost not only the services of those Indians who had deserted, but also those of David Jones, who many years later told his grandniece that 'he was so crushed by the terrible blow and disgusted with the apathy of Burgoyne in refusing to punish the miscreant' that he and his brother asked for their discharge and were refused. They deserted, David having first rescued the precious relic of his betrothed from the savages, and returned to the Canadian wilderness, which he had never been known to leave, except upon one mysterious occasion. David Jones presumably believed that Jane had been murdered.

VIII *New York*

Burgoyne stood on the banks of the Hudson River, which provided an uninterrupted waterway to Albany and New York. Following his capture of Ticonderoga, he had written on August 6th from Fort Edward a gay letter to Howe, stating that he expected to reach Albany by August 23rd. He was in high spirits and he expressed no desire for or expectation of cooperation from the southern army. Howe received Burgoyne's letter on August 16th, three weeks after he had sailed from New York on his expedition to Philadelphia. It confirmed his belief that Burgoyne could reach Albany on his own.

In July a faint chance remained that Howe could be persuaded to abandon his disastrous plan to invade Pennsylvania by sea, and to co-operate with the invasion from the north or, at least, to leave in New York a force strong enough to create a diversion should Burgoyne need to be rescued.

Sir Henry Clinton reached New York on July 5th. He had sailed from England on April 29th, following a stay of several weeks during which he had discussed with Germain the strategy for the forthcoming season. He warned Germain that Howe could not, as he hoped, capture Philadelphia and return to New York in time to co-operate with Burgoyne. Although Clinton stressed the danger of a 'miscarriage unless Burgoyne was supported, Germain failed to employ him to carry to Howe explicit orders which might have cleared up the misunderstanding about the intention of the northern invasion and the part Howe was expected to play.

Unless Clinton could persuade Howe to change his plan at the last minute, the ill-defined Grand Strategy, intended to end the war in 1777, would deteriorate into a series of unre-

lated and objectless operations. Carleton with 3000 men would
defend Canada from a non-existent invasion threat; Burgoyne
with 10,000 men would force his way to Albany, where his
lines of communication dangerously over-extended, and unsupported from the south, he would either be crushed by Washington who might hurry north to prevent the severance of the
colonies, or starved into submission by a locally raised army.
St Leger, at best, would join and sink with him; Howe, with
13,000 regular soldiers, would triumphantly capture the rebel
capital, without bringing the cautious Washington to a decisive
battle; Clinton would garrison New York with a force too
weak to help Burgoyne should he get into difficulties, an eventuality that no one, other than Clinton, thought possible.
There would be no junction of armies on the Hudson. Nor
would Howe, 300 miles away in Pennsylvania, be in a position
to chase Washington and catch him—or the northern American
army—between two fires.

Howe was not ignorant of the fact that the junction of the
two armies on the line of the Hudson was contemplated;
though whether they were actually to join, or merely to co-
operate, had never been defined. He ignored the possibility
that the threat to divide the colonies might force the elusive
Washington to fight a decisive battle, the best chance the British had of subjugating the rebels and winning the war quickly.
Howe took the gloomy view that the war could not be won
in 1777.

Clinton, unfortunately, was the last person likely to make
Howe change his mind. From the beginning of the war the two
major-generals had clashed. Clinton was, like Howe, an aristo-
crat, for his father was the younger brother of the Earl of Lincoln, and he shared with his chief, and with Burgoyne, an overwhelming ambition to succeed. The realization that he was the
obvious successor, should Howe fail and be relieved of his command, bred distrust between the two men; the haughty and
taciturn Howe, who resented advice from subordinates who

did not share his responsibility, and the inconsistent and touchy subordinate, who was inclined to act boldly, even to disobey, yet always remaining fearful of the consequences. Clinton's remark, which he had made in the hearing of Lord Cornwallis, that he would gladly prefer the command of three companies at a distance from Howe to serving in any capacity under him, had been duly reported. It did not endear him to his superior officer.

Clinton had been advised by his friend General William Phillips to 'gulp and swallow' and to 'avoid jarring' Howe, but he pressed his arguments, in his own words, 'oftener than was agreeable'. He considered himself Howe's equal in military judgment, and he felt slighted because Howe had ignored him in the past, and mortified because, although he had been offered and had refused the appointment, Burgoyne, who was his junior in rank, had been 'placed in the high road to glory and enjoying all the agremens of an active and separate command'. Clinton disliked playing second fiddle to Howe and did not enjoy the prospect of doing Burgoyne's job for him. He saw himself left without the smallest prospect of 'either doing anything to serve my country or to advance my own fame'. It is an insight to his character that, after he had achieved supreme command, Clinton wrote a history of the war in order to justify his own actions.

Howe's proposed plan of campaign was, Clinton believed, a strategic stupidity. While Howe penned up his army in a cul-de-sac, Washington would be free either to move against Burgoyne or to capture New York which Clinton was expected to hold with a 'damned starved defensive' and without the means to help Burgoyne, should that become necessary.

Clinton doubted that Burgoyne could reach Albany unaided; for, as he wrote on July 11th to Lord Harvey, the American Northern Department 'may have been so reinforced as to be able to hold against Burgoyne long before he gets to Albany'. Howe, on the contrary, believed that Burgoyne stood in danger only if Washington went north; in which case, as he informed Germain on July 16th, he would speedily follow. Washington would be a 'blockhead', he thought, if he did not ignore Howe and exert his whole force against Burgoyne, or New York.

Clinton saw further than Howe. He wished to impale Washington on the horns of a dilemma; whether to intervene to prevent the loss of his communications with New England, knowing full well that a British advance would endanger them, or to prevent the advance by putting his whole army in jeopardy.

For three weeks, Clinton hammered at Howe to abandon his expedition against Philadelphia, and to act upon the Hudson. Howe answered that his plan had been approved at home, and that he expected to find at Philadelphia friends who would facilitate his capture of the city. He had received no orders to co-operate with Burgoyne, who had been warned not to expect aid from the south. Convinced of the validity of his argument, Clinton persuaded himself that Howe was wavering or, even, that his proposed expedition to the south was a blind. 'Though he was pleased to say that he was going to sea with the first northerly wind, I would expect to see him return with the first southerly blast and run up the North River [the Hudson]'.

Clinton did not believe that Howe was serious in his intention to go to Philadelphia, until he heard of him off the mouth of the Delaware River. 'By some cursed fatality, we could never draw together,' Clinton remarked, following his early conversations with Howe, about which, on the advice of Phillips, he made notes. In these talks 'every past grievance, misunderstanding and petty annoyance' was raked up. Clinton believed that Howe was making a blunder, for he feared that Burgoyne would be checked and threatened with destruction by Washington, and that Howe would be forced to abandon his gains in order to march to his rescue, which he might be too late to achieve. A great opportunity, he felt, was being missed.

Although Howe acted correctly, he showed no imagination, and he failed to foresee the logical consequences of his actions. He deliberately postponed the fulfilment of the Grand Strategy, of which he was one of the fathers, in order to capture Philadelphia, a place of no strategic importance.

Howe sailed from New York on July 23rd, taking with him 13,000 regular troops, to oppose Washington's estimated 11,000 men. At Clinton's request, Howe had, reluctantly, augmented his 6095 effectives and 1117 sick men by 'three thin battalions' and the promise of the return of a fourth battalion, after he had landed in Pennsylvania. The New York garrison included 3000 newly-raised Loyalists.

After the fleet had sailed, Clinton received a letter from Howe expressing his doubts whether he could return the Fourth Brigade as he had promised, adding: 'But, if you can in the meantime make any diversion in favour of General Burgoyne's approaching Albany, I need not point out the utility of such a measure.' Clinton could make an offensive move, if he did not thereby endanger the safety of New York.

Howe's sudden earnestness to co-operate with Burgoyne seems strange. If a rescue operation was required, he had given Clinton a hint to that purpose, and had put it on record. But he had failed to provide him with a force strong enough to force its way pu the Hudson to Albany.

Burgoyne was on his own.

ix *Fort Stanwix*

Sir William Howe had embarked his troops, put to sea, and vanished. His conduct perplexed and disturbed Washington who, expecting that he would sail up the Hudson, had moved his army to the west bank of that river. That Howe would abandon Burgoyne was astonishing and unaccountable and, until he was fully satisfied of it, 'I cannot help casting my eyes behind me,' Washington informed Gates on August 1st. As Washington told Putman who was stationed at Peekskill, the importance of preventing Howe from 'getting possession of the Highlands by a *coup de main* is infinite to America', for he considered that a junction of the two armies would have the most fatal results'. Howe's move to the south might be a feint to draw him from the Hudson. On July 31st, the British fleet had been sighted in Delaware Bay, had put to sea again and had disappeared; Philadelphia seemed to be Howe's objective. Leaving a division at Morristown, within forty-five miles of Peekskill, Washington marched the greater part of his army to Coryell's Ferry on the Delaware, eighty miles from Peekskill and thirty-three miles north of Philadelphia.

In the Northern Department, Schuyler had been joined by Generals Arnold and Lincoln (Washington had sent them north in response to Schuyler's request for more New England officers), whose arrival, however, failed to prevent the desertion of 700 Massachusetts militiamen. Schuyler retreated from Saratoga to Stillwater, and he himself went to Albany, where he owned a town house. He reached it on August 6th, and learned that Colonel St Leger was threatening Fort Stanwix at the farther end of the Mohawk valley, 120 miles from Albany. The Committee of Tyron County requested reinforcements.

Schuyler had written to Washington the day before saying that he might be able to hold Burgoyne, whose next move he awaited, if he was reinforced; 'but, if I should be asked from whence I expect reinforcements, I should be at a loss for an answer, not having heard a word from Massachusetts on my repeated application, nor am I certain that Connecticut will afford any succour. Our Continental force is daily decreasing by desertion, sickness and loss in encounters with the enemy, and not a man in the Militia now with me will remain above one week longer, and, while our force is diminishing, the enemy is augmented by a constant acquisition of Tories but, if by any measure we could be put in a situation of attacking the enemy and giving them a repulse, their retreat could be so extremely difficult that, in all probability, they would lose the greater part of their army.' Schuyler feared that a Tory rising in Tyron County, in the Mohawk valley, could spread throughout the Colonies.

St Leger had left Montreal on June 23rd, sailed 300 miles up the St Lawrence and across Lake Ontario, and reached Oswago on July 25th. Leaving the lake, he advanced by way of Lake Oneida and Wood Creek, and approached Fort Stanwix (which, although it has been renamed Fort Schuyler, is usually referred to by its former name) on August 3rd. St Leger was a zealous and experienced soldier, aged forty, who had fought at Louisburg and Quebec in the earlier war. He had with him a mixed force of European, American, and Indian troops: 200 British infantrymen; 100 German *chasseurs*; 100 Tory rangers under the command of Colonel John Butler; the Royal Greens, a Tory regiment raised by Sir John Johnson, the son of the famous and recently deceased Sir William Johnson who during his lifetime had dominated the Mohawk valley; and about 900 Mohawk and Seneca Indians, led by chief Joseph Brant, whose sister had married Sir William Johnson. The force was equipped with small cannon only: two six-pounders, two three-pounders, and four 4.4-inch mortars, and forty artillerymen. The purpose of the expedition was more political than military, for the British hoped that the appearance of regular troops would induce the Loyalists in the Mohawk valley to rise in favour of the King.

The Mohawk valley was of great strategic importance. It was not only the gateway to the west, but also the abode of the greatest Indian power on the continent—the Confederacy of the Six Nations. The tribes making up this Confederacy included the Mohawks, the Iroquois, and the Senecas who had fought for the British against the French thirty years before. Now, one tribe (the Oneidas), actively supported the rebels, and others were wavering. The loyalties of the people of European stock were divided. The majority of the settlers answered the call of the rebel leader, Nicholas Herkimer, the colonel of the Militia of Tyron County, whose brother had joined the British and marched with St Leger, a fact of some importance for it created undeserved suspicion of Nicholas's loyalty to the rebel cause.

Fort Stanwix stood on the right bank of the Mohawk River and had been built, during the previous war, to dominate the portage from Wood Creek. It had fallen into ruins and had been partly repaired in 1777 by its garrison of 500 Continentals. These were commanded by Colonel Peter Gansevoort, who came from Albany; his second-in-command was the fiery New Yorker, Lieutenant-Colonel Marinus Willett. Towards the end of July they were warned by friendly Indians of St Leger's approach. Those loyal to the Crown advised St Leger that the fort was strongly defended by 600 men. Refusing to delay he pressed on hoping to capture it by surprise; but he threw away his chance by parading his troops in full view of the garrison, thus disclosing that his white troops were inferior in numbers to those of the garrison, which had been reinforced by 200 men, the escort of a convoy carrying supplies for six weeks which had reached the fort a few hours before St Leger's arrival. The hideous war-cries of the Indians boded ill for the garrison should they be forced, or be persuaded, to surrender.

Failing to inflict damage on the sod-work and pallisading of the fort, St Leger withdrew his troops, forming two camps, one on the high ground to the north of the fort, and the other to cover the lower landing on the river, to its south. The Indians were strung out along the low swampy ground in between the two camps, along a frontage of 5000 yards.

Learning of the threat to Fort Stanwix, Nicholas Herkimer called out the militia of Tyron County, summoning all men capable of bearing arms between the ages of sixteen and sixty to join him at Fort Drayton, about thirty miles down the Mohawk River from the fort. It was vital to destroy St Leger's force before the Tories rose in its favour, Herkimer told his men; the presence of his brother with the invaders made them distrustful of his leadership. Nonetheless, the militia, 850 white men with sixty Oneidas, marched from Fort Drayton on August 4th, taking with them 400 ox-carts carrying supplies for the fort. They crossed the Mohawk near the site of the present village of Oriskany, twelve miles below Fort Stanwix. Early on August 5th, Herkimer sent three messengers ahead to get into the fort to warn Colonel Gansevoort of his approach and to request a diversion to distract the besiegers.

That day an Indian reached the British camp, carrying a message from Molly Brant, the widow of Sir William Johnson, warning her brother of Herkimer's advance. Realizing his peril, for he guessed that Herkimer would be supported by a sally from the fort, and that he would be taken between the two fires, St Leger ordered Colonel Guy Johnson, Sir John's brother, and Chief Brant, to ambush Herkimer's column on its march. They set off with 400 Indians and detachments from the Royal Greens and Colonel Butler's Rangers, to prepare the classic strategem of frontier warfare.

In the absence of the signal from the fort, for the three shots fired by the garrison had not been heard, Herkimer hesitated to advance. On the morning of August 6th he called a council of war, at which he voiced the reason for his hesitation to the anger of his men who taunted him with accusations of cowardice and treachery. Goaded to a course which he deemed unwise, Herkimer gave the order to advance, leading the van himself astride a white horse. He was followed by 600 militiamen, marching in columns of twos, the 400 ox-carts, and by a rearguard of 200 militiamen. The Oneidas acted as scouts to the column, which became strung out over the distance of a mile, astride the rough wagon-track. This track ran on the high ground, above the swampy bottom and through dense woods, and was intersected by ravines, across which the settlers had built causeways of 'corduroy' (logs laid cross-ways).

Six miles from the fort, the road was crossed by a deep ravine, through which ran a little brook (later known as 'Battle Brook'), the marshy bottom of which was passable only by the narrow corduroy causeway. A second, shallower ravine lay 400 yards further on. These narrow defiles were perfect places for ambuscade, as the militiamen should have known. Eager to relieve the fort, however, they marched into the trap. It was about 10 a.m. The Tories and their Indian allies lay in deep cover, and they allowed the head of the column to cross the deep ravine and reach the second, shallower one. Herkimer rode up the higher ground beyond. Unable to contain themselves longer, the Mohawks and Senecas did not wait until the American rearguard, commanded by Colonel Peter Vissicher, has descended into the first ravine. Their excited war-whoops resounded through the woods; and their muskets blazed from behind every rock and tree. Those militiamen who did not fall at the first fire took cover behind trees and the wagons of the convoy, or fled to gain protection from the unengaged rearguard.

Hearing firing from behind, Nicholas Herkimer turned his horse and rode back. The horse was killed and he was wounded in the leg. He pulled off the saddle, placed it against a tree and sat astride, smoking his pipe and firing his musket on his Tory neighbours and their Indian allies. When his man urged him to take cover, he replied, 'I will face the enemy.' The Tyron County Militia formed a circle around a knob of ground. A heavy shower of rain damped the priming of their muskets, and, seizing their opportunity, the Mohawks and Senecas dashed in wielding tomahawks and scalping-knives. The militiamen grouped themselves together in pairs, one man firing while the other reloaded. There were several notable individual encounters: Abraham Quackenboss fought with his Indian friend Bronkahorse and shot him dead; three Tory rangers, pretending to be militiamen, were unmasked and killed by Captain Gardenier; assaulted simultaneously by three Mohawks, Captain Dillenbach brained one with the butt of his musket, shot another, and bayoneted the third.

The tide of battle slowly and almost imperceptibly swung in favour of the Tyron County militiamen, for the Indians, as usual, feared to come to close quarters and preferred to snipe from cover. A message from his brother warned Guy Johnson that a sortie from the fort threatened his rear. Ordering his men to withdraw, he led the retreat, leaving Herkimer and his men technically masters of the field. Their losses had been fearful: 200 killed, 250 wounded, and 200 taken prisoner. With his pipe in his mouth and his Dutch Bible in his hand, Herkimer died from his wounds two weeks after the battle. Among the slain lay the bodies of 150 Tories and Indians. The Indians suffered severely, for many of their braves and chiefs had been killed. Lamenting their losses they returned to camp to find that it had been looted.

In his *Narrative*, which was published by his son in 1831, Colonel Marinus Willett told the story of the sortie from the fort;

'About eleven o'clock three men got into the fort who brought a letter from General Harkaman [Herkimer] of the Tyron County militia, advising us that he was 8 miles off with part of his militia, and proposed to force his way to the fort for our relief. In order to render him what service we could in his march it was agreed that I should make a sally from the fort with 250 men, consisting of one-half Gansevoort's, one-half Massachusetts ditto, and one field-piece (an iron three-pounder).

'Nothing could be more fortunate than this enterprise. We totally routed two of the enemy's encampments, destroyed all the provisions that were in them, brought off upwards of 50 brass kettles and more than 100 blankets (two articles which were much needed), with a quantity of muskets, tomahawks, spears, ammunition, clothing, deerskins, a variety of Indian affairs and 5 colours. The Indians took chiefly to the woods, the rest of the troops then at their posts to the river. I was happy in preventing the men from scalping even the Indians, being desirous, if possible, to teach even the savages humanity; but the men were much better employed, and kept in excellent order.

'From these prisoners we received the first accounts of General Harkaman's [Herkimer's] militia being ambushed on their march, and of a severe battle they had with them about two hours before, which gave reason to think they had for the present given up their design of marching to the fort.'

William Colbraith relates that amongst the scalps taken two 'are supposed to be those of girls, being dressed and the hair plaited'. Sir John Johnson had fled in such a hurry that he left behind his coat and personal papers, so suddenly had the camp been surprised.

The British victory at Oriskany—for Herkimer had been forced to abandon the relief of the fort—was a somewhat hollow one. The Indians were dispirited by their losses and enraged by the plunder of their belongings, which left many possessed only of their breech-cloths. They raised a great clamour, which St Leger sought to turn to good account. Under a flag of truce, he sent officers into the fort to warn the garrison that his Indians were 'vastly exasperated' and, unless the American force surrendered, would massacre all the settlers in the valley. To this message Gansevoort replied with dignity: 'By your uniform you are British officers. Therefore let me tell you that the message you have brought is a degrading one for a British officer to send and by no means reputable for a British officer to carry.' Colonel St Leger, he said, would be responsible for any massacre of the garrison, or of the settlers in the valley, by his Indian allies.

Gansevoort knew that the fort could not be battered into submission by St Leger's paltry artillery; but he feared that, unless relief came, the garrison might be starved into surrender. Colonel Willett carried his plea for help to General Schuyler at Albany. Schuyler had heard of Herkimer's defeat, and, as he told his council of officers, he was prepared to run risks on the Hudson in order to save the Mohawk valley. The New Englanders were suspicious of his motives. 'He intends to weaken the army,' he heard one officer say. It was the most bitter moment of his life: the stem of his pipe snapped between his clenched teeth. But the remark made up his mind for him. He would take sole responsibility, he told his officers. Arnold volunteered to lead the relief force.

Accompanied by 950 Continentals from Brigadier-General Learned's brigade, Arnold marched to Fort Drayton, which he reached on August 21st. The surviving officers of the Tryon County Militia warned him that his small force was insufficient to relieve the fort; and there was the danger of a Tory rising following the reverse at Oriskany. Showing unusual caution, Arnold hesitated. Next day, news came that the British had dug trenches to within 150 yards of the fort's ramparts, under which they were preparing to run a mine. The crisis of the siege was imminent. Meanwhile, the Tory plot had been detected and scotched; several prisoners had been taken and had been condemned to death, among them a half-witted settler named Hon Yost, a nephew of Herkimer's and a relation of Schuyler's.

Hon Yost's madness could be employed, it was suggested, to sow dissension amongst St Leger's Indians, who, with their reverence for mental defectives, regarded him with awe. His life would be spared, Yost was told, if he would go to the British camp and frighten the Indians with exaggerated stories of the strength and proximity of the relief force. Yost threw himself into the game, and with the cunning of the half-wit, suggested improvements. At his request, his coat was shot through to give the impression that he had escaped from captivity, and several Oneidas were sent to corroborate his story. Reaching the British camp, he told the Indians that 'Heap Fighting Chief' (the name by which Arnold was known) had with him more troops than 'the leaves of the trees', that he was advancing rapidly, and that Burgoyne's army had been cut to pieces. The ruse worked. Believing the half-wit's story, the Mohawks and Senecas decamped, making off with the liquor and clothes which they looted from the officers' tents, and crying that the terrible Arnold was coming. Denied further assistance from his Indian allies, St Leger abandoned the siege and retreated, his soldiers struggling through the woods weighed down by their heavy packs. At their side ran their former Indian allies crying 'They are coming, they are coming', and massacring and scalping the stragglers.

On August 23rd, Arnold, who had advanced to within twenty miles of the fort, received a message from Gansevoort that St Leger had fled. He relieved the fort next day, and on the 24th went in pursuit of St Leger, reaching the shores of Lake Oneida as the last British boat pulled away.

Leaving 700 soldiers at Fort Stanwix, Arnold returned to rejoin the main army at Albany. St Leger retreated the way he had come, hoping to follow Burgoyne and join him at Albany.

Meanwhile a second and far more serious reverse had befallen Burgoyne.

X *Bennington*

Following Howe's sudden appearance and mysterious disappearance, off the Delaware Capes, Washington shrank from making an irrevocable move. He committed himself to no more than the despatch of two Continental regiments from Peekskill and Morgan's 500 riflemen from Trenton to strengthen Schuyler at Stillwater, whither he had retreated following Burgoyne's advance to the Hudson. To delay his progress further, and to gain time, Schuyler thought to threaten Burgoyne's flank and rear, a plan that was approved by Washington who wrote: 'The expediency of such a measure appears to me evident; for it would certainly make General Burgoyne very circumspect in his advances if it did not wholly prevent them. It would keep him in continued anxiety for his rear.' Showing almost prophetic vision, he told Schuyler: 'Could we be so happy as to cut off one of his detachments, supposing that it should not exceed four, five, or six hundred men, it would enspirit the people and do away with much of the present anxiety. In such an event they would lose sight of past misfortunes, fly to arms, and afford every aid in their power.'

On July 16th, Schuyler wrote to Seth Warner who, following his retreat from Hubbardton, had remained in the Hampshire Grants, ordering him to protect Vermont, and sending him $4000 which he could ill spare. He told him, 'I am at this moment informed by Captain Fitch that the New Hampshire Militia are marching to join me. It is not my intention, much as I am in want of troops, that they should come hither, as it would expose the country in that quarter to the depredations of the enemy. I therefore enclose you an Order for them to join you.'

Schuyler wrote to the General Court of New Hampshire, urging it to send the State's militia to join Warner, 'who has intelligence that a considerable body of the enemy will attempt to penetrate to Bennington'; and he sent Major-General Lincoln to take command in the Grants, or the State of Vermont as that area had become on January 15th, though not yet recognized as the fourteenth state.

Schuyler was not alone in foreseeing the threat to the Vermont frontier for, on July 18th Ira Allen had appealed to the General Court of New Hampshire, the state next to Vermont to help 'the defenceless inhabitants on the frontier who are heartily disposed to Defend their Liberties', and 'to make a frontier for our State with their own'. In answer to this appeal, Speaker John Langdon pledged: 'We can raise a brigade, and our friend John Stark may be safely entrusted with the command, and we will check Burgoyne.'

Stark was accorded an 'independent command', in which he was not amenable to Congress, or to the orders of the generals of the Continental army. The terms of his appointment reflected the widespread distrust which prevailed after the evacuation of Fort Ticonderoga, and the fear that these generals in whom the people of New England reposed no confidence, would order the New Hampshire Militia to join Schuyler at Stillwater, thus leaving their wives and families 'a prey to the enemy', as Joseph Bartlett, a member of the General Court explained.

Though only in his late forties, Stark was a famed Indian fighter who had marched with Roger's Rangers in the French and Indian war, rising to the rank of captain. He had served with distinction at Bunker Hill and, following Congressional lack of appreciation of his services, he had, on March 22, 1777, returned to his farm on the Merrimac River, 'grieved' that Congress had thought fit 'to promote junior officers over my head'. His acceptance of an independent command was greeted with enthusiasm and by rapid recruitment, as is told by the New Hampshire historian Bouton, in his *History of Concord*:

'As soon as it was decided to raise volunteer companies and place them under the command of Gen. Stark, Col. Hutchins (delegate from Concord) mounted his horse, and travelling all night with all possible haste, reached Concord on Sabbath afternoon, before the close of public service. Dismounting at the meeting-house door, he walked up the aisle of the church while Mr Walker was preaching. Mr Walker paused in his sermon, and said: "Col. Hutchins, are you the bearer of any message?" "Yes", replied the Colonel: "General Burgoyne, with his army, is on his march to Albany. Gen. Stark has offered to take the command of the New Hampshire men; and, if we all turn out, we can cut off Burgoyne's march." Whereupon Rev. Mr Walker said: "My hearers, those of you who are willing to go, better leave at once." At which word all the men in the meeting-house rose and went out. Many immediately enlisted. The whole night was spent in preparation, and a company was ready to march next day.'

On that Sunday, seven companies consisting of 419 men were recruited in the town of Concord. In six days, from July 19th to 24th, 1492 officers and men enlisted to fight under Stark, one in ten of the New Hampshire men of voting age.

Stark sent 700 men to join Warner, reaching Manchester himself with another 300 on August 9th, to find that the New Hampshire Militia had been ordered by Major-General Lincoln to march to Stillwater, and were packed up and ready to go. The threat to Fort Stanwix, and the need to relieve it, had caused Schuyler to change his plan, and the New Hampshire Militia were now to threaten Burgoyne's flank. Stark, however, who may have got wind of von Riedesel's suggestion for a foray against Bennington, prevailed upon Lincoln to persuade

Schuyler to revert to the original plan. He considered himself 'adequate to command his own men', Stark said, and he marched them to Bennington. Schuyler, when he learned of Stark's move, offered to furnish him with five or six hundred more men to enable him to harass the British flank.

This explanation of Stark's otherwise 'insubordinate' move is confirmed by Lincoln who wrote on August 12th to Washington: 'I am to return with the Militia from Massachusetts, New Hampshire, and the Grants, to the northward with the design to fall in the rear of Burgoyne.' He told Stark: 'Our plan is adopted,' and 'a movement is intended from here with part of the army to fall into the enemy's rear'. He should march his militiamen to Cambridge where 'troops from here will join you'. Stark retained his 'independent command', and it became the 'first link', as Thomas Jefferson called it, 'in the chain of successes which issued in the surrender at Saratoga'; for thereby Stark and his men were at Bennington when Colonel Baum's ill-fated expedition neared that village.

Unaware of the storm gathering upon his left, Burgoyne planned a foray into the Connecticut valley to secure the horses he needed so badly, which he believed were 'teeming' in that area. The suggestion came from von Riedesel, who following the battle of Hubbardton had remained at Castleton. He had urged upon Burgoyne the necessity to find horses both to mount his dragoons and to facilitate the movement of the army which, as he informed Duke Ferdinand of Brunswick, 'is unable to advance three miles without waiting about eight or ten days for our necessary supplies to be brought up'. Burgoyne approved the plan and ordered von Riedesel to instruct Lieutenant-Colonel Frederick Baum to lead the expedition, which would be accompanied by Colonel Skene, Burgoyne's 'political adviser'. Burgoyne told Skene:

'I request the favour of you to proceed with Lieut. Col. Baume, upon an Expedition of which he has the Command,

and which will March this Evening, or tomorrow Morning.

'The objects of his Orders are to try the Affectations of the Country: to disconcert the Councils of the Enemy; to mount the Regt. of Riedesel's Dragoons, to compleat Lieut. Col. Peters's Corps, and to procure a large supply of Horses for the use of the Troops, together with Cattle and Carriages.

'The Route marked for this Expedition is to Arlington and Manchester, and in case it should be found that the Enemy is not in too great force upon the Connecticut River it is intended to pass the Mountains to Rockingham and ascend the River, from thence to Brattlebury. Some hours before the Corps marches for Arlington, Col. Peters with all his Men are to set forward for Bennington, and afterwards to join at Arlington.

'Receipts are ordered to be given for all Horses, and Cattle taken from the Country.

'Lieut. Col. Baume is directed to communicate to you the rest of his Instructions, and to consult with you upon all Matters of Intelligence, Negotiation with the Inhabitants, Roads and other means depending upon a knowledge of the Country for carrying his Instructions into Execution.

'I rely upon your Zeal, and Activity, for the fullest assistance, particularly in having it understood in all the Country through which you pass, that the Corps of Lieut. Col. Baume is the first Detachment of the Advanced Guard, and that the whole Army is proceeding to Boston, expecting to be joined upon the Route by the Army from Rhode Island.

'I need not recommend to you to continue the requisites of the Service with ev'ry principle of Humanity in the mode of obtaining them, and it may be proper to inform the Country, that the means to prevent their Cattle and Horses being taken for the future, will be to resist the Enemy, when they shall presume to force them, and drive them Voluntarily to my Camp.'

Skene, with his usual confidence, assured Burgoyne that the country to the eastward 'swarmed with men who wished to take up army for the King', and who 'only want the appearance of a protecting power to shew themselves'.

The instructions to Baum, drawn up by von Riedesel, for 'a secret expedition to the Connecticut river' were amended by Burgoyne in one vital particular. Whereas von Riedesel had proposed that the foray should penetrate the country east of Castleton, Burgoyne directed its movement towards Manchester. To von Riedesel's objection that the change of direction would take Baum towards the enemy rather than behind them, as he had originally proposed, Burgoyne replied that if the detachment was sent too far to the northward, it would be unable to return in time to join the proposed advance to Albany. To prepare for the expedition, Burgoyne marched his army down the eastern bank of the Hudson, to Fort Miller, and he sent Simon Fraser, with the advance guard, to ford the river to Saratoga, in order to threaten Schuyler and deter him from sending troops eastwards when he heard of Baum's expedition. The naval contingent and the artificers were set to work to construct a pontoon bridge, but on August 15th it was swept away by torrential rains. On this occasion, Lieutenant Pellew distinguished himself by plunging into the flood to rescue a boat laden with valuable stores, which otherwise might have been lost.

When, on August 11th, Baum paraded his men, preparatory to marching from Fort Miller, Burgoyne rode up and gave him new verbal instructions, countermanding the previous order. These directed Baum to proceed to Bennington, thirty miles south-east of Fort Edward, where, Burgoyne said, a Tory officer had reported a magazine of provisions and a large number of horses inadequately guarded by three to four hundred men. When von Riedesel learned of this last-minute change of plan which directed the foray even farther to the south he expressed his 'fear and astonishment' in regard to the danger attending it. Burgoyne overruled his representation, and, according to von Riedesel, gave three reasons for the change of plan:

'1st. It would be of great advantage to the army to gather their subsistence from the captured magazine of the enemy, until supplies could be transported to the army sufficient to last for four weeks.

2nd. In case he should move with his whole army against the enemy near Stillwater, General Arnold [Schuyler was still in command] would not be able to send a strong force against Colonel Baum.

3rd. That he had received intelligence that Colonel St Leger was besieging Fort Stanwix, and that Arnold intended to send a considerable force to the relief of this place; therefore, it was of the greatest importance that a detachment of the left wing should make a move and thus intimidate the enemy, and prevent him from sending this force against St Leger.'

Von Riedesel states in his *Memoirs* that Burgoyne was warned of the dangers of the road to Bennington, which ran through dense forests, by a Tory officer who informed him that at least 3000 men were required to reach that village.

Baum marched out with a mixed force of Germans and Tories: 175 dismounted dragoons; less than 200 German infantrymen, chiefly grenadiers and light troops; a squad of Hesse-Hanau artillerymen, with two three-pounders; fifty of Fraser's marksmen; 300 Tories and Canadians; and a small number of Indians—a total, with officers, sergeants, and musicians of about 800 men. Some German women accompanied the expedition; so also did Captain O'Connell, who acted as interpreter for Baum who spoke no English. The choice of Germans to compose the bulk of the force, decided by their position on the left of the line, was unwise, since, heavily encumbered and ponderous as they were, they slowed the march when mobility and speed were essential for an expedition designed to sally deep into enemy country.

Marching the sixteen miles from Battenkill to Cambridge in twelve hours, Baum clashed with a small detachment of rebels, whom he drove off, taking eight prisoners and capturing some carts, wagons, and oxen, but losing the horses which were killed or driven away by the Indians. This circumstance led Baum to suggest to Burgoyne the advisability of paying the Indians for each horse they brought in. From the prisoners Baum learned, as he informed Burgoyne in a letter dated August 13th, that the magazine at Bennington was guarded by 1500 to 1800 of the enemy. Despite this alarming news, Baum pushed on, mounting the watershed between the Batten-kill and Hoosick rivers, and halting four miles short of Bennington.

News of the skirmish at Cambridge, and information that a considerable number of enemy troops were involved, was brought to Stark at Bennington. Realizing that it was no mere Indian raid, he despatched Colonel Greg with 200 men to San Coick's Mill to delay the enemy's advance while he mobilized his troops. He also sent orders to Warner at Manchester to come at once to Bennington, a distance of twenty miles, despatched messengers to rouse the countryside, and rallied his own brigade for action next day.

Baum advanced from Cambridge on August 14th and reached San Coick's Mill, at the confluence of Owl Kill stream and the Hoosick River, at 8 a.m., 'being fired on by the Rebels in their usual way from bushes' before they retreated. A volunteer from Bennington, Eleazer Eggerton, delayed Baum's advance for an hour by staying behind with two companions to break down the bridge. This they accomplished under heavy fire, permitting Colonel Greg's militiamen to fall back on Stark who had advanced four miles from Bennington. Upon learning of Baum's strength, he retreated to within one mile of the village.

From San Coick's Mill, Baum sent word to Burgoyne, informing him that the five prisoners he had taken that morning confirmed that 'from 1500 to 1800 are in Bennington, but are supposed to leave it on our approach', and he stated that 'people are flocking in hourly, but want to be armed; the savages cannot be controlled; they ruin and take away everything they please'.

Baum's dispatch was received by Burgoyne that same evening. He replied at 'seven at night', assuring Baum that 'the accounts you have sent me are very satisfactory, and I have no doubt of every part of your proceeding continuing to be the same', and advising him that, 'should you find the enemy too strongly posted at Bennington, and maintaining such a countenance as may make an attack imprudent', he should hold his ground, and 'I will either support you in force or withdraw you'. The news that the rebels at Bennington numbered between 1500 and 1800 men did not alarm Burgoyne. Yet such numbers were unexpected for, as far as he knew, only the remnant of Warner's force lay on his left flank.

After the bridge had been repaired, Baum continued his pursuit of Greg's men, reaching to within four miles of Bennington before nightfall. Thereupon Stark, as he stated in his report written after the battle, acted thus: 'I drew up my little army in order of battle, but when the enemy hove in sight, they halted on a very advantageous hill or piece of ground I sent out small parties in their front to skirmish with them, which scheme had a good effect. They killed and wounded thirty of the enemy without any loss on our side, but the ground that I was upon did [not] suit for a general action. I marched back about one mile and incamped. Called a counsel, and it was agreed that we should send two detachments in their rear, while the others attacked them in front.'

That night Baum wrote Burgoyne a second letter, asking for reinforcements. It reached the British camp at 6 a.m., and Burgoyne was roused to read it. He sent his aide, Sir Francis Clerke, to von Riedesel, instructing him to send Lieutenant-Colonel von Breymann, with the advance corps, to aid Baum. This order 'much troubled' von Riedesel who asked, and obtained, permission to give von Breymann a few suggestions. In his orders, Burgoyne told von Breymann that he was being sent out 'in consequence of good news received from Baum', and it was left to his judgment whether or not to attack the enemy, after joining Baum, whom he outranked. Von Breymann marched on the morning of August 15th with 550 men and two six-pounder cannon, mounted on carts, as he described later:

'I started, therefore at 9 o'clock; and there not being any teams, I had two ammunition boxes placed upon the artillery wagons. Each soldier carried with him forty cartridges. The crossing of the Battenkill consumed considerable time, for the men had all to wade through the water. The great number of hills, the bottomless roads, and a severe and continuous rain, made the march so tedious that I could scarcely make one-half of an English mile an hour. The cannons and the ammunition wagons had to be drawn up hill one after the other. All this, of course, impeded our march very much; and I was unable to hasten it notwithstanding all of my endeavours. The carts loaded with ammunition upset, and it caused considerable trouble to right them.

'To this, also, was added another difficulty. The guide, whom we had, lost the way and could not find it again. At last, Major Barner found a man who put us back on the right path.

'All these unexpected mishaps prevented me from marching on the enemy on the 15th, as far as Cambridge, and, I, therefore, found myself obliged to encamp seven miles this side of that place.

'Before reaching that place, however, I wrote to Lieutenant Colonel Baum notifying him of my arrival, and sent Lieutenant Hageman with the dispatch.'

It rained all day and von Breymann's men slogged through the mud, halting frequently to dress ranks, as German military pedantry demanded even on the march. The overloaded artillery carts upset, spilling their cannon and stores, and had to be righted and dragged back on to the track. At nightfall von Breymann was still seventeen miles behind Baum. Marching until midnight, Warner's regiment reached to within one mile of Bennington, and Warner himself hurried on ahead to join Stark. At 11 p.m., Lieutenant Hageman reached Baum's camp to report that von Breymann was on his way to help him. During the night, or early next day, Colonel Skene rode back to meet and hurry on von Breymann.

Stark also had a visitor that night. Amongst the militia who had answered his call from the surrounding countryside. came a contingent from the town of Pittsfield, commanded by no less a person than their minister, parson Thomas Allen. Allen entered Stark's cabin and demanded to be allowed to attack the enemy which, previously, he and his men had not been permitted to do. 'Would you go out on this dark and rainy night?' enquired Stark. He told the warlike minister to 'go back to your people, and tell them to get some rest if they can, and if the Lord gives us some sunshine, and I do not give you fighting enough, I will never ask you to come out again.'

At dawn on the 16th the rain was still falling heavily. Baum, with 170 dragoons and twenty of Fraser's marksmen, with one cannon and some Indians under St Luc, were encamped upon the hill which rose to 300 feet. The hill overlooked the Walloomac River, but because of its convex shape, the swampy ground by the river was invisible from its summit. On this low ground, Baum had placed four detachments; one beyond the river, 250 yards south of the bridge, which was defended by 150 Tories who built a breastwork of logs; another to protect the bridge across the river, which was occupied by Canadians under the command of Charles de Lanaudière; another behind the bridge, defended by twenty of Fraser's marksmen and fifty Germans, with the second cannon; and the fourth at the bottom of the hill and to the north of the road, in which he had placed fifty Germans and the rest of the Tories, to prevent an attack on the bridge and road from the rear. The German women

huddled in a little cabin near the bridge, and, to complete the
defence fifty German *chasseurs* had been thrown forward down
the south-eastern flanks of the hill, which later became known
as 'Hessian Hill' and on which a monument to the memorable
battle has been raised.

During the morning, Stark, who had been joined overnight
by contingents of local militia from Vermont and New York,
pursued the plan he had formed to surround and destroy Baum.
His troops numbered over 2000 men, more than double those of
the enemy. Keeping 100 men in reserve, he 'detached Col.
Nichols with 200 men to attack them in the rear. I also sent
Col. Herrick with 300 men in the rear of their right, both to
join, and when joined to attack their rear. I likewise sent the
Colonels Hubbard and Whitney with 200 men on their right,
and sent 100 men in their front, to draw away their attention
that way, and about 3 o'clock we got all ready for the attack.
Col. Nichols began the same, which was followed by all the rest.
The remainder of my little army I pushed up in the front, and
in a few minutes the action began.'

According to legend, which lacks documentary authenti-
cation, Stark said jokingly: 'We'll beat them today or by night
Molly Stark's a widow.'

Whether or not by preconceived design, many of the American militiamen adopted the ruse of pretending to be Tories
coming in to join Baum and Skene. Placing pieces of white
paper in their hats, which identified them as Loyalists, the
simple shirt-sleeved farmers worked their way in between the
scattered enemy posts, infiltrating the position, and mingling
with the men they had come to kill. Though he was warned that
the armed men in shirt-sleeves, whose 'demeanour as well as
their dress and style of equipment plainly and incontestibly
pointed them out as Americans', Baum refused to heed, 'most
of all', stated the Tory leader Jessup, 'because Colonel Skene by
his credulity [allowed] the enemy to acquire a considerable
knowledge of our strength'. Baum, he said, 'allowed people to go

and come from his camp, readily believing their professions of sympathy with the Royal Cause, and imparting to them most fully and completely all information as to his strength and designs'. This course did not meet with the approval of his subordinates. They believed that, concealed beneath the plain manners and open countenances of the visitors, there was a keenness and avidity in collecting facts, and that under the guise of simple questions and a careless listening to the answers, valuable information was being carefully sought for, and too readily obtained.

An aged veteran of the battle, whose story is told by Frederick Kidder and Augustus Gould (*History of New Ipswich*, 1852), describes his fellow militiamen.

'To a man they wore small-clothes, coming down and fastening just below the knee, and long stockings with cowhide shoes ornamented by large buckles, while not a pair of boots graced the company. The coats and waistcoats were loose and of huge dimensions, with colours as various as the barks of oak, sumach and other trees of our hills and swamps could make them and their shirts were all made of flax and, like every other part of the dress, were homespun. On their heads was worn a large round-top and broad-brimmed hat. Their arms were as various as their costume. Here an old soldier carried a heavy Queen's Arm, with which he had done service at the conquest of Canada twenty years previous, while by his side walked a stripling boy, with a Spanish fusée not half its weight or calibre, which his grandfather may have taken at the Havana, while not a few had old French pieces that dated back to the reduction of Louisburg. Instead of the cartridge box, a large powder horn was slung under the arm, and occasionally a bayonet might be seen bristling in the ranks. Some of the swords of the officers had been made by our Province blacksmiths, perhaps from some farming utensil; they looked serviceable, but heavy and uncouth.'

Firing from the flanks notified the infiltrators that the moment had come to throw off their masks. Raising their muskets, they shot down the unsuspecting Germans and Tories whom they had duped. Local tradition relates that the first shot was fired by Jacob Onderkirke of Hooisick; his bullet killed a German major. The posts were attacked on all sides, and the flanking parties wormed their way up Hessian Hill, firing from behind trees at Baum's dragoons who were sheltering behind their crude breastworks. Most of the soldiers in the exposed posts threw down their arms and fled into the woods, and the bridge was quickly occupied by the main contingent led by Stark himself. He dismounted and hitched his brown mare to a fence; but while he was fighting it was stolen, and after the battle he offered a $20 reward for its recovery.

The Tories, who occupied the redoubt to the south of the river, were attacked by an American party led by Ebenezer Webster, the father of the more famous Daniel, which included the warlike Parson Allen. Recognizing some of the Tories who came from his own district, he went forward, stood on a log and exhorted them in his best pulpit manner to defect to the American cause. 'There's Parson Allen. Let's pot him,' came the cry from the redoubt. His neighbour's volley failed to harm Allen, and Webster led the rush over the breastwork. The Tory Captain Peters takes up the story: 'A little before the Loyalists gave way, the rebels rushed with a strong party on the front of the Loyalists which I commanded. As they were coming up, I observed a man fire at me, which I returned. He loaded again as he came up, and discharged again at me, crying out, "Peters, you damn Tory, I have got you." He rushed on me with his bayonet, which entered just below my left breast but was turned by my bones. By this time I was loaded and saw it was a rebel Captain, Jeremiah Post by name, an old school-mate and playfellow, and a cousin of my wife. Though his bayonet was in my body I felt regret at being obliged to destroy him.'

The Tories were forced to abandon their redoubt. The

majority were taken prisoner; some succeeded in escaping down
the road to join von Breymann; and others fled up the hill to
throw in their lot with Baum who was by now fiercely assailed
by Stark's men who had reached the summit. As their assailants
stormed in, the dragoons lumbered off down the hill, running
straight into Stark's reserve, advancing along the road. The
battle became a confused mêlée. Baum and a party of dragoons
put up a stiff fight till their ammunition was exhausted. He
then ordered his men to sling their carbines and fight their way
out with their swords, a manoeuvre which gained them a little
time because of the Americans' lack of bayonets. Baum was
shot through the stomach and fell mortally wounded, and the
dragoons lumbered off into the woods, hotly pursued by their
lightfooted foes.

The battle had lasted for two hours and 'it was the hottest
I ever saw in my life', reported Stark, who in 1759 had stood
with Wolfe on the Plains of Abraham. 'It represented one
continued clap of thunder,' he told General Gates. 'However,
the enemy was obliged to give way, and leave their field-pieces
and all their baggage behind them. They were all invironed
within two breastworks, with their artillery. But our martial
courage proved too hard for them.'

The Americans halted to plunder the enemy's posts, and
several men tried to load and fire the captured cannon: but the
mechanism was beyond their knowledge, until Stark came to
the rescue. Other parties pursued the fleeing dragoons whose
heavy swords and scabbards became entangled in the trees,
bringing them to a halt. Stark ordered his men to rally to secure
the victory, but 'in a few minutes I was informed there was a
large reinforcement on their march within two miles of us.
Luckily for us, that moment Colonel Warner's regiment came
up fresh, who marched on and began the attack afresh.'
Stark ordered a hogshead of rum to be broached to refresh
his exhausted men but, according to Captain Barnes, 'so eager
were they to attack the enemy, upon their being reinforced,

that they tarried not to taste it, but rushed on the enemy with an ardour perhaps unparalleled.' Parson Allen secured a German surgeon's horse, the panniers of which were filled with bottles of wine, which he carried to the wounded soldiers.

Marching through Cambridge where he was joined by the carriages and horses sent back by Skene, von Breymann, making slow progress, his ammunition carts continually breaking down, was met at 2 p.m. by messengers from Skene who asked that a detachment should be sent ahead to secure San Coick's Mill from the enemy. Von Breymann despatched Captain Gleissenberg with an advance guard of eighty men, who found the mill unoccupied, and he himself, with Skene who had joined him, reached it about 4 p.m. Though the battleground was only four miles distant, and the fighting was at that time at its height, von Breymann heard no sound of firing. Several fugitives came in, each telling a different story, one stating that Baum was cut off and in great danger, and another, Captain Campbell, that 'things were not so bad'. Skene was cheerful and inclined to believe him, though von Breymann appears to have had his doubts; 'at this time I knew nothing of his [Baum's] engagement being over. If Colonel Skene knew it, I cannot conceive what his reasons were for concealing it from me. If I had known it, I certainly would not have engaged the enemy.' Von Breymann decided to advance in support of Baum; but in the sultry heat his men, fatigued by their long march, plodded along very slowly. According to Hadden, this gave rise to the rumour, related in the camp after the battle, that a 'pique' between von Breymann and Baum was responsible for the former's tardiness, and that he was heard to say, when he heard the firing ahead: 'We will let them get warm before we reach them.'

Skene led the advance for 1000 yards, but then he noticed some men, some clad in jackets, others in their shirt-sleeves, moving along the hills to the north of the road. Thinking that they were Tories he galloped up the slope crying, 'Are you for

King George?' He reached to within a hundred yards before the militia opened fire, killing his horse, but missing him. Skene continued his story in a letter he wrote subsequently to Lord Dartmouth:

'The Chesseurs advanced near Enough to Return their fire and begin the Action, Major Bernar immediately took to the Side of the Hill on our left Flank and rushed the Enemy so Close, that they retreated before him—Lt. Col. Brymen allways advanced in front to shew his men an Example; unluckily the Granadiers did not Close with the Enemy, but continued flinging away their Ammunition at too great a Distance; the Cannon two Six pounders, advanced within point Blank Grape shot & continued firing for an hour and a half and the Enemy continually retreated for about two Miles, the Country was pretty open on our Right with a River near our flank; on the left was an Easy Hill of Ascent thinly Wooded. Victory was at our command had the Granadiers been Quick on their March; and not Wasted their Ammunition at too Great a Distance, which they wanted when the Sun was Setting; and I endeavoured to supply by Galloping to the Ammunition Cart, which I brought up untill I found them retreating; as Col. Brymen was not with them, I rallied and took the Liberty of halting them, at the Mills of Sancoick, Lt. Col. Brymen was the last man of his party that Arrived in the Night, it was my duty as Commissioner of Supplies to provide Carriages, which I did, and brought the Wounded, and Baggage even to knapsacks.'

Warner's regiment had reached the bridge captured by Skene's men at 5 p.m. and, after stopping to drink at the river, had pushed on along its bank. It was becoming dark and both sides were exhausted. The Germans had fired all their ammunition, many had been killed or wounded, and their artillery horses were either dead or too done-up to be useful.

Von Breymann ordered his contingent to retreat, leaving their cannon behind. Warner's Vermonters followed, Stark observing 'I pushed forward as many of the men as I could to their assistance. The battle continued obstinate on both sides till sunset. The enemy was obliged to retreat. We pursued them till dark. But had daylight lasted one hour longer, we should have taken the whole body of them. We recovered 4 pieces of brass cannon, some hundred stands of arms, 8 brass barrells, drums, several Hessian swords, about seven hundred prisoners. 207 dead on the spot. The number of wounded is as yet unknown. That part of the enemy that made their escape marched all night, and we returned to our camp.'

Stark was unaware that the opportunity to capture nearly all von Breymann's men had been lost. As darkness fell, the retreating Germans, many of who had thrown away their arms, halted and offered to surrender, which they signified by beat of drum, a message that conveyed nothing to their victors who were unversed in European military etiquette. Scattering through the woods, the Germans escaped under cover of darkness, and two-thirds of them reached safety at Cambridge. Fearing that his men would shoot each other in the darkness, Stark called off the pursuit. His victory had been prodigious. Between them, Baum and von Breymann had lost 207 men killed, and 700 prisoners; of Baum's 375 German troops, only nine escaped. The American casualties amounted to thirty killed and forty wounded. An army of rustic marksmen had defeated two armies, composed largely of disciplined regular troops and led by experienced soldiers. Truly, as *Almons Remembrancer* reported, Saturday, August 16th, was a 'memorable' day in American military annals, and 'General Stark will be endeared to us for ever'.

Stark, on his part, paid tribute to his officers and men;

'Too much honour cannot be given to the brave officers and soldiers for gallant behaviour. They fought through the midst of fire and smoke, mounted two breastworks that was well fortified and supported with cannon. I can't particularize any officer as they all behaved with the greatest spirit and bravery.

'Colonel Warner's superior skill in the action was of extraordinary service to me. I would be glad he and his men could be recommended by Congress.'

The prisoners were taken to Bennington. The British and Germans were well treated; but the 170 Tories were tied in pairs, each pair attached to a horse and led away midst the jeers and scoffs of the villagers.

XI *The Hudson*

The disaster at Bennington was a staggering blow, for the heavy losses sustained—one-seventh of the army—had reduced Burgoyne's combat troops to 4500 men, and the foray had gained no horses. As yet Burgoyne did not know that St Leger would fail to capture Fort Stanwix and would retreat, and that there would thus be no diversionary force to assist his approach to Albany. But by now he did know that there would be no junction of armies on the Hudson, and little prospect of aid from New York, for on August 4th he had received Howe's letter dated July 17th, in which he said his intention was for Pennsylvania. The high hopes of early summer had been dashed and in sixty days victory had turned into defeat. Many of the Indians had deserted, and the recruitment of Tories had been disappointing. Only about 400, half of them unarmed, had joined the expedition, and the rest were 'trimmers actuated by self-interest'. In a private letter, written on August 20th, Burgoyne told Germain: 'The great bulk of the country is undoubtedly with Congress in principle and zeal; and their measures are executed with a secrecy and dispatch that are not to be equalled. Wherever the king's forces point, militia to the amount of three or four thousand assemble in twenty-four hours; they bring wih them their subsistence etc., and the alarm over, they return to their farms.'

Had the expedition to Bennington succeeded, he said, he could have effected the junction with St Leger, and 'been now before Albany'. The march to Bennington had been worth hazarding, and he thought the misfortune would have been avoided had 'Mr Breymann marched at the rate of two miles an hour any given twelve hours out of two and thirty'. He told the Secretary of State of the industry of the rebels in driving away cattle and removing corn, and he complained of lack of news from Sir William Howe, to whom he had sent messengers. Two of them had, however, been caught and hanged, and the same fate probably had befallen those from Howe, from whom he had received only one letter.

'No operation, My Lord,' Burgoyne lamented, 'has yet been undertaken in my favour; the highlands have not even been threatened. The consequence is, that Putnam has detached two brigades to Mr Gates, who is now strongly posted near the mouth of the Mohawk River, with an army superior to mine in troops of the Congress, and as many militia as he pleases. He is likewise far from being deficient in artillery, having received all the pieces that were landed from the French ships which got into Boston.'

Washington, he said, had sent 2500 men to Albany, and another 4000 to guard the Highlands. Having recorded his pessimistic view of the situation, Burgoyne examined the future:

'Had I a latitude in my orders, I should think it my duty to wait in this position, or perhaps as far back as Fort Edward, where my communication with Lake George would be perfectly secure, till some event happened to assist my movement forward, but my orders being positive to "force a junction with Sir William Howe", I apprehend I am not at liberty to remain inactive longer than shall be necessary to collect twenty-five days provisions, and to receive the reinforcement of the additional companies, the German drafts and recruits now (and unfortunately only now) on Lake Champlain. The waiting the arrival of this reinforcement is of indispensible necessity, because from the hour I pass the Hudson's River and proceed towards Albany, all safety of communication ceases. I must expect a large body of the enemy from my left will take post behind me. I have put out of the question the waiting longer than the time necessary for the foregoing purposes, because the attempt, then critical, depending on adventure and the fortune that often accompanies it, and hardly justifiable but by orders from the state, would afterwards be consumately desperate. I mean, my Lord, that by moving soon, though I should meet with insurmountable difficulties to my progress, I shall at least have a chance of fighting my way back to Ticonderoga, but the season a little further advanced, the distance increased, and the march unavoidably tardy, because surrounded by enemies a retreat might be shut by impenetrable bars or the elements, and at the same time no possible means of existence remain in the country.

'When I wrote more confidently, I little foresaw that I was to be left to pursue my way through such a tract of country, and hosts of foes, without any co-operation from New York, nor did I then think the garrison of Ticonderoga would fall to my share alone, a dangerous experiment would it be to leave that post in weakness, and too heavy a drain it is upon the life-blood of my force to give it due strength.'

Yet he did not despond, Burgoyne assured Germain. Should he succeed in forcing his way to Albany, and be able to exist there, he would think no more of retreat, but would fortify himself and await Howe's operations. The last paragraph of the letter, however, shows that Burgoyne was beginning to despair of reaching his objective;

'Whatever may be my fate, my Lord, I submit my actions to the breast of the King, and to the candid judgment of my profession, when all the motives become public, and I rest in the confidence, that whatever decision may be passed upon my conduct, my good intent will not be questioned.'

In his Public Dispatch, Burgoyne dismised the reverse at Bennington as 'a common accident of war, independent of any general action, unattended by any loss that could affect the main strength of the army, and little more than the miscarriage of a foraying party'.

Showing unusual perspicacity, Germain called the result of the battle of Bennington 'fatal' and, looking back from hindsight, he described it as the 'cause of all our subsequent misfortunes'.

Unfairly—for to send such unwieldly and ponderous soldiers on the foray had been his own decision—Burgoyne criticized the Germans, an accusation to which von Riedesel replied in his *Memoirs*:

'The English, as usual, endeavoured to lay the entire blame of the ill success of this expedition upon the Germans. Burgoyne had merely made a mistake in selecting only Germans for the attack on Bennington, since, in their opinion, they not only marched too slow but carried too much baggage. The English said that the hats and swords of the dragoons were as heavy as the whole equipment of a British soldier. It is true that justice was done to the bravery of Colonel Baum, but they also said that he did not possess the least knowledge of the country, its people, or its language. But who selected him for this expedition?'

'It was much regretted' in the camp, states Lieutenant Digby, that British troops were not sent in the place of the Germans, a remark that indicates the national jealousies present in the campaign in which the German soldiers served with distinction and bravery (handicapped as they were by heavy equipment and military pedantry), and in which they had no interest. At the end of the campaign, Burgoyne regretted that his force had not been entirely British. Slighted by Burgoyne, who kept him from his counsels, von Riedesel found solace in the arrival of his wife, Frederika, with their three little children, for whose journey from Canada he had obtained Burgoyne's permission. She had written urging and imploring her husband to allow her to join him:

'I told him I had sufficient health and pluck to undertake it, and that no matter what happened he would never hear me murmur, but, on the contrary, I hoped to make myself very useful to him on many occasions. He answered me that as soon as it was possible for women to follow the army, I should certainly be sent for. A little while after he wrote me that my wish would now soon be fulfilled; and just as I, in full anticipation, had got myself ready for the journey, Captain Willoe came to escort me. One can easily imagine how warmly he was welcomed by me.

'Two days after his arrival we set out. A boat which belonged to my husband and another one brought us to Three Rivers. The troops on board of the first boat were commanded by the good sergeant, Burich, who showed me every possible attention, and who, since this time, has always kept an eye upon our baggage. Night overtook us, and we found ourselves obliged to land upon an island. The other boat, which was more heavily laden, and was not so well manned, had not been able to keep up with us. We had, consequently, neither beds nor candles; and that which was the most distressing was, that we had nothing more to eat, for we had taken with us upon the boat, only enough to last us (as we supposed) during the day. Besides, we found upon this island nothing but the four bare walls of a deserted and unfinished house, which was filled with bushes that served as a couch for the night. I covered them with our cloaks, making use, also, of the cushions of the boats; and in this way we had a right good sleep.

'I could not induce Captain Willoe to come into the hut. I saw that he was very much troubled about something, but could not at all make out the cause of it. Meanwhile, I observed a soldier set a pot upon the fire. I asked him what he had in it? "Potatoes, which I have brought with me," he replied. I looked wistfully at them, but he had so few, that I thought it cruel to rob him of them, especially as he seemed so happy in their possession. Finally, however, my intense desire to give some to my children triumphed over my modesty, and I therefore begged, and obtained half, which, at the most, might have been a dozen. At the same time, he handed me out of his pocket two or three small ends of candles, which gave me great joy, as the children were afraid to remain in the dark. I gave him for the whole, a thaler, which made him as happy as myself. In the meantime, I heard Captain Willoe give an order for a fire to be kindled around our building, and for his men to go the rounds the whole night. I heard, also, during the entire night considerable commotion outside, which hindered me a little from sleeping. The following morning as I was at breakfast, which I had spread upon a stone, that served us for a table, I asked the captain, who was eating with me, and who, by the way, had slept in the boat, what was the cause of the noises? He then acknowledged that we had been in great danger, from the fact that this island was *L'Isle à Sonnettes* (Rattlesnake Island), so named on account of many rattlesnakes being found upon it; that he had not known of it until too late; and that when he did become aware of it, he was very much frightened, but still had not dared to sail further in the night on account of the storm. There had been, therefore, nothing left for him to do, but to build a great fire and make considerable noise, hoping in this way to frighten the snakes and keep them off. His knowledge of our danger, however, had kept him from sleeping a wink the whole night. Upon hearing this, I was very much terrified, and remarked to him, that we had immeasurably increased our danger by lying down upon the bushes, in which the snakes like to hide. He acknowledged that I was right, and said that if he had known at the time where we were he would have had all the bushes taken away, or else would have begged us rather to remain in the boat. He had first learned the fact, however, from the people in our other boat, which had overtaken us later in the evening. In the morning we found on every side the skins and slime of these nasty creatures, and accordingly, made haste to finish our breakfast.

'After our morning meal, we were ferried over Lake Champlain, and came at noon to Fort John, where we were received by the commander with kindness and much courtesy. Thus it was everywhere; so much was my husband loved, both by the English and by the inhabitants of the country. Here we again took our boats in order to reach a cutter, upon which we came to Wolf's Island, where we remained the entire night on board the ship. During the night we had a thunderstorm, which appeared to us the more terrible, as it seemed as if we were lying in the bottom of a caldron surrounded by mountains and great trees. The following day we passed Ticonderoga, and about noon arrived at Fort George, where we dined with Colonel Anstruther, an exceedingly good and amiable man, who commanded the 62nd Regiment. In the afternoon we seated ourselves in a calash, and reached Fort Edward on the same day, which was the 14th of August. My husband had actually left this place the day before with the further advance of the army; but as soon as he heard of our arrival, he returned on the 15th, and remained with us until the 16th. On that day he was obliged, to my great sorrow, to rejoin the army. But immediately after the unlucky affair at Bennington, I had the joy of seeing him again with us on the 18th, and spending with him three happy weeks in the greatest tranquillity. A few days after my arrival, news came that we were cut off from Canada. If, therefore, I had not taken advantage of this fortunate opportunity, I would have been obliged to remain behind in Canada, three long years without my husband. The sole circumstance, which led to this—as it proved for us—fortunate determination was as follows. Upon the arrival of milady Ackland at the army, General Burgoyne said to my husband, "General, you shall have your wife here also!" Whereupon he immediately dispatched Captain Willoe for me. We led, during these three weeks, a very pleasant life. The surrounding country was magnificent; and we were encircled by the encampments of the English and German troops. We lived in a building called the Red House [Burgoyne's headquarters]. I had only one room for my husband, myself and my children, in which my husband also slept, and had besides all his writing materials. My women servants slept in a kind of hall. When it was beautifyl weather we took our meals under the trees, but if not, in a barn, upon boards, which we laid upon casks and served as a table. It was at this place that I ate bear's flesh for the first time, and found it of capital flavour. We were often put to it to get any thing to eat; notwithstanding this, however, I was very happy and content, for I was with my children, and beloved by those by whom I was surrounded. There were, if I remember rightly, four or five adjutants staying with us. The evening was spent by the gentlemen in playing cards, and by myself in putting my children to bed.'

Madame von Riedesel called the reverse at Bennington 'this unfortunate event' that 'paralized at once our operations', and, following it, she says, the army remained inactive for three weeks. Burgoyne had kept Howe's dispatch to himself, and even von Riedesel was not let into the secret, that Howe had gone to Pennsylvania, until August 10th. The regimental officers knew only that a messenger had come from New York, and that Burgoyne, on August 10th, had sent Cornet Grant of his own regiment of light dragoons to try to get through to General Clinton at New York. Grant was obliged to return through the woods, records Digby, running great risks, 'to the very great dissatisfaction of General Burgoyne'.

Burgoyne suffered other disappointments; the Tories proved reluctant to join him, and the remainder of the Indians, headed by St Luc who had escaped from Bennington, declared their intention to go home, where the harvest required gathering. Von Riedesel considered that the loss of these Sioux, Sacks,

Foxes, Menominees, Winnebagos, Ottawas, and Chippewas was very serious, 'as the Indians were mainly used as guards at the outposts, the rebels hardly ever dared to come near them, well knowing that the wild men were very cunning, and their eyes and ears very acute. This is proved by the fact that as soon as they had left, the enemy began to molest the outposts and became very troublesome.'

The desertion of the Indians was only partly recompensed by the arrival, on September 4th, of a body of Mohawks, who brought their families, their village having been laid waste by the enemy. Lieutenant Anburey's admirable sense of curiosity supplies us with a description of these Indians, and their method of scalping:

'Upon their arrival I visited them at their encampment, and had an opportunity of observing the mode they adopt in training up their children. They are in a manner amphibious; there were several of the men bathing in the creek, and a number of little children, the eldest could not be more than six years old, and these little creatures had got into the middle of the creek upon planks, which they paddled along, sometimes sitting, then standing on them, and if they overbalance the plank and slip off, with a dexterity almost incredible they get on it again; as to diving, they will keep a considerable time under water, nearly two or three minutes.

'The mode of confining their young infants is by binding them flat on their backs to a board, and as they are swaddled up to their heads, it makes them resemble living mummies; this method of binding their young, I am led to imagine, is the cause of that perfect symmetry among the men. A deformed Indian is rare to be met with; the women would be equally as perfect, but as they grow up they acquire a habit, it being deemed an ornament, of so turning in the feet that their toes almost meet; the squaws, after they have suckled their infants, if they fall asleep, lay them on the ground, if not, they hang the board they are swaddled to on the branch of a tree and swing them till they do; upon a march they tie these boards, with their infants, on their backs.

'When they arrive, as they imagine, in hearing of the camp, they set up the war whoop, as many times as they have number of prisoners. It is difficult to describe . . . and the best idea that I can convey is that it consists in the sound of *whoo, whoo, whoop*! which is continued till the breath is almost exhausted, and then broken off with a sudden elevation of voice; some of them modulate it into notes, by placing the hand before the mouth, but both are heard at a great distance.

'Whenever they scalp, they seize the head of the disabled or dead enemy, and placing one of their feet on the neck, twist their left hand in the hair, by which means they extend the skin that covers the top of the head, and with the other hand draw their scalping knife from their breast, which is always kept in good order for this cruel purpose, a few dextrous strokes of which takes off the part that is termed the scalp; they are so exceedingly expeditious in doing this, that it scarcely exceeds a minute. If the hair is short, and they have no purchase with their hand, they stoop, and with their teeth strip if off; when they have performed this part of their martial virtue, as soon as time permits, they tie with bark or deer's sinews their speaking trophies of blood in a small hoop, to preserve it from putrefaction, painting part of the scalp and the hoop all round with red. These they preserve as monuments of their prowess, and at the same time as proofs of the vengeance they have inflicted on their enemies.

'At one of the Indian encampments, I saw several scalps hanging upon poles in front of their wigwams; one of them had remarkably fine long hair hanging to it. An officer that was with me wanted to purchase it, at which the Indian seemed highly offended, nor would he part with this barbarous trophy, although he was offered so strong a temptation as a bottle of rum.

'The appearance of a dead body . . . is not a pleasing spectacle; but when scalped it is shocking; two, in this situation, we met in our march from Skenesborough to Fort Edward. After so cruel an operation, you could hardly suppose anyone could survive, but when we took possession of Ticonderoga, we found two poor fellows who lay wounded, that had been scalped in the skirmish the day before the Americans abandoned it, and who are in a fair way of recovery. I have seen a person who had been scalped, and was as hearty as ever, but his hair never grew again.

'Should I at any time be unfortunate enough to get wounded, and the Indians come across me with an intention to scalp, it would be my wish to receive at once a *coup de grace* with their tomahawk, which in most instances they mercifully allow.

'This instrument they make great use of in war, for in pursuing an enemy, if they find it impossible to come up with them, they with the utmost dexterity throw, and seldom fail striking it into the skull or back of those they pursue, by that means arresting them in flight. The tomahawk is nothing more than a small hatchett, having either a sharp spike or a cup for tobacco affixed opposite to the part that is intended for cutting, but they are mostly made to answer two purposes, that of a pipe and a hatchet. When they purchase them off the traders, they take off the wooden handle, and substitute in its stead a hollow cane one, which they do in a curious manner'.

These Mohawks, on their arrival at the camp, brought in the four scalps they had taken from seven rebels they had killed in a skirmish along the road. Another party, led by a chief, reached the camp on August 28th. They came from Oswego, having travelled 100 miles through the wilderness, and had retreated with St Leger. They acquainted Burgoyne, of St Leger's intention to return to Canada and he now knew that he could expect no help from that quarter. By that date, states Digby, Burgoyne had decided to sever all kind of communication with Canada. He could not remain inactive; high as was the morale of his troops, desertions were increasing and the officers had proved reluctant to reduce their baggage, for which he himself had failed to set the required example. While Burgoyne wined and dined with his mistress—to Madame von Riedesel's scandalized disapproval—at Duer's House, Fort Miller, his adjutant-general Major Kingston, issued an order forbidding the use of horses and carts for private purposes, with the threat, in the case of officers, of 'cashiering' (i.e. dismissal) with the utmost disgrace, and in that of the soldiers of being tried by court martial for theft.

In another order, designed to deter desertions, Kingston stated:

'The General Zeal of this Army in the Cause of the King and British Constitution is too apparent to admit of suspicion of the Crime of desertion ever entering the Men's Minds, except when they are intoxicated, or imposed upon by Emissaries of the Enemy. There is reason to believe that such Emissaries have dared to intrude themselves in the Camp, and by their Specious promises, false representations and perhaps by Readiness in the German Language have deluded these late Criminals to an Ignominous Death.'

He was referring to the case of four German recruits who had disappeared, and 'it is not doubted but they will be brought in, or scalped'. He promised a reward of $100 for the discovery of any person who tampered with any soldier and persuaded him to desert. The money would be paid on the conviction of the offender, who would be punished by death. A lesser reward of $20 was offered for any deserter, or his scalp, brought in. Despite these rich rewards and the fearful penalties, the rate of desertion rose as the army plunged deeper into enemy territory.

On September 3rd, 300 recruits arrived from Canada, increasing the army to a total of 5500 men. Burgoyne mounted

7a. American rifleman's uniform of the period.

b. North American soldier. By Chappel (*New York Public Library*)

8a. *Right:* C.O. Washington's Life Guard
(*New York Public Library*)

b. *Below left:* Uniform of 62nd British
  Regiment.

c. *Below right:* Uniform of a Brunswick
  Dragoon. (*New York Public Library*)

the eighty remaining German dragoons, and added 100 picked men to Fraser's marksmen, to replace the Indians and to prevent such incidents as when, on September 1st, an outpost manned by thirty Canadians was surprised and taken prisoner by American patrols who became bolder as the danger from Burgoyne's Indians lessened. About that date he was told by an American deserter that the enemy's troops, twenty miles to the south, numbered 14,000 to 15,000, an exaggerated figure which implied that they numbered nearly three times his own army.

The victory at Bennington had elated the Americans. The heartening news of Stark's feat, and of Herkimer's heroic stand at Oriskany, soon to be followed by the glorious news of the relief of Fort Stanwix, spread throughout the colonies. The dark days of uncertainty were over; despair gave way to hope; and, throughout New England, men flocked to join the militia. The harvest had been gathered and the farmers were free, if they so willed, to march 'agin' Burgoyne. 'One more such victory', wrote Washington, 'and we shall have no great cause for anxiety as to the future designs of Britain.' He hoped that New England would rise and crush Burgoyne, he told General Putman, 'as there is not now the least danger of General Howe going to New England'. Howe had landed at the Head of Elk, in Delaware Bay, which proved that his destination was Philadelphia. On August 22nd, the day he heard the news of Bennington, Washington issued a Special Order, expressing his happiness to inform the army 'of the signal victory obtained to the northward'.

General Schuyler also employed the word 'signal' to describe the victory which came too late to revive his shattered reputation. On July 29th, Congress had passed a resolution calling for an inquiry into the loss of Fort Ticonderoga, and had requested Washington to appoint a successor to Schuyler; Gates's intrigues had borne fruit. Upon the commander-in-chief's refusal to do so, Congress voted for Gates who, on August

14th, was accorded almost dictatorial powers, being given authority to suspend officers and appoint others 'until the pleasure of Congress be known'. Gates dawdled on his way to Albany, arriving on the 19th, to become the beneficiary of the great victory. 'Until the country is safe, I shall stifle my resentment', remarked Schuyler when he heard the news of his supersession. He accepted his fall with the philosophy of a great gentleman, expressing his sentiments on September 7th, to Gouveneur Morris, a member of the New York Provincial Congress:

'I thank you for sympathizing with me on my removal from the command in this department at a time when our affairs were at the worst and when no change could happen but what must be for the best. Congress I find faults me for painting in strong colours the situation we were in, and yet I dare say if I had not done it and any capital misfortune had happened they would have asked why they had not been truly informed. But my crime consists in not being a New England man in principle, and unless they alter theirs I hope I never shall be. Gen. Gates is their idol because he is at their direction.'

Morris had given his opinion of Gates, saying, 'The new Commander-in-Chief . . . may, if he please, neglect to ask or disdain to receive advice. But those who know him well, I am sure, will be convinced that he needs it.' On reaching Albany, Gates called a council of war from which he excluded Schuyler, whom he treated with studied rudeness. Even the callow heart of James Wilkinson bled for Schuyler who was 'obliged to resign the fruits of his labours'. To Washington, Schuyler expressed his 'extreme chagrin' that he had been deprived of his command 'at a time when soon, if ever, we shall probably be enabled to meet the enemy'. That Gates reaped where Schuyler had sown is the almost universal opinion of modern military commentators, few of whom have a good word to say of Gates.

His career ended in ignomy; his repellent character alienated everyone with whom he came into contact.

Horatio Gates, it seems, suffered from a sense of inferiority. His mother had been housekeeper to the Duke of Leeds, and scandal related that Horace Walpole, then a child of eleven, had been his father—an unlikely tale that arose probably because Walpole, whose maid was the boy's mother's friend, became Gates's godfather. His lowly birth, on the fringes of the aristocratic world he admired, turned Gates into a snob; he coveted his superiors' rank, and exalted in their downfall, unctuously enjoying their disgrace, yet revelling in the position of superiority it gave him. He had overthrown by his intrigues the aristocratic Schuyler; to fill his cup of joy it remained only to humble the even more aristocratic Burgoyne.

The appointment of Gates to command the Northern Department stimulated recruitment in New England, whose people respected him for his championship of their claim to the Hampshire Grants in opposition to those of New York State, of which Schuyler had been a prominent advocate. Resourceful and bold in the face of disaster, as Schuyler had shown himself, his value as commander in the north had been destroyed by his inability to win friends in the only area from which support could come. Benefiting from Schuyler's tactics which had delayed Burgoyne for seven vital weeks, Gates set out to placate Stark, praising his great victory, asking his advice, and deploring his lack of promotion. He also sought to win over Arnold, Schuyler's friend, who was popular with the New Englanders and commanded their loyalty. With their help, Gates told these officers, 'We can try our best with Burgoyne'.

The situation that confronted Gates seemed little better than that which had been relinquished by Schuyler, who, on August 19th, expressed his 'pity' for his successor. Burgoyne was only twenty miles away, and Stark and Arnold were engaged to the east and west. Gates's army numbered only 4500 rank and file; perhaps 6000 men in all according to Wilkinson's estimate.

But the victory at Bennington had dispelled the gloom and defeatism which had been induced by earlier defeats and retreats, and had resulted from everyone's failure to take seriously the threat posed by Burgoyne's advance from Canada. Schuyler retired to Albany, embittered against his successor, in whose camp he left two active partisans who, whether or not he encouraged them, awaited an opportunity to undermine Gates's position.

Gates considered himself in no immediate danger from Burgoyne, and within a few days his army was reinforced by the arrival of Morgan's riflemen (the *élite* of the Continental army), 500 frontiersmen from Pennsylvania, Maryland, Virginia and the Jerseys, commanded by Daniel Morgan and his two trusted officers, Lieutenant-Colonel Richard Butler and Major Morris. To this force, which at the end of its long march over bad roads and through stifling heat, numbered only 331 'effectives', Gates added 250 sharpshooters commanded by Major H. Dearborn—who had campaigned with Morgan and Arnold in Canada—about whom he said, 'A more determined officer never wore a sword'.

Morgan was a legendary hero, and his men carried a precise weapon, the Kentucky rifle, which was vastly superior to the rifles carried by some of von Riedesel's Germans. Some unknown genius had substituted for the cumbersome method, whereby European soldiers rapped the ramrod with a little mallet in order to thrust home the bullet, the use of small pieces of greased leather, which were kept in a cavity in the stock, and were wrapped round the bullet. A few taps with the light ramrod pushed the bullet against the powder, to which the greased patch adhered, securing bullet and powder and gripping the rifling-grooves. With this rifle it was possible to hit a target accurately at twice the range of the smooth-bore musket, which at one hundred yards' range was only fifty per cent effective. And the speed of reloading was double that of the ordinary rifle. Armed with this unique weapon, Morgan's men were able to adopt the frontier tactic in which they excelled—aimed fire from cover—and to pick off the disciplined troops who had been trained for volley-firing at close range.

Daniel Morgan was a natural leader of men, an impetuous, fiery character, a frontier hero, who had been born in 1736. He had volunteered at the age of twenty, in the early days of the French and Indian war, and had joined Braddock's army as a wagon-driver. Although this was a civilian occupation, it rendered him amenable to military law, of which he fell foul. A British officer struck him with his sword; the quick-tempered Morgan struck him back, and was sentenced to 500 lashes of the cat-o'-nine-tails, a punishment he miraculously survived. So well did he prosper that within two years he rose to commissioned rank. He was severely wounded in the war, and on its conclusion in 1763, he returned to Virginia where he became a farmer, a noted gambler, a heavy drinker and a crack shot. The injustice he had received from the British still rankled and in 1774 he joined the rebel cause. He raised and marched his corps of ninety-six frontiersmen to the relief of Boston, a distance of 600 miles which they covered at an average of twenty-eight and a half miles a day. He accompanied Arnold on his march to Quebec, where he was captured by the British, who dangled a colonel's commission before his eyes to induce him to desert the rebel cause. Spurning the offer, he was exchanged, and was commissioned by Washington Colonel of the riflemen, whose regiment came to be known by his name.

On August 27th, when the hoped-for militia from New England failed to arrive, Gates designated Morgan's riflemen as the army's advance guard. Arnold returned triumphant with 1200 men on September 1st, and Gates sent Lincoln into Vermont to hang on Burgoyne's left flank, and to take advantage of any opportunity of keeping him in check.

Following the battle of Bennington, Burgoyne sent a letter, carried by Doctor Wood under a flag of truce, to Gates, protesting at the treatment accorded to wounded prisoners, and alleging that the Tories had been refused quarter when they offered to surrender. Gates, in his reply, complained of the horrible cruelties committed by Burgoyne's Indians, saying, 'that the famous Lieutenant-General Burgoyne, in whom the fine gentleman is united with the soldier and the scholar, should hire the savages of America to scalp Europeans and the descendants of Europeans, nay, more, that he should pay a price for every scalp so barbarously taken, is more than will be believed in England, until authenticated facts shall in every gazette convince mankind of the truth of this horrid tale.'

Gates called particular attention to the scalping of Jane MacCrea, whom he described as 'a country girl, of honest family in circumstances of mediocracy, without either beauty or accomplishments', who, he alleged, had been killed in a dispute 'as to the right of property in the person of the captive'. After he had written this letter, states Wilkinson, Gates read it to him and Lincoln, who, when pressed, gave their opinion that it was 'too personal', whereupon the 'old gentleman' replied with characteristic bluntness, 'My God, I don't believe either of you can mend it,' and sent it off. Gates allowed Doctor Wood to visit the wounded men.

Burgoyne, at the start of the campaign, had reluctantly accepted the Indians whose recruitment Germain had demanded, and whose employment had been favoured by many Englishmen as 'the most effective means of reducing the rebels to subjection'. On his return home, Burgoyne put the blame for Jane McCrea's murder on La Corne St Luc, who bore an evil reputation based on his activities with the French in the earlier war.

The legend of British barbarity was fostered by Benjamin Franklin, who accomplished his purpose by a hoax. He wrote a letter to a Boston newspaper in the name of an imaginary'Captain Gerrish', describing his interception of eight bales of American scalps, allegedly sent to Canada by a Seneca chief, including those of eighty-eight women, 193 boys, 211 girls, and twenty-nine infants. With the letter, he enclosed another written in English, which stated: 'We wish you to send these scalps over the water to the great king that he may regard them and be refreshed; and that he may see our faithfulness in destroying his enemies and be convinced that his presents have not been made to ungrateful people.' The scalps, 'Captain Gerrish' said, had been placed on exhibition in Boston where 'thousands of people are flocking to see them'.

On September 8th, Gates moved his army from the mouth of the Mohawk River, marching it thirteen miles northwards to Stillwater. The ground here was examined for entrenchments by Colonel Koscivszko, who condemned the position as untenable. Wilkinson claims that, at his suggestion, but more probably at the suggestion of a local farmer named Neilson, the army then advanced three more miles, where Wilkinson had noticed a narrow defile formed by a spur of the hills jutting out close and towards the river. The digging of a line of trenches was begun on September 12th on the steep and thickly-wooded bluff, known as Bemis Heights after the man who owned the tavern on the river bank.

Stark remained in Vermont following his victory at Bennington, because, he informed Lincoln, his men thought themselves slighted by the letter which he wrote to the Council of Massachusetts, describing the battle. When Gates asked Stark to move his men down the Hudson, he replied that he had only 800 effectives, and that 'the task is too hard for me in my present circumstances'. The whole of Burgoyne's army lay on his side of the river, and Stark felt that Gates 'may as well tell me to go and attack General Burgoyne with my brigade, as to desire me to march between him and the army'. Later Stark complained that his numbers had been reduced by measles to 700 effectives, and that he had not sufficient transport to move them. He was ready and willing to go 'if I can be supported'. He still did not move when Gates wrote on September 9th, begging him not to tarnish the glory of Bennington.

Gates's army had been strengthened by the arrival of Morgan and the return of Arnold, and his forces now numbered about 7000 men. He believed that Burgoyne must either advance to attack him or retreat to Ticonderoga before the winter snows and frost cut him off from Canada. From the prisoners taken at Bennington, he learned that Burgoyne had left strong detachments to protect his line of supply; and one of Warner's sergeants, who had escaped from Ticonderoga, told him that the fort was weakly held and that most of the Indians had deserted.

The desertion of the Indians enabled Gates to gather more precise information about the enemy's strength and intentions. A reconnaissance party, of which Wilkinson was a member, set out on September 12th, reached Saratoga, and returned with several prisoners, who stated that Burgoyne had abandoned his communications with Canada, and meant to 'prosecute his march to Albany, agreeable to his instructions'. 'Our labours on the fortifications of our camp were redoubled,' says Wilkinson, 'in consequence of this advice, and calls for militia were transmitted to all quarters; the greater number of Burgoyne's Indians had long before deserted him, and the few who remained had lost their spirit or enterprise; this circumstance gave our riflemen so decided a superiority that on his approach he could not make a motion without our knowledge, nor peep beyond his guards with safety.'

According to Wilkinson the condition of the two armies was now precisely reversed, for the Americans now enjoyed all the advantages which the British had formerly derived from 'a cloud of barbarians'.

XII *Swords Farm*

The heavy losses sustained at Bennington, St Leger's retreat, and the disappointing news from Howe failed to shake Burgoyne's resolution. Knowing that his troops were dwindling in numbers while those of the enemy were probably increasing, that ahead lay a hostile countryside, that the season was growing late, that once he crossed the Hudson his retreat would be cut off and his supply line from Canada severed, that Howe had gone to Pennsylvania, and that there was little prospect of support from the south, he refused to deviate from his purpose to reach Albany in fulfilment of his orders which he deemed mandatory and peremptory. He refused to admit that his instructions gave him any latitude, or the discretion to act as circumstances might dictate. It is strange in the light of his knowledge that the Grand Strategy for a junction of armies in the Hudson had collapsed, that he emphasized in his subsequent attempt at self-justification that his advance from Canada was part of a pre-arranged and interlocking plan which he feared to jeopardize.

Spurred by pride and vanity, and driven by ambition, Burgoyne had claimed that he could reach Albany on his own, he was thus caught on the horns of a dilemma of his own making. If he achieved his objective he would be hailed as a bold man, and would be richly rewarded; he would be condemned as rash if he failed. If he adopted the wise course, and retreated, he would lose the King's favour, as Carleton had done. To advance was Burgoyne's desperate answer to a rapidly deteriorating situation. He gambled on winning a decisive victory.

To reach Albany, which stood on the west bank, Burgoyne needed to cross the Hudson River. If he continued down the eastern bank, the marshes and creeks would force wide detours, requiring him to leave his *bateaux* on the river unprotected. He decided to cross above Battenkill to Saratoga (the modern Schuylerville), whence a good road ran along the western bank to Albany, and to that end he built up supplies to last for thirty days.

The park of artillery was brought from Fort George, the *bateaux* which had been conveyed overland were launched in the river, and, on September 6th, Digby recorded: 'It was then expected we should shortly move as the magazines of provisions and other stores were mostly up, and our new bridge over the Hudson River was near finished. Our removal from that post was also very necessary, in respect of procuring forage, which began then to turn very scarce; indeed I wonder we did so well, as it was amazing the great quantity of hay, Indian corn, etc., we were obliged to provide.'

By September 9th the new bridge was finished, and some of the wounded from Ticonderoga had recovered sufficiently to rejoin the army. Digby noted that the weather was beginning to turn cold in the mornings and evenings. The soldiers were still wearing their summer uniforms. Their heavy winter apparel had been left at Ticonderoga whither the officers had been forced to return their marquees, sleeping instead in ordinary soldier's tents. Next day, Digby heard that the enemy were on the move, advancing nearer, and had been joined by some thousands of militiamen.

Von Riedesel brought the Germans from Fort Edward and the army advanced three miles to Battenkill. As the British and German troops advanced, says von Riedesel, the rebel army withdrew their scouts from Saratoga. They nevertheless sent some detachments to reconnoitre the British camp, which obliged Fraser and von Breymann to keep their corps under arms all night, and forced Burgoyne to dig some entrenchments with the utmost haste. Von Riedesel had first designed to send his family back to Canada, but 'was dissuaded by the prayers of my wife', who begged to be allowed to follow his fortunes in the same way as other officers' wives.

Madame von Riedesel, who was grateful for the permission to follow the army, was able to continue her story:

'We made only small day's marches, and were very often sick; yet always contented at being allowed to follow. I had still the satisfaction of daily seeing my husband. A great part of my baggage I had sent back, and had kept only a small summer wardrobe. In the beginning all went well. We cherished the sweet hope of a sure victory, and of coming into the "promised land"; and when we passed the Hudson River, and General Burgoyne said, "The English never lose ground," our spirits were greatly exhilarated. But that which displeased me was, that the wives of all the officers belonging to the expedition, knew beforehand everything that was to happen; and this seemed the more singular to me, as I had observed, when in the armies of the Duke Ferdinand, during the Seven Years War, with how much secrecy everything was conducted. But here, on the contrary, the Americans were apprised beforehand of all our intentions; so that at every place where we came they already awaited us; a circumstance which hurt us exceedingly.'

According to von Riedesel, the ladies followed in carriages a day's march behind the army, and got along as well as they could. 'General Burgoyne was so certain of victory that the ladies were in high spirits,' he states, a remark which is supported by his wife's happy narrative:

'I lived in a pretty well-built house, in which I had a large room. The doors and the wainscot were of solid cedar, a wood that is very common in this vicinity. They burn it frequently, especially when there are many midges around, as these insects cannot stand the odour of it. It is said, however, that its smoke

is very injurious to the nerves, so much so, indeed, as to cause
women with child to bring forth prematurely. As we were to
march farther, I had a large calash made for me, in which I,
my children, and both my women servants had seats; and in
this manner I followed the army, in the midst of the soldiers,
who were merry, singing songs, and burning with a desire for
victory. We passed through boundless forests and magnificent
tracts of country, which, however, were abandoned by all the
inhabitants, who fled before us, and reinforced the army of
the American general, Gates. In the sequel this cost us dearly,
for every one of them was a soldier by nature, and could shoot
very well; besides, the thought of fighting for their fatherland
and their freedom, inspired them with still greater courage'.

Led by Brigadier-General Simon Fraser with the advance
guard, the British troops marched past General Burgoyne with
colours flying and bands playing and crossed the river on September 13th. The Germans followed next day, whereupon the
bridge of boats was broken up, and the *bateaux* were floated
down river. Simon Fraser led his men to the heights above the
Fishkill creek, which entered the Hudson below the village of
Saratoga. The chief house in the village was Philip Schuyler's
mansion, and this was taken over by Burgoyne and his staff.
The soldiers reaped the harvest which Kitty Schuyler had found
too wet to burn before she abandoned the estate. Burgoyne had
crossed his Rubicon, and severed his connection with Canada,
to the dismay of some of his officers whom he had not consulted,
but apparently to the satisfaction of others, for the Earl of
Harington remarked in Parliament in 1778 that General Burgoyne's reputation 'would not have stood very high, either
with the army, the country, or the enemy, if he had halted at
Fort Edward'.

Burgoyne now commanded about 4600 effective regular
soldiers, 2500 of them British, and 1800 Germans, together
with the 300 recruits who had recently joined, about 800 Cana-

dians and Tories, and 80 Indians. These, with about 300 sailors, *bateau*-men, artificers, artillerymen, and Canadian drivers, brought the total strength to 5000 men. The artillery comprised thirty-five guns of various calibres and six mortars. That Burgoyne was not yet satisfied with the unauthorized use of the army's carts is clear from the reference in his General Order of the 14th, to 'enormous mismanagement'.

Learning that a party of rebels, 200 strong, had been seen near the camp, Burgoyne sent Simon Fraser forward to intercept them, but he failed to find them in the dense woods on the heights above the river. That night the revels' evening guns were heard distinctly. Next day, the army advanced three miles to Dovecot (the modern Coveville), marching blindly along the road below the wooded heights, the trees on which were turning scarlet and gold. The Americans had broken down the bridges across the many creeks and streams which intersected the meadows between the river bank and the heights. That night, Burgoyne issued a Standing Order, which was to apply for the remainder of the campaign, that all pickets and guards were to be under arms an hour before daylight every morning, and to remain so until it was completely dark, and that the army was to be 'in such a state as to be fit for instant action'. Deprived of his Indian scouts, Burgoyne had no knowledge of the American position, and he knew only that they were in strength a few miles ahead.

Burgoyne moved his headquarters to Dovecot, and the army encamped on the heights above the river, where Lieutenant Anburey found an incident to record:

'Our situation, as being the advanced post of the army was frequently so very alert that we seldom slept out of our clothes. In one of these situations a tent, in which Major Acland and Lady Harriet were asleep, suddenly caught fire; the Major's orderly sergeant, with great danger of suffocation, dragged out the first person he got hold of, which was the Major. It providentially happened that in the same instant Lady Harriet, without knowing what she did, and perhaps not perfectly awake made her escape by creeping under the walls in the back part of the tent, and upon recovering her senses, conceive what her feelings must be when the first object she beheld was the Major, in the midst of the flames, in search of her! The sergeant again saved him, but the Major's face and body was burnt in a very severe manner: everything they had with them in the tent was consumed. This accident was occasioned by a favourite Newfoundland dog, who being very restless, overset a table on which a candle was burning (the Major always had a light in his tent during the night, when our situation required it), and it rolling to the walls of the tent, instantly set them on fire.'

Digby noticed that Lady Acland bore the disaster with a degree of steadfastness and resolution worthy of a campaigner.

On the morning of the 16th, the sound of distant drums indicated that the enemy were advancing. At 11 a.m. Burgoyne, who was accompanied by Generals Phillips, von Riedesel and Simon Fraser, reconnoitred ahead with 2000 soldiers and six guns, while the remainder of the troops occupied themselves with repairing bridges under cover of strong detachments. Burgoyne returned at 8 p.m. without having seen the enemy. The bridges having been repaired, the army renewed its march next day, encamping that night at Swords Farm, unaware that the enemy were only four miles ahead. From Swords Farm a wagon-track led up the heights to the west and across the plateau which was occupied by the advance guard.

Owing to the destruction of bridges, the road ahead was impassable for an army, and it could advance no further until they had been repaired. On the afternoon of September 18th, records von Riedesel, four regiments of the enemy, with banners, could plainly be seen. Three were hidden behind the hills, and two behind some woods on the plain.

Warning of the American reconnaissance had been given by a deserter who reached the British camp—though not in time to prevent considerable loss amongst a party of soldiers who had straggled ahead in search of potatoes. They were gathering them in a field when they were surprised by the enemy scouting party which fired, killing and wounding about thirty men, when, says Anburey, they might with care have surrounded and taken the whole party prisoners. He was led to remark that 'such cruel and unjustifiable conduct can have no good tendency, while it serves greatly to increase hatred, and a thirst for revenge'.

The total number of killed and missing was fourteen, an unnecessary loss which called forth Burgoyne's reproach:

'The Lieut. Genl. will no longer bear to lose Men, for the pitiful consideration of Potatoes, or Forage. The Life of the Soldier is the property of the King, and since neither Friendly Admonitions, repeated Injunctions, nor Corporal punishments have effect, after what has happened, the Army is now to be informed, and it is not doubted the Commanding Officers will do it solemnly, that the first Soldier caught beyond the Advanced Centinels of the Army, will be instantly Hanged.'

This incident disclosed to Burgoyne that the enemy were not far away, and that they occupied a position on the heights which dominated the road by the river. He decided to make a reconnaissance in force to determine their position and strength and, if possible, to turn their left flank.

While Burgoyne groped in the dark, Gates learned from his scouts the progress of the enemy. He sat secure in the fortifications constructed by Colonel Kosciuszko on Bemis Heights. From his reconnaissance on September 14th, Wilkinson brought back three prisoners, soldiers of the 20th Regiment, who stated that General Burgoyne intended to march to Albany, information that was confirmed by two German deserters. On September 18th, Gates sent Arnold out to reconnoitre; and, that night,

Colonel Colburn of the Continental army, returned from a lone reconnaissance to report that, by climbing a tree on the eastern bank of the river, he observed that Burgoyne had struck his tents and was preparing to advance. 'The crisis is near,' Colburn told Gates. Another scouting party, led by Colonel Benjamin Warren of the Massachusetts Militia, discovered the enemy in too large a number 'to pick a wrangle with'.

Gates commanded an army which numbered between 7000 and 10,000 men, composed of both Continentals and militia. This was considerably less than were mustered after the surrender in October when the 'Returns' show that his army was composed of 10,395 Continentals and 11,968 militia, many of whom had arrived after September 19th when only 4970 men were engaged: 1810 from Massachusetts, 1408 from New Hampshire, 652 from New York, 600 from Connecticut, and Morgan's 500 riflemen who, though called Viginians, had been drawn from other states as well.

The American right wing, which covered the heights above the Hudson, was commanded by General John Glover, who had with him Brigadier-General John Patterson and Colonel John Nixon. The centre, which was composed of New Yorkers under Colonel James Livingstone and the Massachusetts regiments, was commanded by General Ebenezer Learned; and the left wing was commanded by Benedict Arnold, and was composed of New Hampshire Continentals and New York and Connecticut militia. Morgan's riflemen and Dearborn's light infantry were also placed on the left wing, though whether or not they were part of Arnold's command, or were directly responsible to Gates, was uncertain.

Gates suffered a disappointment at the behaviour of Stark's men. The story is told by James Wilkinson who failed to elucidate the ambiguous part played by Stark himself. Burgoyne's advance, states Wilkinson, had induced Gates to order the junction of the militia from the Hampshire Grants with the main body, and:

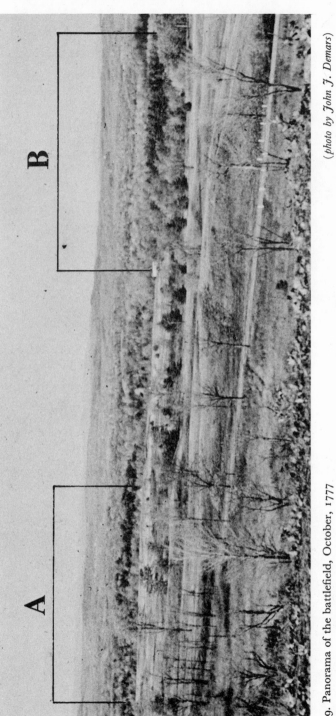

9. Panorama of the battlefield, October, 1777

(photo by John J. Demars)

(A) Breymann Redoubt
(B) Balcarres Redoubt – Freeman's Farm.

10*a*. Looking eastward from the Visitors' Centre, Saratoga.
(*Niagara Mohawk Power Corp.*)

b. Looking eastward from the summit of the Great Redoubt.
(*Saratoga National Historical Park*)

'In consequence of which General Stark, by easy marches and a circuitous route, reached headquarters with his corps on the morning of the 18th, the day preceding the action. The army was animated by the arrival of a band of citizen-soldiers who had conquered the Germans and killed their commander near Bennington; but the term of service, for which these men were engaged, expired with the day, and every exertion was made, to induce them, to wait the event of an action, which was daily expected; but to the exhortations of the commander-in-chief, and the persuasions of many other officers, no decisive reply could be obtained. General Stark and his subordinates *"thought it proper, and necessary* that they should adhere to the service", but I observed they employed no influence to promote the end, which was in effect to discourage it; the men communicated with each other in whispers, and a buzz was heard around their fires; for they had neither unpacked the baggage which they carried on their backs, nor laid down to repose; I left this hord of hardy freemen about 11 o'clock, determined to watch the result, and about 5 minutes after 12, I discovered them in motion, the aid-de-camp of the General called for the parole, to pass the guards of the camp, and I verily believe neither officer nor private was left behind; nor could they have been beyond the sound of action when it began, yet not a man returned. This punctuality of the father, the husband and the son, who till their own ground and enjoy the sweets of domestic life, is not reprehensible, since it is enjoined by an irresistible impulse of nature. These citizens had fought once, and having served the term of their engagement, were desirous to tell the tale of "feats performed", and look into their private affairs, after which they were ready again to take arms'.

Whatever is the truth behind the many controversies affecting Gates's command, he occupied a strong position on Bemis Heights, the plateau that rose above the river and which so squeezed the road to Albany as to make it necessary for the invaders to turn the rebel position before they could advance further. From the river bank the fortifications dominated the road and river, and turned northwards and westwards, forming three-sides of a box. Gates's front was protected by a deep ravine, running parallel to his line, at the apex of which stood the barn which had been built by a farmer named Neilson. The ground in front was closely wooded and criss-crossed by small creeks and wagon-tracks, one of which led to a clearing where stood the small farm-house formerly occupied by a farmer named Freeman. Gates's left was protected by more woods and by steep ground, on which now stands the Visitors' Centre of the National Park Service, which gives a panoramic view of the battleground.

On the plateau, from the bluffs overlooking the river, to the west of Neilson's barn, Kosciuszko had constructed earthworks and breastworks made of trunks of trees, logs, and rails, and the barn had been turned into a rude fort, protected by a powerful battery. To the left of this knoll rose another smaller one, which had been partly fortified. The ground over which the two battles of September 19th and October 7th were fought was far more wooded and broken than it is today. Rough and rolling, it was intersected by deep, wooded ravines, and only small patches had been cleared for cultivation. Wilkinson's description of the battleground may help us to visualize the terrain:

'General Gates's right occupied the brow of the hill near the river, with which it was connected by a deep intrenchment; his camp, in the form of a segment of a great circle, the convex towards the enemy, extended rather obliquely to his rear, about three-fourths of a mile to a knoll occupied by his left; his front was covered from the right to the left of the centre, by a sharp ravine running parallel with his line and closely wooded: from thence to the knoll at his extreme left, the ground was level and had been partially cleared, some of the trees being felled and others girdled, beyond which in front of his left flank, and extending to the enemy's right, there were several small fields in very imperfect cultivation, the surface broken and obstructed with stumps and fallen timber, and the whole bounded on the west by a steep eminence. The extremities of this camp were defended by strong batteries, and the interval was strengthened by a breastwork without intrenchments, constructed of the bodies of felled trees, logs and rails, with an additional battery at an opening left of the centre. The right was almost impracticable; the left difficult of approach.

'The intermediate space between the adverse armies on the low grounds of the river was open and in cultivation; the high land was clothed in its native woods, with the exception of three or four small, newly opened and deserted farms, separated by intervals of woodland, and bordering on the flanks of the two armies, most remote from the river; the principal of these was an oblong field, belonging to a person of the name of Freeman; there was also, exclusive of the ravines fronting the respective camps, a third ravine, about mid-way between them, running at right angles to the river. The intervening forest rendered it utterly impracticable to obtain a front view of the American position, or any part of the British except its left near the river.'

Gates's position was very strong. To gain a decisive victory, he needed only to stand fast and allow Burgoyne to batter his head against his defences. Prudently, Gates awaited attack; he was the only commander on either side who could lose the war in one afternoon.

XIII *Freeman's Farm*

To reach Albany, Burgoyne had to defeat Gates and sweep him from his path. The Americans blocked the only road and there was no way round except through the impenetrable forest-clad hills to the west. Deprived of his Indian scouts, who had hitherto thrown an impregnable screen around his troops, Burgoyne had no knowledge of the American position. They, on the other hand, knew of his every move from the intelligence of their scouts who, in the absence of the Indians, swarmed around the British camp, observing it from the tree-tops. Advance was imperative, and Burgoyne determined to probe the American position, hoping to turn its left wing and drive it into the river. With his now numerically inferior force, he set his army an impossible task. To dislodge the Americans from their strong position, he required three times as many men; his powerful train of siege-guns was inadequate to do the job alone, for, as it proved, the marksmanship of the rebels decimated the gunners long before the guns could reach within range of the fortifications on Bemis Heights.

Thick fog and rain on the morning of September 19th delayed Burgoyne's advance until 8 o'clock, when the army moved out of camp in three columns; the right wing led by Simon Fraser; the centre, with which Burgoyne himself went, by Briga-dier-General Hamilton; and the left by von Riedesel, who was accompanied by the second-in-command, Major-General Phillips. The right wing was composed of the *élite* of the British troops, the Grenadier Battalion, the Light Infantry Battalion, and the 24th Regiment, numbering in all 900 men, to which had been added von Breymann's advance corps, about 500 men, and all the auxiliaries, consisting of 800 Canadians and Tories.

THE BATTLE of FREEMAN'S FARM
September 19th ≈ 1777

Sword House

FRASER

BURGOYNE

Great Ravine

Freeman's Farm

VON RIEDESEL

Middle Ravine

MORGAN
LEARNED
POOR

HUDSON RIVER

LEARNED

ARNOLD
POOR

Neilson's Barn

PATTERSON

GLOVER

GATES

N

Bemis Tavern

SCALE IN MILES

0   ¼   ½   1

Four six-pounders and four three-pounders had been allotted to this column which may also have included some of the remaining Indians.

The centre column comprised four British regiments, the 9th, 21st, 62nd, and 20th, 1100 rank and file, together with the artillerymen in charge of the six six-pounders. Von Riedesel's column advanced along the river road, with the three remaining German regiments and Captain Pausch's Hesse-Hanau artillery, made up of six six-pounders and two three-pounders. Six companies of the British 47th Regiment and the Hesse-Hanau Regiment remained in camp to guard the baggage, *bateaux*, and reserve artillery. Excluding von Riedesel's column, which was intended to threaten and hold down the American's right wing, a little more than 2000 soldiers, each supplied with sixty rounds of ammunition, mounted the Heights. The two columns marched through the woods, the plan being that once they had reached their positions they would advance in parallel on a signal from Burgoyne, who would order the firing of three guns.

Fraser, having the longer way to go, marched first, making a large circuit through the woods with the object of gaining an advantageous position to the west of the centre column. This centre column followed the wagon-track across the plateau, turning southward where Fraser had continued westward, and crossing the Great Ravine, where it again turned westward. About noon, it reached a position to the northward of the fifteen-acre patch which had been cleared by Freeman, the poor farmer whose name became famous as the owner of the land upon which the encounter took place that day. This clearing had been made on a promontory of ground between the Great Ravine and the north fork of Mill Creek, and it extended 350 yards from north to south, sloping from east to west. To give Fraser time to reach his position, the centre column halted, while a picket advanced to investigate the tiny cabin in the centre of the clearing.

Von Riedesel, following the river road, advanced about two miles, halting to repair three bridges under fire, and reaching the point whence a second wagon-track ran westward over the plateau. We shall hear of him again later in the day, when he came to Burgoyne's rescue.

As early as 8 o'clock, Gates learned from Colonel Colburn that the enemy had struck the chief part of their tents on the plain near the river, had crossed the gully at the gorge of the Great Ravine, and were ascending the heights in a direction towards the American left. The cautious Gates proposed to stand behind his fortifications; the fiery Arnold persuaded him to send Colonel Morgan and his riflemen and Colonel Dearborn and his light infantry into the woods in front of Bemis Heights, to retard the British advance and cripple them as much as possible. It was good advice since, as Arnold claimed, it would have been dangerous to allow the enemy to approach unopposed to within artillery range of the camp. The British were adept at siege tactics, while in the woods their method of waging war by brave shoulder-to-shoulder advance and disciplined volley-firing would be at a disadvantage against American individual marksmanship and ability to take cover. Furthermore, if Morgan and Dearborn were forced to retreat, they had a fortified camp on which to fall back. On the other hand if the British were allowed to storm the American lines and broke them, the retreating army would have nothing to fall back upon, and its retreat might easily degenerate into a rout.

The events of the battle fought on September 19th proved that Arnold was right. It is possible that, had Gates allowed him to support Morgan more energetically and to take personal charge of the attack, the Americans might have gained a decisive victory that day.

What part Arnold played in the battle, once it was joined, is uncertain, for the evidence is ambiguous. The contemporary historians of the campaign fail to agree on the question of his personal involvement, though they are unanimous in giving credit to his division which bore the brunt of the fighting. While it seems inconsistent with Arnold's volatile and fiery nature that he should remain in camp, a listless observer of the scene of which he was in direct charge when his every inclination must have been urging him to join in, it seems that, contrary to the recollection of Captain E. Wakefield of Dearborn's Light Infantry, who spoke from personal knowledge, Arnold, in the words of historian Edward Bancroft, 'was not on the field'.

The evidence is conflicting. Bancroft added 'so witnesses Wilkinson, whom Marshall knew personally and believed'. Yet Marshall himself states 'reinforcements were continually brought up and, about 4 o'clock, Arnold, with nine Continental regiments and Morgan's corps, was completely engaged with the whole right wing of the British army. The conflict was extremely severe and only terminated with the day.'

William Gordon a contemporary historian, declares that: 'Arnold's division was out in the action, but he himself did not lead them; he remained in camp the whole time.' Edmund Stedman, an equally good authority, says, "The enemy were led to the battle by General Arnold, who distinguished himself in an extraordinary manner.' Henry B. Dawson, a careful historian, and B. J. Lossing, who specialized in the study of the campaign, concur with Marshall. Hoffman Nickerson, who devoted a long appendix to 'Arnold's Presence in Action September 19', believed that the evidence is in favour of Arnold's presence in action'.

The evicence of the participants and eye-witnesses is equally conflicting. Colonel Varick, Schuyler's friend and Arnold's aide, gives Arnold credit not merely for superintending the field operations of his division, but also of leading them in person, and he is supported by Arnold's other aide, Livingstone. Colonel Henry Dearborn, who belonged to Arnold's division, does not allude to Arnold, whereas he mentions several minor figures in the action, and Dr Thacher, who treated the wounded, and Jeduthan Baldwin, who fought in the action, are silent about Arnold's participation. Wilkinson avers that 'not a single General Officer was on the field of battle the 19th September, until the evening when General Learned was ordered out', and he describes, as we shall learn, how Gates sent him to recall Arnold after he had impetuously galloped towards the sound of the guns. In a letter written to General St Clair on September 21st, Wilkinson said 'General Arnold was not out of camp during the whole action.' The young Neilson, who had been brought up by his father at the scene of the battle (where Father Neilson had acted as guide to the American troops) and learned its traditions, makes no specific statement about Arnold's involvement other than to say that his presence on the field was 'well known at the time', and 'confirmed by a number who were present'.

Arnold himself, in his letter of complaint to Gates about the General's inadequate praise for his division, which he wrote after the battle, failed to make clear the part he had played in the action, other than to state that 'before the action was over, I found it necessary to send out the whole of my division to support the attack'.

Yet, according to Captain Wakefield, Arnold was personally involved. Quoted by Reuben Aldridge Guild, *Chaplain Smith and the Baptists*, (American Baptist Publishing Society 1885), Wakefield states:

'A persistent effort has been made from the day of the battle to rob Arnold of the glory. Being attached to Dearborn's Light Infantry, which had a conspicuous part in the battles of the 19th of September and the 7th of October, I had the opportunity of witnessing the principal movements of both, and therefore speak from personal knowledge.

'I shall never forget the opening scene of the first day's conflict. The riflemen and light infantry were ordered to clear the woods of the Indians. Arnold rode up and, with his sword pointing to the enemy emerging from the woods into an opening partially cleared, covered with stumps and fallen timber, addressing Morgan, he said, "Colonel Morgan, you and I have seen too many redskins to be deceived by that garb of paint and feathers; they are asses in lions' skins, Canadians and Tories, let your riflemen cure them of their borrowed plumes.'

'And so they did; for in less than fifteen minutes the "Wagon Boy", with his Virginia riflemen, sent the painted devils with a howl back to the British lines. Morgan was in his glory, catching the inspiration of Arnold, as he thrilled his men; when he hurled them against the enemy, he astonished the English and Germans with the deadly fire of his rifles.

'Nothing could exceed the bravery of Arnold on this day; he seemed the very genius of war. Infuriated by the conflict and maddened by Gates' refusal to send reinforcements, which he repeatedly called for, and knowing he was meeting the brunt of the battle, he seemed inspired with the fury of a demon.'

The debate is clouded by Arnold's subsequent treasonable actions, and, for a century at least, there was little disposition by historians to do him justice. In recent years the tendency has swung the other way, showing Arnold personally leading the American force at the battle of Freeman's Farm, and, due possibly to the accepted dislike of Gates, Arnold has frequently been accorded the honour of winning the victories on both September 19th and October 7th.

This attitude does Horatio Gates scant justice. While it is certain that he benefited on September 19th from Arnold's advice and gave him no credit for it, Gates feared Arnold's impetuosity, as he had good reason to. Listening to Arnold's passionate demands for a 'complete and general victory over the enemy', Gates may have recalled how, when Naval Commander on Lake Champlain in 1776, Arnold had ignored his orders to play a defensive role, and had thereby, however heroically, lost the American fleet at Valcour Island. Gates kept his rash subordinate under his own eyes at headquarters, at the rear of Bemis Heights, where, as Wilkinson recalled, the orders were 'worked out by both commanders'. Though it was not an amicable process, the violent row between the two men did not flare up until after the battle, when it seems it may have been precipitated by Arnold's tactless act in appointing as his aide Colonel Varick, who had quarrelled with Gates.

Arnold played a decisive part in the battle of September 19th. On October 7th his role was heroic and possibly dangerous. Although Gates commanded the victorious army, he needed to gain time while his forces were augmented, and those of the enemy diminished; and to him must go the credit for the defeat of Burgoyne. Morgan was the great hero of the battle; his hardy frontiersmen, clad in their coon-skin caps and fringed hunting-shirts, fired the shots that decimated the British ranks.

At Arnold's suggestion and on Gates's agreement, Morgan and Dearborn marched out of camp to seek the enemy. They moved along the wagon-track that ran northwards from Bemis Heights, and, after about a mile, reached the woods that surrounded the southern and south-western side of Freeman's cleared patch, the northward extremity of which had been reached by the British centre column, while Fraser's corps had occupied ground to the westward, which was also cloaked by woods. Approaching this area, Morgan divided his force into separate bodies, in order to comb the woods effectively. Both sides were unaware that their forces were converging. About 12.30 p.m., Wilkinson, who stood by Gates's side, heard the report of small arms which indicated that Morgan's corps was engaged in 'front of our left'. The battle, he says, was 'perfectly accidental' for 'neither General meditated an attack at this time'. It was not Gates's policy to court action, for the defences of his camp were not half-completed, and reinforcements were arriving daily.

In the action on September 19th, the British centre column was engaged by the American left division, and the fighting occupied three phases. Simon Fraser's column played little part in the action, and von Riedesel became engaged late in the day when, by his speedy arrival at the scene of conflict, he staved off a British defeat. As is true of the whole campaign, we are told far more by the British diarists and generals than by their American counterparts who, when they wrote at all, confined their remarks to the most general statements. The British and German writers described both what they saw for themselves, and what they were told by others, frequently without reference to times or places.

The action, which lasted until nightfall, became a confused struggle which, except on Freeman's clearing, took place in dense woods and on ground which the Marquis de Chastellux (one of the Comte de Rochambeau's officers) found in 1780 to be 'so intersected and covered, that it is impossible either to conceive or to discover the smallest resemblance between it and the plans given to the public by General Burgoyne'.

From the British centre column which, having crossed the Great Ravine, had halted on the edge of Freeman's clearing, a picket commanded by Major Forbes was sent to reconnoitre the cabin. There he was attacked, in his own words, 'with great vigour from behind railed fences' by Morgan's riflemen, who about the same time came into contact with Canadians of Simon Fraser's column. The Americans' aimed rifle fire was so deadly that every officer of the picket, Forbes included, and many of its men were instantly killed or wounded. The survivors fled, pursued eagerly by the riflemen who, overrunning the clearing, came face to face with the main body of the British centre column. They scattered and retreated across the clearing to take shelter in the woods, where they were discovered by Colonel Wilkinson who, despite Gates's orders, had found an excuse to go forward in search of intelligence:

'I put spurs to my horse, and directed by the sound, had entered the wood about an hundred rods, when the fire suddenly ceased: I however pursued my course, and the first officer I fell in with was Major Dearborn who, with great animation and not a little warmth, was forming thirty or forty file of his infantry: I exchanged a few words with him, passed on and met Major Morris alone, who was never so sprightly as under a hot fire; from him I learnt that the corps was advancing by files in two lines, when they unexpectedly fell upon a picket of the enemy, which they almost instantly forced, and pursuing the fugitives, their front had as unexpectedly fallen in with the British line; that several officers and men had been made prisoners, and that to save himself, he had been obliged to push his horse through the ranks of the enemy, and escaped by a circuitous route. To shew me where the action commenced, he leaped a fence into the abandoned field of Freeman, choked up with weeds, and led me to the cabin which had been occupied by the British picket, but was then almost encircled with dead; he then cautioned me to keep a look out for the enemy, who he observed could not be far from us; and as I never admired exposition from which neither advantage nor honour could be derived, I crossed the angle of the field, leapt the fence, and just before me on a ridge discovered Lieutenant-Colonel Butler with three men, all *tree'd*; from him I learnt that they had "caught a Scotch prize", that having forced the picket, they had closed with the British line, had been instantly routed, and from the suddenness of the shock and the nature of the ground, were broken and scattered in all directions; he repeated Morris's caution to me, and remarked that the enemy's sharpshooters were on the opposite side of the ravine, and that being on horseback, I should attract a shot. We changed our position, and the Colonel inquired what were Morgan's orders, and informed me that he had seen a heavy column moving towards our left. I then turned about to regain the camp, and report to the General, when my ears were saluted by an uncommon noise, which I approached, and perceived Colonel Morgan attended by two men only, who with a *turkey call* (an instrument for decoying the wild turkey) was collecting his dispersed troops. The moment I cme up to him, he hurst into tears, and exclaimed, "I am ruined, by G–d! Major Morris ran on so rapidly with the front, that they were beaten before I could up with the rear, and my men are scattered God knows where." I remarked to the Colonel that he had a long day before him to retrieve an inauspicious beginning, and informed him where I had seen his field officers, which appeared to cheer him, and we parted.'

Noticing that Morgan, when marching to the scene of action, brought up the rear of his corps, Wilkinson inquired the reason, and was told by Morgan that his motive was 'to see that every man did duty, and that cowards did not lag behind, whilst brave men were fighting'. Wilkinson rode back to camp to ask Gates to order up reinforcements, while Morgan rallied his men.

The first phase of the action was over by 1 p.m. The retreat of the survivors of the British picket had been covered by a detachment of light infantry sent from the right column, but not before a number of British soldiers had been killed by their own men, who fired without orders. The firing at Freeman's Farm had been heard by General Phillips down by the river. Believing that it was the start of a general action, he galloped onto the plateau to investigate, taking with him Major Williams with four pieces of artillery. Some time after one o'clock Burgoyne ordered the firing of the three signal guns, to notify the wing columns that it was time to advance. The British centre column moved up the slope on to the pro-montory and across the clearing to Freeman's cabin, the three regiments extending, the 21st on the right, the 62nd in the centre, and the 20th on the left. The 9th Regiment was held in reserve.

Probably before phase two of the action in the centre began or possibly synchronizing with it, Morgan's and Dearborn's men clashed with Simon Fraser's column which had taken position on rising ground to the westward of Freeman's Farm, from where it was concealed by the dense woods. For this action we rely on Lieutenant Anburey, who joined the advance of the 24th Regiment which Fraser had sent to cover Major Forbes's retreat;

'A batman of General Fraser's rescued from the Indians an officer of the Americans, one Captain Van Swearingham, of Colonel Morgan's Virginia riflemen; they were on the point of stripping him, which the man prevented, and recovered his pocket book from them, containing all his papers of consequence and his commission. He offered the soldier all his *paper* dollars and lamented that he had no *hard* ones to reward him with.

'The batman brought him up to General Fraser (who now had come up to the two companies he had detached) when he interrogated him concerning the enemy, but could obtain no other answer than that their army was commanded by Generals Gates and Arnold. General Fraser, exceedingly provoked that he could gain no intelligence, told him if he did not immediately inform him as to the exact situation of the enemy he would hang him up directly; the officer, with the most undaunted firmness, replied, 'You may if you please'. The General, perceiving he could make nothing of him, rode off, leaving him in the custody of Lieutenant Dunbar of the artillery.

'My servant, just at this period, arrived with my canteen, which was rather fortunate, as we stood in need of some refreshment after our march through the woods and this little skirmish; I requested Dunbar, with his prisoner, to partake of it, and sitting down upon a tree, we asked this Captain a variety of questions, to which he always gave evasive answers, and we both observed he was in great spirits; at last I said to him, "Captain, do you think we shall have any more work upon our hands today?" to which he replied, "Yes, yes, you'll have business enough, for there are many hundreds all round you now." He had hardly spoken the words, than from a wood a little way in our front there came an excessive heavy fire. Dunbar ran to his guns, saying "Anburey, you must take charge of the Captain". There being only one officer besides myself with the company, I committed him to the custody of a sergeant, to convey him to the house where the rest of the prisoners were, with particular orders, as the General had desired, that he should not be ill-treated. I then hastened to my company, on joining of which I met a number of the men who were retiring wounded, and at this time the firing of the enemy was suppressed by the artillery.'

As a result of the information brought back by Wilkinson, Gates first sent out the New Hampshire Continentals, the regiments of Scammel and Cilley, and later five more regiments which successively took position on Morgan's left. The New Hampshire men, on their arrival, poured a withering fire upon the massed British regiments standing shoulder to shoulder in the clearing around Freeman's cabin. They suffered severely from the marksmanship of the Americans, being unable to fire effectively in return against their elusive opponents, many of whom had perched themselves in trees where, against the autumn foliage, their frontier-shirts were indistinguishable from the background. In face of this fire, the British retreated slowly across the clearing, rallying again and again to drive back their pursuers who, said the Earl of Balcarres, 'behaved with great obstinacy and courage'. As more and more American reinforcements came up, the action extended to the right and left of the clearing, as Anburey reports:

'We heard a most tremendous firing upon our left, where we were attacked in great force, and at the very first fire Lieutenant Don of the 21st Regiment received a ball through his heart. I am sure it will never be erased from my memory;

for when he was wounded, he sprang from the ground nearly as high as a man. The party that had attacked us were again driven in by our cannon, but the fire raged most furiously on our left, and the enemy were marching to turn their right flank, when they met the advanced corps, posted in a wood, who repulsed them. From that time, which was about three o'clock, till after sunset, the enemy, who were continually supplied with fresh troops, most vigorously attacked the British line: the stress lay upon the 20th, 21st, and 62nd Regiments, most part of which were engaged for near four hours without intermission. The grenadiers and 24th Regiment, as well as part of the light infantry, were at times engaged. In the conflict the advanced corps could only act partially and occasionally, as it was deemed unadvisable to evacuate the heights where they were advantageously posted.

Next day, Anburey learned of an incident of this stage of the battle, which he found worthy of record:

'In the course of the last action, Lieutenant Hervey, of the 62nd, a youth of sixteen, and nephew to the Adjutant-General of the same name, received several wounds and was repeatedly ordered off the field by Colonel Anstruthers, but his heroic ardour would not allow him to quit battle while he could stand and see his brave lads fighting beside him. A ball striking one of his legs, his removal became absolutely necessary, and while they were conveying him away, another wounded him mortally. In this situation the Surgeon recommended him to take a powerful dose of opium, to avoid a seven or eight hours life of most exquisite torture; this he immediately consented to, and when the Colonel entered the tent with Major Harnage, who were both wounded, they asked whether he had any affairs they could settle for him? His reply was that being a minor, everything was already adjusted; but he had one request, which he had just enough life to utter: "Tell my uncle I died like a soldier!"'

Sergeant Lamb was an observer of both engagements, those in which the British right and centre columns were involved:

'The Americans being incapable from the nature of the country, of perceiving the different combinations of the march, advanced a strong column, with a view of turning the British line upon the right; here they met the grenadiers and light infantry, who gave them a tremendous fire. Finding that it was impossible to penetrate the line at this point, they immediately countermarched and directed their principal effort to the centre. Here the conflict was dreadful; for four hours a constant blaze of fire was kept up, and both armies seemed to be determined on death or victory.

'Men, and particularly offcers, dropped every moment on each side. Several of the Americans placed themselves in high trees, and as often as they could distinguish a British officer's uniform, took him off by deliberately aiming at his person. Reinforcements successively arrived and strengthened the American line.'

Lieutenant William Digby, of the Shropshire Regiment, appears also to have participated in or observed both engagements, if they can be separated in place and time:

'About half past one [he wrote], the fire seemed to slacken a little; but it was only to come on with double force, as between 2 and 3 the action became general on their side. From the situation of the ground, and their being perfectly acquainted with it, the whole of our troops could not be brought to engage together, which was a very material disadvantage, though everything possible was tried to remedy that inconvenience, but to no effect. Such an explosion of fire I never had any idea of before, and the heavy artillery joining in concert like great peals of thunder, assisted by the echoes of the woods, almost deafened us with the noise. To an unconcerned spectator, it must have had the most awful and glorious appearance, the different battalions moving to relieve each other, some being pressed and almost broke by their superior numbers. The crash of cannon and musketry never ceased till darkness parted us, when they retired to their camp, leaving us masters of the field, but it was a dear-bought victory if I can give it that name, as we lost many brave men. The 62nd had scarce 10 men a company left, and other regiments suffered much, and no very great advantage, honour excepted, was gained by the day.'

In respect to this stage of the action, the Earl of Harrington told the House of Commons in 1778: that the British line was formed with the utmost regularity; that, at the General's orders, different attempts were made to charge the enemy with bayonets; that all failed but the last, when the British troops finally drove them from the field; and that the action was disputed very obstinately by the enemy.

If not an actual participant, Wilkinson was another eye-witness who recorded his observations:

'The theatre of action was such, that although the combatants changed ground a dozen times in the course of the day, the contest terminated on the spot where it began. This may be explained in a few words. The British line was formed on an eminence in a thin pine wood, having before it Freeman's farm, an oblong field stretching from the centre towards its right, the ground in front sloping gently down to the verge of this field, which was bordered on the opposite side by a close wood; the sanguinary scene lay in the cleared ground, between the eminence occupied by the enemy and the wood just described; the fire of our marksmen from this wood was too deadly to be withstood by the enemy in line, and then they gave way and broke, our men rushing from their covert, pursued them to the entrance, where, having their flanks protected, they rallied, and charging in turn drove us back into the wood, from whence a dreadful fire would again force them to fall back; and in this manner did the battle fluctuate, like waves of a stormy sea; with alternate advantages for four hours without one moment's intermission. The British artillery fell into our possession at every charge, but we could neither turn the pieces upon the enemy, nor bring them off; the wood prevented the last, and the want of a match the first, as the lint stock was invariably carried off, and the rapidity of the transitions did not allow us time to provide one. The slaughter of this brigade of artillerists was remarkable, the captain and thirty-six men being killed or wounded out of forty-eight. It was truly a gallant conflict, in which death by familiarity lost its terrors, and certainly a drawn battle, as night alone terminated it; the British army keeping its ground in rear of the field of action, and our corps, when they could no longer distinguish objects, retiring to their own camp.'

Erroneously, it was reported to Gates that General Burgoyne had been killed. The mistake was occasioned by the fall from his horse of Captain Green whose richly embroidered saddle-cloth persuaded the rifleman who had shot him that he had killed Burgoyne himself. Burgoyne, who was unscathed, said in his report of the action: 'The enemy had with their army great numbers of marksmen, armed with rifle-barrel pieces; these, during an engagement, hovered upon the flanks in small detachments, and were very expert in securing themselves and in shifting their ground. In this action many placed themselves in high trees in the rear of their lines, and there was seldom a minute's interval of smoke in any part of our line, without officers being taken off by a single shot.'

The spice of the action was provided by the British artillery, of which Lieutenant Hadden was the only officer who was not either killed or wounded. Of the forty-eight artillerymen engaged, thirty-six became casualties. Early in the engagement (around 2 p.m.), Hadden was ordered by his superior officer, Captain Jones, to train a gun on Freeman's cabin and fire a shot through it, presumably to ensure that no enemy were lurking within. By then Morgan's riflemen had retreated to the woods, and the artillery, guarded by the 62nd Regiment, occupied the clearing, Hadden taking charge of two guns on the infantry's left. During the next three hours he lost nineteen of his twenty artillerymen, as the guns were successively lost to and regained from the enemy. Hadden applied to Brigadier-General Hamilton for help, which that officer could not supply, and Hadden was forced to remain inactive until the arrival of the additional artillerymen brought by General Phillips. Time and again Hadden's guns were silenced, before the infantrymen could recapture them, actions in which the 62nd Regiment lost 187 men killed and wounded and twenty-five taken prisoner. Captain Jones was severely wounded Supporting him in his arms, Hadden carried him back to a hut, which was already so filled with wounded that he could not find a place on which to lay him. Jones died that night.

With the British guns periodically silenced, the rebels might have won the field had not General Phillips arrived with four additional pieces. Loading them with grapeshot, Major Williams directed their fire into the trees amongst which the Americans were lurking, between their charges, holding them down at little more than musketry range. Simultaneously Burgoyne threw in the 20th Regiment on the left of the hard-pressed 62nd, and it succeeded in clearing the woods at the side of the clearing—a fortunate occurrence, for it enabled von Riedesel to attack the American right, unhindered and virtually unobserved.

The battle across and around the clearing swayed to and fro for several hours. That night Colonel Dearborn noted in his diary: 'On this Day has been fought one of the Greatest Battles that Ever was fought in America, and I trust we have Convinced the British Butchers that the Cowardly yankees Can, and when there is a Call for it, will, fight.'

General Glover, on the other hand, found both sides equally courageous:

'Both armies seemed determined to conquer or die. One continual blaze without any intermission till dark, when by consent of both parties it ceased. During which time we several times drove them, took the ground, passing over great numbers of their dead and wounded. Took one field prize, but the woods and brush were so thick, and being close pushed by another party of the enemy coming up, was obliged to give up our prize. The enemy in turn sometimes drove us. They were bold, intrepid, and fought like heroes, and I do assure you, Sirs, our men were equally bold and courageous and fought like men fighting for their all.'

Despite Phillip's intervention, American fire-power and numbers were beginning to tell. Successively Arnold sent out the Connecticut Militia commanded by Colonels Broeck, Cook, and Latimer; three New Hampshire regiments, those of Cilley, Hale and Scammel; Henry Livingstone's and Van Courtland's New Yorkers; and finally Brigadier-General Learned's Brigade, consisting of Bailey's, Weston's, and Jackson's Massachusetts regiments, James Livingstone's New Yorkers, together with Marshall's Regiment of Patterson's Brigade, and the Massachusetts Line. Arnold had despatched more troops than Gates thought wise, and he declared that no more should go, less the camp be jeopardized. His opinion was confirmed by his quartermaster-general, Colonel Morgan Lewis, who rode up to report that, though as yet undecided, the action was going well. Whereupon Arnold exclaimed, 'My God, I will soon put an end to it,' and, clapping spurs to his horse, galloped off at high speed. Fearing that Arnold, by some rash act, might do mischief, Gates sent Wilkinson to recall him, an order which Arnold obeyed. Lacking Arnold's direction, Learned's brigade, the last to be sent out, went astray and instead of joining the action in the centre, where its presence might have been decisive, blundered off to the left, where it became engaged with the British right wing to no useful purpose.

Even without Arnold's guiding hand, the British centre column was in danger of being annihilated. Von Riedesel tells the story of his intervention. He had heard the firing since 1 p.m., and in consequence he had collected his men to be ready for any eventuality:

'Towards two o'clcok in the afternoon Major Bloomfield of the artillery returned. He had accompanied Phillips on his reconnoitring expedition, and had now been sent back by him to Riedesel with the report that the Brunswick light troops belonging to the advance guard of the right wing were already hotly engaged with the enemy, that the latter were drawn up in order of battle, and that a general engagement would take place that very afternoon. Major Bloomfield was accordingly directed to bring back with him a few heavy guns from the artillery train, for the support of the right wing; but scarcely had he left, when the fire of musketry began anew. Riedesel, having as yet heard nothing from Burgonye, immediately dispatched Captain Willoe to the latter, at the same time posting his men so that he could not be taken by surprise. It was of the utmost importance that the ground between bridges Nos. 1 and 2 should be held, as upon that depended the salvation of the entire army. Here were the artillery and the supply train; in fact, here, near Taylor's house (situated about 3½ miles south of Fish Creek and about 100 rods north of the road that led from the meadows on to the plateau) was the main position. This point was occupied by the regiment Riedesel, which had for its support two six-pounders, under Captain Pausch, posted in an advantageous position, a little in advance. Some Indians, running across the woods and mountains from the right wing, reported that a few regiments of the enemy had marched to within a short distance of the left wing. This story, moreover, was the more credible, as some rebel patrols, who had been seen on the plain, had shot the horse of a dragoon while acting as sentry. In the meantime, the firing lasted until five o'clcok in the afternoon, when Captain Willoe returned with a message from Burgoyne to the effect that Riedesel, after reinforcing his rest of his troops and attack the flank of the enemy near Freeman's farm. Riedesel, accordingly, immediately selected for this purpose two companies from the regiment Rhetz, and the whole of his own regiment, together with two cannons—their places being filled by the remaining three companies of the regiment Rhetz. Leaving Bridagier Specht with the 47th and the heavy artillery in command on the river, Riedesel took the road behind bridge No. 2, and crossed the new one No. 3, leading to the plain. Here he stationed a guard. After crossing the bridge he hastened, with two companies of the regiment Rhetz as an advanced guard, as quickly as possible on a road, one and half English miles long, through the woods till he arrived on an eminence, from the top of which he could see the engagement of the right wing. The enemy were posted on a corner of the woods, having on his right flank for a defence a deep muddy ditch, the bank of which had been rendered inaccessible by stones, underbrush and barricades. In front of this corner of the forest, and entirely surrounded by dense woods, was a vacant space, on which the English regiments were drawn up in line. The struggle was for the possession of this vacant space, on which, by the way, Freeman's farm was situated. It had already been in possession of both parties, and now served as a support for the left flank of the English right wing, the right flank being covered by the corps of Fraser and Breymann. The 9th served as a reserve.

'When General Riedesel arrived on the eminence, the battle was raging the fiercest. The Americans, far superior in numbers, had, for the sixth time, hurled fresh troops against the three

English regiments—the 20th, 21st and 62nd. The guns on this wing were already silenced, there being no more ammunition and all the artillerymen having been either killed or wounded. The three brave English regiments had been, by the steady fire of fresh relays of the enemy, thinned down to one-half, and now formed a small band surrounded by heaps of dead and wounded. This was the scene presented to the view of Riedesel on his arrival on the height. Every moment he expected to see the little band either captured or annihilated by the Americans. Quickly, and without waiting for the rest of his troops—with drums beating and his men shouting "hurrah!"—he attacked the enemy on the double quick. Posting his troops at the edge of the above mentioned ditch, he sent such a well-directed volley among the Americans, that those troops who were coming out of the woods, and about to fall upon the English, were startled and turned back. The British, animated with fresh courage, pressed forward at the point of the bayonet Meanwhile, Captain Pausch arrived with his guns at the right moment, and forming into line with the English, opened fire with grapeshot. The regiment Riedesel also arrived at the nick of time, and, joining the two companies on the ditch, considerably extended the line of fire.

'The English had thrown a bridge across the ditch for the purpose of keeping up the necessary connection with the left wing. General Riedesel, therefore, after posting his two companies on the edge of the ditch, galloped toward the bridge, in order to confer with Generals Burgoyne and Phillips. Thence he sent orders to his troops to do their best to cross the ditch and unite with the English. The Brunswickers, having succeeded in spite of its apparent impossibility in accomplishing this feat, immediately poured another volley of musketry into the enemy's flank, accompanying it with a "hurrah!" This was the turning point; for the English and Germans, throwing themselves upon the enemy in the woods, repulsed them. Scarcely, however, was the engagement over in this quarter, when firing began again on the right. A few Americans brigades had endeavoured to surround the right wing, but Lieutenant Colonel Breymann, being on his guard, received them with a vigorous fire, and compelled them to retreat after a few discharges. General Fraser who was a witness of this, gives the most splendid acknowledgements to the German troops in a general circular to all the English generals.'

'Thus had General Riedesel,' says that General himself, 'with his German troops, once more saved the English from a great misfortune, having unquestionably, decided the engagement in their favour. Notwithstanding, however, the praise which the German troops received for their bravery on this occasion, General Burgoyne, and a few other English commanders, regarded the German general with secret envy. Indeed, they would gladly have passed over his merits, had such a thing been possible. British pride did not desire the acknowledgement of bravery other than their own, as we shall see more plainly in the future.'

The day had been saved. 'During the night,' says Lieutenant Digby, 'we remained in our ranks, and though we heard the groans of our wounded and dying at a small distance, yet could not assist them till morning, not knowing the position of the enemy, and expecting the action would be renewed at daybreak. Sleep was a stranger to us, but we were all in good spirits and ready to obey with cheerfulness any orders the general might issue before morning dawned.'

Writing several weeks after the battle, Lieutenant Anburey commented:

'Notwithstanding the glory of the day remains on our side. I am fearful the real advantages resulting from this land fought battle will rest on that of the Americans, our army being so much weakened by this engagement as not to be of sufficient strength to venture forth and improve the victory, which may, in the end, put a stop to our intended expedition; the only apparent benefit gained is that we keep possession of the ground where the engagement began.

'The courage and obstinacy with which the Americans fought were the astonishment of everyone, and we now become fully convinced they are not that contemptible enemy we had hitherto imagined them, incapable of standing a regular engagement, and that they would only fight behind strong and powerful works.'

The British casualties had been severe. Burgoyne had lost a third of his force and had gained nothing. Of the 62nd Regiment only sixty men remained standing. In his returns, Major Kingston noted the killed, wounded and missing as 556, including two lieutenant-colonels, three majors, nine captains, fourteen lieutenants, seven ensigns, twenty-six sergeants, six drummers, and 489 rank and file. The high proportion of officers killed and wounded was attributed by Anburey to the great execution of Morgan's riflemen who directed their fire against them in particular: 'In every interval of smoke they were sure to take off some, as the riflemen has posted themselves in high trees.'

The dead were buried in deep pits on the field of battle, and, though sought by the National Park Service, they have never been located. Anburey describes his experiences in command of a burial party:

'The day after our late engagement, I had as unpleasant a duty as can fall to the lot of an officer, the command of the party sent out to bury the dead and bring in the wounded, and as we encamped on the spot where the three British regiments had been engaged, they were very numerous. . . . I, however, observed a little more decency than some parties had done, who left heads, legs and arms above ground. No other distinction is paid to officer or soldier than that the officers are put in a hole by themselves. Our army abounded with young officers in the subaltern line and in the course of this unpleasant duty, three of the 20th Regiment were interred together, the age of the eldest not exceeding seventeen. This friendly office to the dead, though it greatly affects the feelings, was nothing to the scene in bringing in the wounded; the one were past all pain, the other in the most excruciating torments, sending forth deadful groans. They had remained out all night, and from the loss of blood and want of nourishment, were upon the point of expiring with faintness: some of them begged they might lie and die, others again were insensible, some upon the least movement were put in the most horrid tortures, and all had near a mile to be conveyed to the hospitals; others at their last gasp, who for want of our timely assistance must have inevitably expired. These poor creatures, perishing with cold and weltering in their blood, displayed such a scene, it must be a heart of adamant that could not be affected at it, even to a degree of weakness.'

The wounded were carried back to the base camp, and some were taken to the small, uninhabited hut in which the wives of von Riedesel, Major Acland, Major Harnage, and Lieutenant Reynell had taken shelter at the start of the action, as the Baroness describes:

'On the 19th September, there was an affair between the two armies, which, it is true, ended to our advantage; although we were, nevertheless, obliged to make a halt at a place called Freeman's farm. I was an eye witness of the whole affair, and as I knew that my husband was in the midst of it, I was full of care and anguish, and shivered at every shot, for I could hear everything. I saw a great number of wounded, and what was still more harrowing, they even brought three of them into the house where I was. One of these was Major Harnage, the husband of a lady of our company; another, a lieutenant, whose wife, also, was of our acquaintance; and the third, a young English officer of the name of Young. Major Harnage, with his wife, lived in a room next to mine. He had received a shot through the lower part of the bowels, from which he suffered exceedingly. A few days after our arrival, I heard plaintive moans in another room near me, and learned that they came from Young. the young English officer just mentioned, who was lying very low.

'I went to him and found him lying on a little straw, for he had lost his camp equipage. He was a young man, probably eighteen or nineteen years old; and, actually, the own nephew of the Mr Young, whom I had known, and the only son of his parents. It was only for this reason that he grieved; on account of his own sufferings he uttered no complaint. He had bled considerably, and they wished to take off his leg, but he could not bring his mind to it, and now mortification had set in. I sent him pillows and coverings, and my women servants a mattress. I redoubled my care of him, and visited him every day, for which I received from the sufferer a thousand blessings. Finally, they attempted the amputation of the limb, but it was too late, and he died a few days afterwards. As he occupied an apartment close to mine and the walls were very thin, I could hear his last groans through the partition of my room.'

In his official report of the action, in which he had played a conspicuous and, according to several diarists, a courageous part, Burgoyne paid tribute to the discipline and bravery of his men, which he said had been exemplary. He paid grudging tribute to von Riedesel who 'had exerted himself' to bring up part of the left wing and 'arrived in time to charge the enemy with regularity and bravery'. In common with his contemporaries, both British and German, Burgoyne failed to observe the remarkable feature of the battle of Freeman's Farm—the introduction of a new method of warfare—the tactics of Morgan's sharpshooters. Clad in dress indistinguishable from their background, they skirmished in line, taking accurate fire with their rifled and quick-loading pieces. On September

189

19, 1777, medieval and modern methods of warfare had clashed for the first time. It took Europeans more than a century to perceive the advantages of the method of fighting, that the Americans had learned in their frontier wars against the Red Indians.

XIV *Neilson's Barn*

Unknown to Burgoyne, the American camp on the morning following the battle was in turmoil. The troops who had borne the brunt of the fighting were exhausted, and the whole army was short of ammunition, there being less than forty rounds per man. Schuyler, in Albany, went round collecting the lead from windows, and sent it to Bemis Heights. The day dawned thick and misty, and the Americans stood behind their breastworks, expecting any moment that Burgoyne's soldiers would zoom out of the mists. About 7 a.m. a British deserter, a corporal from the 62nd Regiment, reached the American lines. He was brought to Colonel Wilkinson who noticed his blackened face, discoloured from uncapping cartridges with his teeth. Interrogated, he declared:

... that he had been in the whole of the action the day before, that after night all the wounded and the women had been removed to the encampment and hospital tents near the river, and that fresh ammunition had been served to the troops who had been engaged (as a proof of which he showed his cartridge box with 60 rounds); that he had left the ranks not 15 minutes before, pretending an occasion of nature; that the whole army was under arms, and orders had been given for the attack of our lines; that the mutiny act had been read at the head of each corps, and that they expected to march in ten minutes. He appeared to be much alarmed, and begged to be discharged with a pass, declaring that we should have the grenadiers at our lines on the left, in fifteen minutes.'

Wilkinson states that full credit was given to the report, and 'our lines were manned, and the troops exhorted; but we were badly fitted to defend works, or meet the close rencontre; the late hour at which the action closed the day before, the fatigue of officers and men, and the defects of our organization, had prevented the left wing from drawing ammunition, and we could not boast of more than a bayonet for every three muskets; the fog obscured every object at the short distance of twenty yards. We passed an hour of awful expectation and suspense, during which, hope, fear and anxiety played on the imagination many could hear the movement of the enemy, and others could discern through the floating mist the advance of their column; but between eight and nine o'clock the sun dispersed the vapour, and we had no enemy in view; the report of the deserter was discredited, and the troops dismissed; and yet his information was cirumstantially correct, as is proved by the following authentic facts.'

According to Wilkinson, Major-General Phillips, who was a captive at Boston told him in the following summer 'After the affair of the 19th September terminated, General Burgoyne determined to attack you the next morning on your left, with his whole force; our wounded, and sick, and women had been disposed of at the river; the army was formed early on the morning of the 20th, and we waited only for the dispersion of the fog, when General Fraser observed to General Burgoyne, that the grenadiers and light infantry who were to lead the attack, appeared fatigued by the duty of the preceding day, and that if he would suspend the operation until the next morning, he was persuaded they would carry the attack with more vivacity. Burgoyne yielded to the proposition of Fraser; the orders were countermanded, and the corps returned to camp.'

These 'facts' reported by Wilkinson seem of doubtful validity. It is improbable that Fraser's men were fatigued as they had played little part in the battle at Freeman's Farm, and Digby states that both Fraser and Phillips advised the renewal of the attack on the morning of the 20th. Burgoyne, because the hospitals were full and the magazines had not been properly secured, postponed it to the 21st, and the golden opportunity was missed. On that day, a message which changed Burgoyne's mind arrived from General Clinton.

If Burgoyne had attacked the American camp on the 20th or 21st as he had originally intended, says Wilkinson, 'his force would have enabled him to lead a column of 5000 rank and file against our left, where the ground was most favourable to his approach; whilst a feint on our right, by the plain near the river, would have kept every man at this station within our extensive lines; and under such advantages on his side, it is highly probable, he would have gained a decisive victory, and taken our artillery and baggage; for although our numbers in rank and file exceeded six thousand, the sick, casualties, and contingencies of the service, would not have left us more than five thousand five hundred men for defence; and from the formation of our camp, by penetrating on the left, he would have cut off our right.'

Wilkinson's appraisal of the American fear of the renewal of the battle, and their preparations for retreat, are confirmed by the diaries kept by Colonel Henry Dearborn, and Ephraim Squire, a sergeant of the Connecticut Line. Dearborn says that, on September 20th, he expected a 'General Battle this day' and on the 22nd he was still 'hourly expecting a General battle'. Squire noted:

20th—Today ordered to strike our tents at 3 o'clock p.m. hourly expecting the enemy to force our lines.
21stst—Sunday. Much expecting the enemy, struck tents ready to march.
22nd—We still expect the enemy.
23rd—Today about 12 p.m. we are alarmed by the enemy's firing.
24th—Today ordered to strike our tents.

Captain Benjamin Warren, on the other hand, remarks that the British deserter from the 62nd Regiment also reported that

General Burgoyne had been mortally wounded, that his second-in-command had been killed on the spot, and that 'most of their regimental officers and soldiers were either killed or wounded, and he thought it the safest way to desert to us'— hardly a picture that foreshadowed a renewal of the conflict. That afternoon, Warren sent out a party which brought in the bodies of several of the American dead and wounded, including that of Colonel Colburn, the scout leader. On his return to camp, he reported that 'the loss of the enemy is very great; the field was covered with dead almost for several acres'. Warren described the battle of the previous day as 'the hottest and longest that was ever fought in America'.

Wilkinson contented himself with a visit to the British wounded who had been brought into the camp, discovering 'a charming youth not more than 16 years old, lying among them; feeble, faint, pale and stiff in his gore, the delicacy of his aspect, and the quality of his clothing attracted my attention, and on enquiry I found he was an Ensign Phillips; he told me he had fallen by a wound in his leg or thigh, and as he lay on the ground was shot through the body by an army follower, a murderous villain, who avowed the dead, but I forgot his name; the moans of this hapless youth affected me to tears; I raised him from the straw on which he lay, took him in my arms and removed him to a tent, where every comfort was provided and every attention paid to him, but his wounds were mortal, and he expired on the 21st; when his name was first mentioned to General Gates, he exclaimed, "Just Heaven! he may be the nephew of my wife," but the fact was otherwise.'

The British were in no condition to renew the battle. Burgoyne's army had been badly mauled, and to no useful purpose. In respect to the action on September 19th, Digby says, 'No great advantage, honour excepted, was gained that day,' and Anburey states, 'It is as if we had conquered only to preserve our reputation, for we have reaped little advantage, from our invincible efforts. 'We have gained little more by the

victory than honour,' he added. Though they remained masters
of the field, the British had won a Pyrrhic victory, for they
could ill afford the severe losses they had sustained.

Burgoyne must have been aware that he had failed in his
attempt to shake the Americans, and that time was gainst him.
'It was soon found', he reported in his next public dispatch,
completion of which he delayed until October 20th, 'that honour
excepted, no fruits were attained by the preceding victory; the
enemy working with redoubled ardour to strengthen their left;
their right was already unattackable'.

Nevertheless, Burgoyne put a brave face on the situation,
claiming victory in the two letters he wrote to Brigadier-General
Powell, who commanded at Ticonderoga. Neither letter reached
its destination for, as Wilkinson reports, they fell into American
hands. Lieutenant Hardin had been sent out to take a prisoner
and pick up intelligence, and on his return, near Saratoga on
the 22nd, 'he met an Indian courier in a path on the summit of
a sharp ridge; they were within a few paces, presented and
fired at the same instant; the Indian fell, and Hardin escaped
with a scratch of his antagonist's ball on his left side; the letters
of Burgoyne to Powell, and several others were found in the
shot pouch of the dead Indian, and delivered by the Lieutenant
at headquarters'. These captured letters suggested that
Burgoyne was putting the best complexion he could on a
disastrous setback.

Burgoyne's decision to postpone the renewal of the attack
was due to the arrival, on the night of the 21st, of a message
in cipher from Clinton at New York, dated September 12th:

'You know my good will and are not ignorant of my poverty.
If you think 2000 men can assist you effectually, I will make a
push at Montgomery in about ten days. But ever jealous of my
flanks if they make a move in force on either of them I must
return to save this important post. I expect reinforcements
every day. Let me know what you wish.'

That night, Burgoyne sent the messenger, Sergeant Daniel Taylor, back to Clinton, and on the following night he despatched two further messengers, Captain Thomas Scott of the 53rd Regiment, and Captain Alexander Campbell of the 62nd Regiment. Some confusion surrounds Taylor's fate, it being said that he was captured on his journey to Clinton, whereas it appears that he reached Fort Montgomery and was intercepted on his return to Burgoyne. Scott, following an adventurous journey in which he kept to the woods by day, stole a horse for one night's ride, and persuaded a friendly farmer to row him across river concealed in a canoe, got through safely to Clinton, carrying this letter;

'Have lost the old cypher, but being sure from the tenor of your letter you meant it so to be read, I have made it out— An attack, or the menace of an attack, upon Montgomery, must be of great use, as it will draw away a part of this force, and I will follow them close. Do it my dear friend directly.

'*Yours ever faithfully*,
'*J. B.*'

The other messenger, Captain Campbell, carried a duplicate of this letter, with a verbal explanation, which Clinton recorded:

'Burgoyne's army did not exceed 5000 men, having lost 500 or 600 in the action on the nineteenth; but the rebel army was very strongly posted to the amount of above 12,000 men within a mile and half of his army, and had perhaps another considerable body hanging in the rear; that his provisions would not last him longer than till the 20th of October, his communication with Canada being entirely cut off; that altogether he had no doubt of being able to force his way to Albany, yet, being uncertain he could subsist after he got there, he wished before he attempted it to know whether I could open a communication with that town, at what time I expected to be there, and whether I could procure supplies from New York for him afterwards, requesting I would send him as soon as possible by triplicate my most explicit orders, either to attack the enemy or to retreat across the lakes while they were still clear of ice— hinting at the same time that he would not have relinquished his communication with them had he not expected a co-operated army at Albany. This account of General Burgoyne's real condition, which I had neither heard of nor suspected until the present moment, filled my mind with the most anxious reflections. As matters were cirumstant, I greatly feared it was too late. I therefore despatched a messenger to General Burgoyne to let him know where we were.'

Upon doubtful prospect of aid from the south, Burgoyne postponed the renewal of the battle. While he awaited a favourable reply from Clinton, he entrenched his army upon the heights, constructing three redoubts, the strongest of which, named the Great Redoubt, formed a citadel above the river. The Earl of Balcarres with the light Infantry occupied Freeman's Farm, and von Breymann took position on a small height of land to the north. The British and German regiments extended across the plateau and down to the river bank.

On September 21st, the British heard a great noise of cheering and a salute of thirteen guns from the American camp. Several days elapsed before they learned the significance of the celebration: the considerable success gained at Fort Ticonderoga by General Lincoln's men. On September 28th Gates released a prisoner, Cornet Graef of the German dragoons, who brought the news to Burgoyne.

Learning that Fort Ticonderoga was weakly held, Lincoln, who, following the battle of Bennington, had remained on Burgoyne's eastern flank, sent three contingents, each 500 strong, commanded by Colonels Woodbridge, Johnson, and John Brown, to attempt to cut Burgoyne's line of communication from Canada and to destroy his bases. While Woodbridge proceeded to Skenesborough, which had been abandoned by the British, Johnson closed in on Mount Independence in order to create a diversion for Brown. Brown, on route to Ticonderoga, mopped up the small garrison at Fort George and moved up the lake, lying concealed for two days near Fort Ticonderoga, which he had helped to capture in 1775. Brigadier-General Powell's garrison, consisting of the German regiment of Prince Frederick and the British 53rd Regiment, about 900 men in all, was taken by surprise when Brown, on September 18th, rushed the Lake George landing and stormed the Old French Lines. He captured the blockhouse at the sawmills, after a stout resistance by Lieutenant Lord, and overpowered the small garrison on Mount Defiance. To cover Brown's attack, Johnson kept up a cannonade on Mount Independence, thereby fully engaging its garrison. Brown took 315 prisoners chiefly from the 53rd Regiment, and released more than 100 American prisoners who had been held in the old fort since the battle of Hubbardton. His demand for the surrender of the fort, an audacious bluff, was rejected by Powell who declared that he would defend it to the last man. Before he departed on September 22nd, Brown destroyed 200 *bateaux*, seventeen armed sloops, and a quantity of stores. On his return journey down the lake he attacked the British post on Diamond Island, twenty-five miles south of Ticonderoga, where he was repulsed with considerable loss by Captain Aubrey, who commanded two companies of the 42nd Regiment. The attacks on the British posts were notable achievements which demonstrated the ease with which a stronger force, equipped with siege artillery, could sever Burgoyne's tenous link with Canada.

On Brown's return to Pawlett, Lincoln, followed later by his 2000 men, marched to Bemis Heights, where his arrival was welcomed by Gates who had lost the services of the commander of his left wing. Benedict Arnold sat in his tent, nursing a grievance against his commander-in-chief.

Consideration of the famous quarrel between Arnold and

Gates has been obscured by Arnold's subsequent behaviour, and possibly, by failure to evalute the evidence, which consists of the Gates–Arnold correspondence and the letters written by Arnold's young aides, Richard Varick and Henry Brockholst Livingstone. These two, as partisans of the discredited Schuyler, may have hoped to inflame the dispute in order to discredit Gates and to vindicate their former chief whom they, and others, believed had been supplanted as a result of Gates's intrigues. Varick and Livingstone were not unbiased spectators of the row, and it is possible that they provoked and widened the clash of two incompatible personalities, the smug and conceited Gates and the temperamental Arnold, a man who, obsessed with his own virtues thirsted for glory.

Until the evening of September 19th no cloud darkened the horizon. Arnold and Gates disagreed amicably about the measures to be taken, even when they argued about the number of troops which should be engaged in the battle. It is true that Wilkinson, who appears to have taken an unusually passive part in the affair, had remarked on September 2nd that 'General Gates despises a certain pompous little fellow', but there is no other hint of previous hostility between the two generals other than Arnold's disregard of Gates's orders in the previous summer. On the day of the battle Arnold's impetuosity had been curbed, and his desire to renew the action next morning had been rejected by Gates who wisely perceived that his role lay in delaying the advance of Burgoyne, who would soon run short of supplies, rather than risk a pitched battle.

The rupture came on September 22nd when, in his report to Congress, Gates failed specifically to give credit to Arnold's division, assigning the glory of the action 'entirely to the valour of the Rifle Regiment and corps of Light Infantry under the command of Colonel Morgan'. His commander-in-chief's failure to accord him the honour and renown he craved infuriated Arnold. He took as a studied insult Gates's subsequent action in transferring Morgan's corps, which had functioned as part of his division, to his own command. He stormed into Gates's headquarters, and high words were exchanged. Arnold waxed hot and angry, shouting accusations and insults, to which Gates replied with sarcasm. Arnold threatened to leave the Northern Department. Gates pointed out that, on July 11th, Arnold had resigned his command and had never withdrawn his resignation; it had been suspended at his own request. It was doubtful, therefore, whether he still held the rank of major-general, and he, Gates, was not obliged to give him a command. He could have a pass to leave the Department whenever he wanted it.

Gates's calm acceptance of his threat to leave the Northern Department wounded Arnold's pride, and, unwise as Gates may have been (for Arnold's services as an intrepid fighter and a popular leader were valuable), he was entirely justified in his treatment of his unruly subordinate who was prepared, from pique, to leave the army in the lurch in the face of the enemy. Gates, it seems, may have been provoked beyond endurance.

Arnold had needlessly insulted his commander-in-chief by his action on the night of the 19th, when he appointed to his personal staff Richard Varick, who had quarrelled over dinner with Gates. Varick had taken exception to 'words that had dropped from Gates's mouth', and, springing to his feet, had offered his resignation as muster-master of the army. He would sooner see Gates 'drawn and quartered' than serve him further, he told Schuyler in the letter he wrote that night. Arnold he would cheerfully serve.

Varick and Livingstone inflamed Arnold's mortification, and they may have turned an unfortunate situation, which could have been remedied, into a sordid and dangerous altercation which they described gleefully, and probably inaccurately, in their letters to Schuyler at Albany. The latter adopted an attitude of unctious superiority, and accepted the rift between Arnold and his hated rival with unconcealed pleasure, making no effort to curb the enthusiasm of his young partisans.

Arnold returned to his tent after the stormy interview and wrote Gates a long letter, in which he rehearsed his grievances, stating that he was conscious of no offence or neglect of duty, of which, it may be remarked, he had not been accused. As he appeared to be of little consequence to the army of the Northern Department, said Arnold, he requested a pass to Philadelphia, where he proposed to join General Washington and 'may possibly have it in my power to serve my country'. To this letter Gates replied on September 23rd, enclosing a letter addressed to John Hancock, the President of Congress, which Arnold rejected in a second letter which clearly indicates his state of mind:

'Camp Stillwater, Sept. 23, 1777

'*Sir,*

'When I wrote you yesterday I thought myself entitled to an answer, and that you would at least have condescended to acquaint me with the reasons which have induced you to treat me with affront and indignity, in public manner which I mentioned and which has been observed by many gentlemen of the army; I am conscious of none, but if I have been guilty of any crimes deserving such treatment, I wish to have them pointed out, that I may have an opportunity of vindicating my conduct. I know no reason for your conduct unless I have been traduced by some designing *villain.*

'I requested permission for myself and aides to go to Philadelphia, instead of which you have sent me a letter to the honourable John Hancock, esq'. which I have returned. If you have any letters for that gentleman which you think proper to send sealed, I will take charge of them. I once more request your permission for myself and aides to pass to Philadelphia.

'*I am Sir,*
'*Your obedient servant,*
'*B. Arnold.*

'*Hon. Major-General Gates.*'

Arnold did not really want a pass; he hoped that Gates would offer a reconciliation. To Arnold's letter Gates replied in mild terms, denying any intention to give insult and enclosing a Common Pass. A little exercise of common sense on Arnold's part might have healed the breach; but Varick and Livingstone stoked the flames of his resentment. On September 22nd, Varick had informed Schuyler that 'matters between Generals Gates and Arnold are got to such a pitch, that I have the fullest assurance Arnold will quit the Northern Department in a day or two', and he himself would stay no longer. He added, 'This I am certain of, that Arnold has all the credit of the action on the 19th, for he was ordering out troops to it, while the other was in Dr Pott's tent backbiting his neighbours.'

Thus, according to Varick's interpretation of the battle, Arnold's aggressiveness had been responsible for engaging the British in the first place; and, if he had not been denied more troops, he would have defeated Burgoyne. Schuyler replied that Gates 'will probably be indebted to him [Arnold] for the glory he may acquire by a victory, but perhaps he is so very sure of success that he does not wish the other to come in for a share of it'.

On the same day Livingstone wrote Schuyler a letter which is remarkable for its similarity in expression to Arnold's own words:

'I am much distressed at Gen. Arnold's determination to retire from the army at this important crisis. His presence was never more necessary. He is the life and soul of the troops. Believe me, Sir, to him and to him alone is due the honour of our late victory. Whatever share his superiors may claim they are entitled to none. He enjoys the confidence and affection of officers and soldiers. They would, to a man, follow him to conquest or death. His absence will dishearten them to such a degree as to render them of but little service.'

Arnold's spirit, said Livingstone, Schuyler's one-time aides could not brook the repeated indignities he received from Fate, and he emphasized that 'the reason for the present disagreement between two old cronies is simply this—*Arnold is your friend*'. He himself, he said, could no longer submit to the command of a man whom he abhorred from the very bottom of his soul. He ended with the enigmatic remark, 'A cloud is gathering and may ere long burst on his [Gates's] head.'

Both Gates and Arnold believed that others were poisoning the other's mind in order to make reconciliation impossible and to promote discord. Livingstone told Schuyler, 'It has been several times insinuated by the Commander-in-Chief of General Arnold that his mind had been *poisoned and prejudiced* by some of his Family and I have been pointed out as the Person who had this *undue* influence over him.'

Arnold, on his part, claimed that he was 'being traduced by some designing villain', usually identified as James Wilkinson, who seems to have played no significant role in the controversy. If he had done so, he could hardly have refrained from claiming credit in his self-laudatory *Memoirs*, in which he refers only to a 'difference' that 'took place betweeen General Gates and General Arnold, which terminated in a public quarrel, and may be traced to official presumption and conscious superiority on one side, and an arrogant spirit and impatience of command on the other. General Gates had, by a violent exertion of power, screened Arnold from disgrace the preceding campaign, and Arnold conceived he had by his voluntary perils and the *éclat*, acquired in the command of the fleet on Lake Champlain, cancelled the obligation. Gates trusted to the confidence of Congress for the support of his authority, and Arnold relied on feats of arms and intrepidity of character for popular patronage. With such pretensions, the smallest spark of collision sufficed to light up the flames of discord.'

Livingstone wrote again to Schuyler on the 24th:

'Gen. Arnold's intention to quit this department is made public and has caused great uneasiness among the soldiery. To induce him to stay, General Poor proposed an Address from the general officers and colonels of his division, returning him thanks for his past service and particularly for his conduct during the late action and requesting his stay. The Address was framed, and consented to by Poor's officers. Those of Gen. Learned refused. They acquiesced in the propriety of the measure, but were afraid of giving umbrage to General Gates.'

There is no extant evidence other than the statement contained in Livingstone's letter that the officers of the Northern Department attempted (and, according to Livingstone, were too weak), to intervene in the dispute in order to bring about a reconciliation; and Livingstone's assertion, on the following day in a further letter to his old chief, that he hoped that the officers would unite in preventing Arnold from leaving, is equally unsupported. He described their failure to do so in unflattering terms, and he praised Arnold's determination to accept no compromise, which Gates seems to have suggested by a messenger. Major Chester, the envoy, who told Arnold that overtures were necessary on his part and 'the first step towards an accommodation would be to get rid of Livingstone', a remark which so infuriated that gentleman that he could hardly contain himself.

According to Livingstone, Arnold consented to remain in the camp because he had been so requested by a letter signed by all the general officers. It seems more probable that Arnold never intended to leave. He did not do so when, on September 24th, he found Lincoln giving orders to his division. He challenged Lincoln's authority, which the latter agreed he did not yet have. The authority was confirmed next day in Gates's General Order, which appointed Lincoln to command of the right wing. This order provoked Varick to remark: 'Arnold is determined not to suffer anyone to interfere with his division and says it will be certain death to any officer who does it in action, if it be not settled before.'

Goaded to fury by what he considered to be unjustified treatment, but loath to leave as long as the chance of winning glory remained, the sensitive Arnold stayed in camp, ignored by Gates. to whom he wrote again:

Camp Stillwater, October 1, 1777

'Notwithstanding the repeated ill treatment I have met with, and continued daily to receive, treated only as a cypher in the army, never consulted or acquainted with one occurrence in the army, which I know only by accident, while I have every reason to think your treatment proceeds from a spirit of jealousy, and that I have every thing to fear from the malice of my enemies, conscious of my own innocency and integrity, I am determined to sacrifice my feelings, present peace and quiet, to the public good, and continue in the army at this critical juncture, when my country needs every support.

'I beg leave to say, that when Congress sent me into this department at the request of his excellency General Washington, they thought me of some consequence, and I believe expected the commander-in-chief, would consult with me, or at least would have taken my opinion on public matters. I think it my duty (which nothing shall deter me from doing) to acquaint you the army are clamorous for action. The militia who compose a great part of the army are already threatening to go home. One fortnight's inaction will, I make no doubt, lessen your army by sickness and defection at least four thousand men, in which time the enemy may be reinforced or make good their retreat.

'I have reason to think, from intelligence since received, that had we improved the 20th of September it might have ruined the enemy, that is past, let me intreat you to improve the present time.

'I hope you will not impute this hint to a wish to command the army, or to outshine you, when I assure you it proceeds

205

from my zeal for the cause of my country in which I expect to rise or fall.

'*I am, Sir*'
'*Your humble servant,*
'*B. Arnold.*

'*Hon. Major-general Gates.*'

Contrary to Arnold's statement, the militia were not threatening to leave, but were in fact pouring into Gates's camp, eager to repel Burgoyne's advance. It was improbable that Burgoyne would be reinforced, and unlikely that he would retreat. Gates had formed this correct estimate of his opponent, of whom he said, 'Despair may dictate to him to risk all upon one throw; he is an old gambler, and in time has seen all the chances.' 'In a fortnight at furthest', he told Washington on October 5th, 'he must decide whether he will rashly risque at an infinite disadvantage to force my camp or retreat to his den,' and in a letter to the President of Congress he spoke of Burgoyne's 'distressed condition', adding that he was taking every means not only to distress him, but to cut off his retreat.

By October 7th, the strength of the rebel army had increased to 10,000 men, who now included a band of Oneida Indians. These Wilkinson thought, would turn upon the enemy 'the vengeance which they had prepared to inflict upon us'. Almost daily they brought in scalps and prisoners. Benjamin Warren recorded in his diary on September 25th, 'Indians brought in 27 regulars and Hessians, also tories who were given up to them to buffet'', by which he probably meant that the wretched loyalists were made to run the gauntlet. Between September 29th and October 6th. Colonel Dearborn noted the arrival in camp of deserters and prisoners to the number of at least sixty-four.

Having determined to await news of Clinton's advance on which he had staked his future, Burgoyne heard on September

27th the unwelcome news that one of his messengers had been detected and hanged. Three days later, he received more heartening news; St Leger, having retreated to Canada, had reached Ticonderoga, though the courier carrying the letter announcing his arrival had been intercepted by the watchful Lieutenant Hardin. St Leger's second messenger, who had been obliged to make his way through the woods in order to elude the vigilance of the enemy's war parties, informed Burgoyne that the Brunswick recruits had arrived at Ticonderoga, where Powell would hold them to reinforce his depleted garrison. St Leger, whose contingent had been greatly reduced by Carleton on its return to Canada remained at Ticonderoga and made no move to join Burgoyne.

In the British camp, Digby heard a confused rumour that Clinton was on his way, coming up river, which led him to remark that 'General Burgoyne was too ready to believe any report in our favour'. All communication with Canada was cut off, he says, and 'some thought we should be ordered to retreat suddenly under cover of night; others believed that Burgoyne would try another action first'. As Burgoyne's soldiers became increasingly dismayed, Gates's men became correspondingly confident. Early in October they learned that Stark had captured Fort Edward and was on his way down river with 1000 militiamen.

On October 3rd, Burgoyne was forced to cut the rations to a third; the soldiers had no winter clothing, and the nights were getting cold. Desertions mounted; those who were caught were either hanged or sentenced to 1000 lashes. These punishments failed to deter others, many of whom were caught and scalped by the enemy's Indians.

Though continuously on active duty, Anburey found time to write his Journal;

'Our present situation is far from being an inactive one, the armies being so near that not a night passes but there is firing and continual attacks upon the advanced pickets especially those of the Germans. It seems to be the plan of the enemy to harass us by constant attacks, which they are enabled to do without fatiguing their army, from the great superiority of their numbers.

'We are now become so habituated to fire that the soldiers seem to be indifferent to it, and eat and sleep when it is very near them; the officers rest in their clothes, and the field officers are up frequently in the night. The enemy, in front of our quarter-guard, with hearing, are cutting trees and making works, and when I have had this guard, I have been visited by most of the field-officers, to listen to them. . . . The enemy had the assurance to bring down a small piece of cannon to fire as their morning gun, so near to our quarter-guard that the wadding rebounded against the works.

'We have within these few evenings, exclusive of other alarms, been under arms most of the night, as there has been a great noise, like the howling of dogs, upon the right of our encampment; it was imagined the enemy set it up to deceive us, while they were meditating some attack. The two first nights this noise was heard, General Fraser thought it to have been the dogs belonging to the officers, and an order was given for the dogs to be confined within the tents; any that were seen running about, the Provost had orders to hang them. The next night the noise was much greater, when a detachment of Canadians and Provincials were sent out to reconnoitre, and it proved to have arisen from large droves of wolves that came after the dead bodies; they were similar to a pack of hounds, for one setting up a cry, they all joined, and when they approached a corpse, their noise was hideous till they had scratched it up.'

Of the military diarists, General von Riedesel alone supplies a detailed account of the occurrences of this time. He says that, in order to fill the thinned ranks of the three English regiments

11. View eastwards to Freeman's Farm; scene of the opening battle, September 19, 1777. (*Saratoga National Historical Park*)

12a. Panoramic view of the battlefield as it is today. (*Photo: R. K. Dean*)

b. John Neilson House, used as quarters by American officers. (*Photo: R. K. Dean*)

which had borne the brunt of the engagement on the 19th, the provincials were incorporated, upon the written promise that they would be dismissed by December 25th; and, following the battle, that Burgoyne ordered the construction of a pontoon bridge across the Hudson to facilitate communication with the opposite bank. Although von Riedesel heard of the arrival of Clinton's message, he was not informed of its contents, though camp rumour reported that Howe had sent a corps up the Hudson, under Clinton's command, for the purpose of getting in the rear of the Americans.

On the 23rd, Burgoyne sent the Brunswick captain, Gerlach, with a strong detachment of provincials, on a reconnoitring expedition to the opposite bank of the Hudson, for the purpose of ascertaining more exactly the real position of the enemy, and to ascertain if something could not be done against the enemy's right wing. On his return, Gerlach reported that he had been beyond the right wing of the Americans, but could not find out their position, other than that he supposed they were encamped in two lines.

That day the servant of the late Colonel Baum, who had been given his liberty by General Gates, reached the camp — a circumstance, says von Riedesel, 'which caused the man to break forth in such laudations that it was feared the fellow might induce some of the soldiers to desert'. He was followed by several American deserters who reported that General Howe had lately gained some advantage over Washington, whose army was in dissolution. As we shall learn, Howe defeated Washington at Brandywine and Germantown, but on both occasions Washington succeeded in extricating his army.

General Burgoyne's situation, considered von Riedesel, was becoming more dangerous. The outposts were more and more molested; the army was weakened by sick and wounded and the need to send out detachments while the enemy swarmed in the rear. In consequence of the close proximity of the enemy, the soldiers had but little rest. 'But that which weakened the army still more was the growing desertions.' The Americans, says von Riedesel, sent agents in to the camp:

'who endeavoured to induce the soldiers, by all kinds of representations, to desert; and it being already known that the Americans treated their prisoners very kindly, and that they were not as strict in their discipline as the Europeans, the agents here and there found a willing ear. The want, moreover, of everything to which the English soldier especially was accustomed, and the hard service, made matters worse yet. There were already, besides the sick who were with the regiment, eight hundred men in the hospital, the most of whom were wounded.'

Both armies endeavoured to reconnoitre the enemy's position, the Americans having the greater success. One of their patrols had the audacity to penetrate 500 yards behind British headquarters, where it surprised a party of soldiers digging potatoes and carried them off as prisoners 'in the very faces of their comrades'. As the days went by, and no word was received from Clinton, Burgoyne began to be 'seriously alarmed', von Riedesel says.

On the evening of October 4th, Burgoyne called his Generals, Phillips and von Riedesel, and Simon Fraser, in to a council of war and explained the position. The provisions were becoming exhausted; the season was growing late; they were outnumbered by the enemy whose position the scouts had been unable to reconnoitre; and there was no news of Clinton. To extricate his army from its predicament, Burgoyne proposed a bold plan: leaving 800 men to guard the camp and bridge, he would take 4000 in an attempt to surround the enemy's left flank. This proportion, says von Riedesel, caused considerable argument, for the question arose 'whether eight hundred men would be sufficient for the purpose assigned them. The safety of the whole army depended upon this; for if this force should be beaten and the bridges in its rear taken, then the entire army would be completely cut off, and even if this detachment held its ground the position might still be lost—since, as three or four days were necessary to get round through the woods and pathless thickets, the enemy would have abundance of time to mass his force on this spot, when he would, in all probability, capture the men and destroy the two bridges—the only means of retreat. Such a hazardous undertaking must be thoroughly considered; and it was, therefore, agreed to inspect carefully on the next day the fortifications in that place, and the surrounding country.'

Following this reconnaissance, the council met again. Von Riedesel gave his opinion that it would be impossible to reach the enemy's rear in one day, and it would be better to recross the Hudson and reoccupy the old position behind the Battenkill, where the communication with Canada could be regained, and there await news of Clinton. Fraser agreed with von Riedesel, and Phillips refused to give an opinion. But Burgoyne would not hear of retreat, which he considered would be disgraceful. He said, according to von Riedesel, that 'on the 7th, he would undertake another great reconnoitring expedition against the enemy's left wing, to ascertain definitely his position, and whether it would be advisable to attack him. Should the latter be the case, he intended to advance on the enemy on the 8th with his entire army; but if he should not think an attack advisable then he would, on the 11th, march back to the Battenkill.'

In both camps the tension amounted. The October days were warm and gentle, the woods aflame with the golden tints of the Indian summer. Only the cold nights gave foretaste of the approaching winter, when the ground would be deep in snow, and the rivers and lakes frozen. Within a few weeks the weather would make retreat impossible. At Freeman's Farm, Burgoyne gazed southward, listening for the sound of the guns which would herald Clinton's approach. A mile and a half away, on

Saratoga

Bemis Heights, Gates knew, as Burgoyne did not, that Clinton had advanced up the Hudson and had pierced the Highlands barrier. On October 8th Clinton sent Captain Campbell back to Burgoyne, carrying an encouraging message. The American General Putnam also sent a courier galloping northwards; on reaching Bemis Heights he warned Gates to 'prepare for the worst'.

xv *The Highlands*

At his headquarters on Manhattan Island, New York, Sir Henry Clinton thought about Burgoyne's predicament. He was still at Saratoga, hoping to 'force his way to Albany', and worrying about how he would provision his army once he had reached his objective. Although Clinton did not yet know of Burgoyne's reverse at Freeman's Farm, and, despite his 'damned starved defensive', he concluded that Burgoyne might 'be in want of a little diversion'. Much as he had preferred 'the necessity for a co-operation with Burgoyne' to Howe's move to the southward, Clinton did not have the strength to force a junction of armies. In late September he proposed only to help Burgoyne once he had reached his objective. That Clinton believed that Burgoyne might be in trouble is indicated by his two letters to Lord Harvey, the adjutant-general, in which he referred to his proposed advance up the Hudson as 'a desperate attempt on a desperate occasion', and 'indeed it looks a little desperate, but the times may possibly require such an exertion'.

Clinton had been authorized by Howe to 'make any diversion in favour of General Burgoyne approaching Albany', but he needed to await the arrival of the long overdue transports bringing reinforcements from England before he dared to leave New York, where he had a hundred miles of perimeter to defend. When the transports arrived on September 29th, only 1700 of the 3000 troops they brought were fit for duty. These increased Clinton's effective strength to 2700 British and 4200 German regulars, or about 7000 men in all, excluding the 3000 strong Tory contingent. Allocating 4000 men to guard New York City, Clinton prepared 3000 for a push up the Hudson.

Saratoga

The possibility of a threat to New York City by General Washington was less than Clinton imagined, for Washington had been defeated by Howe at Brandywine on September 16th. Though he had succeeded in extricating his army, Washington had been unable to prevent Howe's entry into Philadelphia on September 29th. On the previous day he had learned of Gates's success at Freeman's Farm, and of Brown's achievement at Ticonderoga, which led him to issue a General Order congratulating the Northern Army.

Following his failure to halt Howe, Washington had written to Gates requesting the return of Morgan's riflemen, if their services could be dispensed with, to which Gates replied on October 5;

'Since the action of the 19th ultimo, the enemy have kept the ground they occupied the morning of that day, and fortified their camp; the advanced sentries of my pickets are posted within shot of and opposite to the enemy's; neither side have given ground an inch. In this situation, your excellency would not wish me to part with the corps the army of General Burgoyne are most afraid of. From the best intelligence he has not more than three weeks' provisions in store; it will take him at least eight days to get back to Ticonderoga; so that in a fortnight at furthest, he must decide, whether he will really risk at infinite disadvantage to force my camp or retreat to his den: in either case, I must have the fairest prospect to be able to reinforce your excellency in a more considerable manner than by a single regiment.'

On October 4th, Washington suffered another reverse at Germantown, but once again Howe failed to follow up his advantage.

If Clinton still hesitated to thrust up the Hudson, Burgoyne's message, sent on September 23rd, convinced him of the urgency of the enterprise. Burgoyne expressed his hope for 'an attack or even the menace of an attack upon Fort Montgomery, to draw away part of the enemy's force', and he went on:

'But should you not be, from inevitable and cross circumstances, able to carry it within the time required, even the keeping it besieged will check the enemy and consequently will help. Should Gates venture and be rash and ignorant enough to detach to support Putnam, he will give me very fair game (and I conceive he cannot be in hopes if he fails of success to be supported elsewhere) which I shall not hesitate to seize—depend upon me to exert every nerve and I shall have 5000 to follow him. Lose no opportunity to correspond with me as no time or place will be difficult for such emissaries as you employ. Gates little suspects how near they are to his person.'

On October 3rd, Clinton embarked 3000 troops on sixty transports and sailed up river, escorted by the vessels of Commodore Hotham's squadron.

Forty miles north of New York City, the Highlands, a narrow range of rocky hills through which flowed the Hudson River, formed an impenetrable barrier to an army which did not command the river. The importance of this narrow river-defile had been appreciated by the Americans, who had built two forts, named Clinton and Montgomery, to command the narrows. In May 1777, General Washington had sent Major-General Putnam, a skilled frontier fighter who had fought in the French and Indian war, to command at Peekskill, on the eastern bank of the river, four miles south of Fort Clinton, and seven miles from Fort Montgomery. Both forts stood on the western bank and neither of which had been completed by the end of September. Another small fort had been constructed on Constitution Island further up river, and a boom of logs and a chain had been stretched across the river above Montgomery. From heights of 200 and 150 feet, Forts Clinton and Montgomery commanded the river, but neither had been designed to resist assault from the rear.

These forts were weakly garrisoned. Most of the Continental regiments had been taken from Putnam to strengthen Washington, and in early October he commanded a force composed of 1000 Continentals and 400 militiamen. Upon receiving a report of Sir Henry Clinton's proposed advance, Governor George Clinton of New York had ordered out the state's militia as far north as Poughkeepsie, but many men had been allowed to return home to complete the harvest.

Sir Henry Clinton reached Veerplanck's Point on October 5th, where, in order to make a feint at Peekskill, he landed some of his troops. There he was joined by Captains Scott and Campbell. Campbell brought the verbal message from Burgoyne which stated that his provisions would last to October 29th, and asked whether he should advance or retreat. To this Clinton replied:

'That not having received any instructions from the Commander-in-Chief to the Northern Army, and unacquainted even of his intentions concerning the operations of that army, excepting his wishes that they should get to Albany, Sir Henry Clinton cannot presume to give any orders to General Burgoyne. General Burgoyne could not suppose that Sir Henry Clinton had any idea of penetrating to Albany with the small force he mentioned in his last letter.'

This letter, which represented Clinton's realistic view, for he was still south of the Highlands, and 100 miles from Albany, was carried by Campbell who reached Burgoyne's camp on the night of October 16th. Captain Scott also set out to rejoin Burgoyne, and, hearing of his surrender, returned to Clinton.

Sir Henry Clinton's threat to Peekskill deceived Putnam, who weakened the garrisons of the forts, reducing them to 600 men, to strengthen his own force. Leaving 1000 men at Veerplanck's Point, Clinton, under cover of the morning mists, ferried 2000 troops across the river, landing them on the western bank at Stony Point. Between there and Fort Clinton and Montgomery, repectively seven and twelve miles to the northward, rose precipitous, forest-clad heights intersected by deep and impassable ravines. One narrow path led through the hills, Clinton had been told by the local Tory, Brom Springster, who offered to guide the assault on the rear of the forts. This pass, over the 'Timp', 850 feet high, encircled the Dunderberg mountain, 1100 feet and had been left unguarded by the Americans.

Forty miles to the north, at Esopus (the modern Kingston), Governor George Clinton learned of Sir Henry Clinton's progress. Proroguing the meeting of the State Legislature over which he was presiding, he hurried to take command at Fort Montgomery, ordering the militiamen to reassemble, and sending his elder brother James to command at Fort Clinton.

On reaching Fort Montgomery on the evening of the 5th, and learning of the British landing at Stony Point, Governor Clinton sent out thirty men under Major Logan to reconnoitre and, if possible, to take and hold the summit of the pass before the British reached it. They were too late, for by 8 a.m. on the 6th the British were over it. Governor Clinton also sent a message to Putnam asking for help, but it was not delivered.

Having surmounted the pass, Sir Henry Clinton divided his forces into two bodies. He ordered Lieutenant-Colonel Campbell to make the seven-mile detour behind Bear Mountain to assault Fort Montgomery from the rear with the British 52nd and 57th Regiments, each composed of 450 men, and with 400 Tories. And he ordered General Vaughan, with the 63rd and 26th Regiments, one company of the 71st, a squadron of dismounted dragoons, and some Hessian *chasseurs*, about 1200 men in all, first to cover Campbell's advance, and, when he was in position, to attack Fort Clinton. Meanwhile, the pass was held by General Tyron with the 7th Regiment and a Hessian regiment, with orders to participate in the assaults once they had begun.

Following Major Logan's retreat, Governor Clinton despatched Colonels Brown and McLaghey, with 200 men, to halt Colonel Campbell's column at the deep Hell Hole ravine. In his subsequent report to the Council of New York, the Governor said that the party behaved with great spirit but were obliged to give way to superior force. Colonel Lamb, sent out with a twelve-pounder and sixty men, kept his gun in full play until his men 'were drove off with fixed bayonets', losing their cannon. The Americans retreated to their fort at about 2 p.m. and, about 4.30 p.m., both forts were simultaneously stormed at the point of the bayonet. Colonel Campbell was killed at Fort Montgomery leading his men, who in revenge massacred many of the garrison. At Fort Clinton the survivors escaped under cover of darkness. Governor Clinton scrambled down a precipice to reach the river-bank, where he found his brother who had been bayoneted in the thigh. Though he refused to endanger an already overloaded skiff, he was pushed into it by his brother who, catching and mounting a loose horse, galloped off making his way over the mountains, where he was joined next day by the Governor.

The American loss—killed, wounded or prisoners—was 300 men, and 100 cannon. According to Comodore Hotham, the British lost forty killed and 150 wounded. They followed up their victory by destroying the boom and chain, which barred the river, and burning the American flotilla which, because of the strong north wind's forcing the vessels against the boom, had been unable to escape. General Putnam retired to the heights above Peekskill; and the small garrison at Fort Constitution, six miles up river, set fire to and abandoned their fortifications.

Sir Henry Clinton had pierced the Highlands barrier on the day of Burgoyne's second defeat, but he was still 100 miles south of Albany.

Clinton had not intended to do more than destroy the forts and return to New York, but as he described in his book *The American Rebellion*, 'a fair prospect opening of our being able to remove every obstruction as far as Albany, I began to extend my views beyond the limits they were first confined to'. Clinton's disinclination to progress further, due to the small number of men who would be available after he had garrisoned the captured forts and secured his communications with New York, was overcome by the receipt of a letter from General Pigot who commanded at Rhode Island, offering to spare 1000 men. 'I began', Clinton says, 'to entertain hopes that I should even be able to support General Burgoyne, should he incline to force his way to Albany'.

Availing himself of Pigot's offer to send 1000 men to New York, Clinton dispatched General Vaughan with 2000 men, under the escort of Sir James Wallace with naval galleys, and with six months' provisions for 5000 men, to run up river and to 'feel his way to General Burgoyne and do his utmost to assist his operations, or even join him if required'.

Vaughan's force sailed up to Esopus, which it burned, and proceeded up river to Livingstone Manors within forty-four miles of Albany and eighty miles of Saratoga, where the vessels were obliged to come to anchor because the pilots absolutely refused to take further charge of them. Vaughan reported that he had not been able to communicate with General Burgoyne, and that the Americans were massing 5000 and 1000 troops on his right and left flanks; and, says Clinton, 'all accounts agreed in representing his [Vaughan's] situation as desperate'.

Sir Henry Clinton tells the remainder of the sad story;

'Though this intelligence destroyed all my hopes of being in the least serviceable to the northern army, whose fate I now feared was inevitable, it yet was very much my wish to be able to retain the footing we were now possessed of in the Highlands. Every view of that sort was, however, dissipated by my next dispatches from the Commander in Chief, as I was thereby ordered to send him *without delay* the Seventh, Twenty-sixth and Sixty-third Regiments, two battalions of Anspach and [the] Seventeenth Dragoons, together with all the recruits and recovered men belonging to the southern army and the Jagers and artillerymen which came by the English fleet—*even notwithstanding I might be gone up the North River, agreeable to the intimation I had given him of my intentions in my letter of the 29th of September*—except I should be on the eve of accomplishing some very material and essential stroke, being left at liberty *in that case* to proceed upon it *provided I judged it might be executed in a few days after the receipt of his letters.*

'These orders being too explicit to be misunderstood or obedience to them even delayed, and several of the corps with General Vaughan being particularized in them, I wrote to that general officer on the 22nd of October to direct him to return with all speed. And, receiving soon afterward another order from Sir William Howe to dismantle Fort Clinton, I was under the mortifying necessity of relinquishing the Highlands and all the other passes over the Hudson, to be reoccupied by the rebels whenever they saw proper. For even had General Burgoyne been fortunately in a situation to have availed himself of my success and been tempted to trust to my support at the time I received these orders, I believe there is no military man who will not allow that I should have had no small difficulty in reconciling the delay an effort of that consequence must have necessarily occasioned with the obedience I owed to so explicit and pressing an order from my Commander in Chief'.

Clinton evacuated the Highlands and returned to New York on October 26th.

On October 8th, following his capture of the American forts, Clinton had sent another message to Burgoyne:

'*Nous voici*—and nothing between us but Gates. I sincerely hope this *little* success of ours may facilitate your operations. In answer to your letter of the 28th of September by C. C. [i.e. Captain Campbell] I shall only say I cannot presume to order, or even advise, for reasons obvious. I heartily wish you success.'

This message was carried by Sergeant Daniel Taylor. He reached Esopus on October 10th and, being deceived by the similar name of the American general, thought that he had caught up with Sir Henry Clinton. He was taken prisoner, as Samuel Richards of the Connecticut Line explains;

'. . . he fell in with a small scouting party of ours under the command of a sergeant of Webb's regiment, who with his men were dressed in British uniform which had been captured in a transport ship. Their speech and appearance being the same, and our sergeant managing with the utmost address, proposed themselves to General Clinton, who, our sergeant said, was out from the fort and not far off.

'On seeing the American General Clinton, he instantly discovered that he was deceived and swallowed something hastily, which, being noticed, the General ordered the regimental surgeon to administer a strong emetic, which in its powerful operation occasioned in his throwing up a silver ball of the size of a pistol ball, which on being cleansed and opened, was found to contain the note. He was tried the next day and the proof being full and complete was condemned and executed as a spy'.

Whether or not this is the true version of Taylor's fate is uncertain, for Dr Thacher states that the sergeant of that name fell into American hands on his way from Burgoyne to Clinton.

Clinton had done too little, and left it too late, to help Burgoyne, but with the small force at his disposal he had achieved a notable success, and had shown greater energy than any other British general.

XVI *Bemis Heights*

On the morning of October 7th, Madame von Riedesel had just sat down to breakfast at Burgoyne's headquarters, when suddenly—'my husband, with the whole general staff, decamped.' He informed her that there was to be a reconnaissance, which did not surprise her as that often happened. But this one was different, and Madame von Riedesel, looking back after the elapse of several months, remarked that 'our misfortunes may be said to date from this moment'. She made her way homeward to the Smith House, meeting many savages in war-dress, armed with guns. To her question, where they were going, they cried, 'War. War.' She had hardly reached her house before she heard firing, which by degrees became constantly heavier until, finally, the noise became frightful.

At eleven o'clock that morning, Burgoyne had marched from camp with 1500 picked men and ten cannon, intending to advance through the thick woods south-westward of Freeman's Farm, with the object of reconnoitring the enemy position which as yet, no officer had observed. If an attempt to turn the American left then appeared feasible, Burgoyne proposed to make the attack next day. Although Lieutenant Anburey says that the movement to the enemy's left was made 'not only to discover whether there was the possibility of forcing a passage', but also 'if necessary to advance or dislodge the enemy', it is improbable that Burgoyne could have hoped to accomplish both purposes without employing the greater part of the 4500 men whom he had left to guard his camp.

Nor could Burgoyne have intended, as is frequently suggested, to occupy the small height on the extreme left of Bemis Heights, the existence of which he could hardly have known, as Gates's fortified position was completely screened by woods from Freeman's Farm, the farthest British advance point. This small knoll and most certainly been fortified and occupied by the Americans since September 19th, if not before, and it was commanded by the batteries facing west from Neilson's barn.

Before they were spotted and intercepted, the British and German troops, having advanced beyond the two redoubts, which were named after the Earl of Balcarres and Colonel von Breymann and stood at the western end of the line, reached two small clearings. These may be identified as the Chatfield and Munger farms, which lay halfway between Freeman's Farm and Bemis Heights, and midway between the Middle Ravine and the south fork of Mill Creek. The foragers were put to work to gather the unharvested wheat, while Burgoyne and his officers mounted to the roofs of two small cabins, whence they peered through their spyglasses into the trees ahead, in a vain attempt to discern the enemy's position.

Burgoyne had left the bulk of his army to guard the provisions, stores and boats drawn up on the river bank, under the command of Brigadier-Generals Hamilton, Specht and Gall, taking with him Major-Generals Phillips and von Riedesel and Brigadier Simon Fraser. Having reached the two clearings and reconnoitred the front, Burgoyne made no advance, taking up a defensive position by extending his troops on a front of 1000 yards, sending Captain Fraser with his rangers, and the Tory and Canadian auxiliaries and some Indians, to make a detour through the woods on the right. He positioned Simon Fraser with the 24th Regiment, and the Light Infantry under the Earl of Balcarres on the right of the line; von Riedesel in the centre with von Breymann's grenadiers, with whom went Captain Pausch with two twelve-pounder guns and two six-pounders; and Major Acland on the left with the British grenadiers and the artillery commanded by Major Griffith Williams. The flanks rested on woods, suited to shelter a lurking enemy, the right being protected by a rail-fence and the left by a small rivulet. The clearing stood on a gentle slope, and on the far right rose a densely wooded hill. According to von Riedesel, the reconnaissance force stood its ground for an hour and a half before it was attacked.

The British advance had already been observed, and reported to Gates who, like Burgoyne and his officers, heard the American advance guard beating to arms. Obtaining Gates's permission, Wilkinson mounted his horse and rode off to enquire the cause. Being unable to obtain information at the guard post, he proceeded from the camp and, ascending a gentle acclivity, perceived, about half a mile ahead, several columns of the enemy entering a field of uncut wheat, beyond a small rivulet (probably the southern fork of Mill Creek). Even without his glass, he could see distinctly their every movement:

'After entering the field, they displayed, formed the line, and sat down in double ranks with their arms between their legs. Foragers then proceeded to cut the wheat or standing straw, and I soon after observed several officers, mounted on the top of a cabin, from whence with their glasses they were endeavouring to reconnoitre our left, which was concealed from their view by intervening woods'.

Having satisfied himself, after fifteen minutes' attentive observation, that no attack was meditated, Wilkinson returned to camp and reported to Gates who asked what appeared to be the intentions of the enemy.

'They are foraging, and endeavouring to reconnoitre your left; and I think, Sir, they offer you battle.'

'What is the nature of the ground, and what your opinion?'

'Their front is open, and their flanks rest on woods, under cover of which they may be attacked; their right is skirted by a lofty height. I would indulge them'.

'Well, then, order on Morgan to begin the game'.

Wilkinson waited upon the Colonel. Morgan, who suggested

13a. Storming of Breymann Redoubt: a reconstruction at Saratoga. (*Photo: R. K. Dean*

b. Morgan rallies his riflemen by a turkey call: a reconstruction at Saratoga. (*Photo: R. K. Dean*)

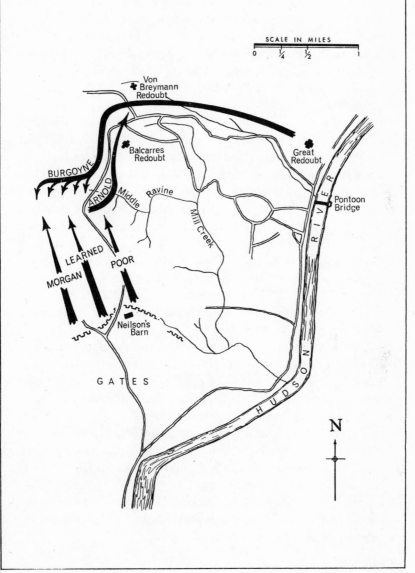

THE BATTLE of BEMIS HEIGHTS
October 7th ≈ 1777

SCALE IN MILES

0   ¼   ½   1

Von Breymann Redoubt

Balcarres Redoubt

Great Redoubt

BURGOYNE

ARNOLD

Middle   Ravine

Mill Creek

Pontoon Bridge

LEARNED

POOR

MORGAN

RIVER

Neilson's Barn

GATES

HUDSON

N

the plan which Gates approved, whereby the British were attacked simultaneously right, front and left. While Morgan circled round through the woods to gain the height on the British right, Enoch Poor would fall upon their left, and Ebenezer Learned would assault the centre once the flank attack had developed. Of the 10000 men whom by now he may have commanded, Gates, during that afternoon, probably committed upwards of 9200, some of them Continentals, some militiamen, who derived from five different states: New York—4201, Masachussetts—2710, New Hampshire—1408, Connecticut—401, and Virginia (the place of origin of Morgan's riflemen, many of whom were Irishmen)—500. Poor and Learned each commanded five regiments. Poor's forces included three New Hampshire regiments, led by Colonels Joseph Cilley, George Reid (in place of Nathan Hale who had been taken prisoner at Hubbardton), and Alexander Scammel, and two New York regiments, led by Colonels Philip Van Courtlandt and Henry B. Livingstone. Learned's command consisted of the 2nd, 7th, 8th, and 9th Massachusetts Regiments and James Livingstone's New York Regiment. Later in the day, 3000 Albany County Militia were also engaged, under the command of Colonel Ten Broeck, and part of Patterson's brigade.

The battle, which it is convenient to call the Battle of Bemis Heights, progressed in two phases from the first onset to the death of Simon Fraser; and from the intervention of General Arnold, of whose equivocal part in the battle we shall hear later. Overwhelmed by American numerical superiority, firepower, confidence, and enthusiasm, the British and German regulars gave way, falling back upon the Balcarres and Breymann redoubts, against which Arnold led assaults which closed the action that had been won already by Morgan, Poor, Learned, and Colonel John Brooks. Gates remained in camp on Bemis Heights, receiving reports of the battle, not one incident of which he personally observed.

The engagement began between 2.30 and 3 p.m. Having gained the height to the north, Morgan's riflemen and Dearborn's light infantry poured down, in Wilkinson's words 'like a torrent' on the British right wing, attacking it in front and rear. Morgan, it seems, had been delayed by the need to mop up Captain Fraser's auxiliaries, whom he sent flying through the woods. Meanwhile Poor had engaged Major Acland's grenadiers on the left, as has been planned, before Learned assaulted von Riedesel's troops. Within a few minutes the whole British–German line of 1500 men was under assault by five or six times their number.

Poor led his brigade steadily up the slope, in face of deadly volleys of musketry fire and a fusilade of grape-shot on the British left, his men holding their fire until they reached the crest on which stood the grenadiers, drawn up in line and standing shoulder to shoulder, and Major Williams's guns. Into their serried ranks Poor's New Yorkers and New Hampshire soldiers poured a close-range, rapid fire, mowing down the grenadiers and decimating the gunners. The grenadiers fired back, taking heavy toll of the Americans who excited to madness by the galling fire of the terrible grenadiers, sprang to their feet and, with a great shout, swept over the guns, killing the gunners and their horses, and rolling back the grenadiers who, outnumbered by three to one, disintegrated into small groups, fighting back to back. Lieutenant Digby, who took over command of his company on the death of Captain Wight, says, 'Our cannon were surrounded and taken—the men and horses being killed..which gave them additional spirits, and they rushed on with loud shouts, when we drove them back a little with so great a loss to ourselves, that it evidently appeared a retreat was the only thing left for us. They still advanced under a storm of grape-shot.' By the end of the day, Digby's company which had marched from Canada fifty strong, was reduced to four men. Poor's soldiers were twice thrown back; they charged again with fierce impetuosity, taking and relinquishing

227

one cannon five times until, in the end, they carried it off in triumph.

Galloping fiercely amongst the disordered ranks in an endeavour to wheel the grenadiers to the rearward, and encouraging his men by voice and example, Major Acland was shot through both legs. Seeing their leader fall, the grenadiers retreated up the slope, leaving the ground strewn with their dead and wounded. Wilkinson, who had joined in the attack, says that within a square of one to fifteen yards, he counted eighteen grenadiers in the agony of death, and saw three officers propped against tree trunks, two of them mortally wounded, bleeding and almost speechless.

Poor's amateur soldiers had defeated the *élite* of the British army. The experience so excited the courageous Colonel Cilley that he sat himself astraddle the brass twelve-pounder, exalting in its capture, a show of exuberance which Wilkinson as much applauded as he was sharply to rebuke the barbarism of a surgeon, a man 'of great worth', who was dressing the wounds of one of the officers. Raising his blood-besmeared hands in a frenzy of patriotism, the surgeon exclaimed, 'Wilkinson, I have dipt my hands in British blood'. Wilkinson stepped over the dead and wounded, hearing one exclaim, 'Protect me, Sir, against this boy.' Turning his eyes 'it was my fortune to arrest the purpose of a lad, thirteen or fourteen years old, in the act of taking aim at a wounded officer who lay in the angle of a worm fence. Inquiring his rank, he answered, "I had the honour to command the grenadiers".'

The wounded officer was Major Acland. When he saw his men retreating, he had requested Captain Simpson of the 31st Regiment, an intimate friend, to help him back to camp. Simpson, who was a very stout man, carried the large and heavy Acland on his back, under heavy fire until, closely pressed by the enemy, he was obliged to abandon him. Acland called to his passing men, offering fifty guineas reward to anyone who would save him, and a large grenadier carried him upon his back, until they too were overtaken by the enemy. Wilkinson saved both their lives. Dismounting from his horse, he and his servant lifted Acland on to a horse and carried him back to the American camp, where we shall hear of him again.

The rout of the British grenadiers, and the capture of several of Major Williams's guns, exposed the left flank of von Riedesel's Brunswickers who, simultaneously with the British grenadiers, had been under assault during the fifty-two minutes that this phase of the battle lasted. The conflict extended along the whole line.

On the right, Morgan and Dearborn fell upon the 24th Regiment, causing it to change front to protect its rear. Though rallied frequently by Balcarres, the soldiers fell back under the deadly fire and the gallant charges of the frontiersmen, reforming behind a rail fence. Observing the regiment's retreat, which threatened the whole line, Burgoyne sent his aide, Sir Francis Clerke, with an order to the artillery to retire, to save the surviving guns. On his way through the melée, Clerke fell severely wounded, and the order was not delivered.

Balcarres's withdrawal on the right, and the demoralization of the grenadiers on the left, had severely weakened the centre, where the 300 gallant Germans coolly and courageously resisted the assaults of Learned's five regiments, who were supported by Ten Broeck and his 3000 Albany County Militia. Ebeneazer Mattoon, an artillery officer in Learned's brigade, describes his part in the action against the centre:

'In a few minutes, Capt. Furnival's company of artillery, in which I was lieutenant, was ordered to march towards the fire, which had now opened upon our pickets in front, the picket consisting of about 300 men. While we were marching, the whole line, up to our picket or front, was engaged. We advanced to a height of ground which brought the enemy in view, and opened our fire. But the enemy's guns, eight in number, and much heavier than ours, rendered our position intenable.

'We then advanced into the line of infantry. Here Lieutenant M'Lane joined me. In our front there was a field of corn, in which the Hessians were secreted. On our advancing towards the corn field, a number of men rose and fired upon us. M'Lane was severely wounded. While I was removing him from the field, the firing still continued without abatement.

'During this time, a tremendous firing was heard on our left. We poured in upon them our canister shot as fast as possible, and the whole line, from left to right, became engaged. The smoke was very dense, and no movements could be seen; but as it soon arose, our infantry appeared to be slowly retreating, and the Hessians slowly advancing, their officers urging them on with their hangers [swords].

'The troops continuing warmly engaged, Col. Johnson's regiment, coming up threw in a heavy fire and compelled the Hessians to retreat. Upon this we advanced with a shout of victory. At the same time Lord Auckland's corps gave way. We proceeded but a short distance before we came upon four pieces of brass cannon, closely surrounded with the dead and dying; at a few yards further we came upon two more. Advancing a little further we were met by a fire from the British infantry, which proved very fatal to one of Col. Johnson's companies, in which were killed one sergeant, one corporal, fourteen privates—and about twenty were wounded.

'They advanced with a quick step, firing as they came on. We returned them a brisk fire of canister shot, not allowing ourselves time even to sponge our pieces. In a short time they ceased firing and advanced upon us with trailed arms. At this juncture Arnold came up with a part of Brooks's regiment, and gave them a most deadly fire, which soon caused them to face about and retreat with a quicker step then they advanced.'

Both von Riedesel and Captain Pausch also described this stage of the battle from personal experience. While the German

general confined himself to saying that 'the enemy threw their
entire force on the centre', which, he states, 'would have maintained its ground, had not Lord Balcarres fallen back on the
right exposing its flank and obliging it to retreat', a move which
led the regiments of Rhetz and Hesse-Hanau to form themselves
into a half-circle. Pausch describes the action in far greater
detail, and in very different terms:

'At this junction, our left wing retreated in the greatest possible
disorder, thereby causing a similar rout among our German
command, which was stationed behind the fence in line of
battle. They retreated—or to speak more plainly—they left
their position without informing me, although I was but fifty
paces in advance of them. Each man for himself, they made
for the bushes. Without knowing it, I kept back the enemy for
a while with my unprotected cannon loaded with shells. How
long before this the infantry had left its position, I cannot tell,
but I saw a great number advance towards our now open left
wing within a distance of about 300 paces. I looked back towards the position still held, as I supposed, by our German infantry, under whose protection I, too, intended to retreat—but
not a man was to be seen. Their right wing was thus in front of
the house I have so often mentioned [presumably one of the
cabins], but all was in disorder, though they still fought the
enemy which continued to advance.'

Finding himself isolated and almost completely surrounded,
Pausch retreated, making his way along the rough track to one
of the cabins where he reposed his two cannon, manned by
the four gunners and one subaltern who survived. He fired,
says Pausch, three wagon-loads of ammunition until the guns
became so heated that it was impossible to lay hands upon them.
Finally, when the right wing was repulsed, Pausch was forced
to relinquish his position and retreat, expecting to meet the

German infantry and with them to make a stand. His hope was quickly dispelled, for the road was occupied by the enemy. Seeing that 'all was irretrievably lost' and that 'it was impossible to save anything', he ordered the remaining gunners to save themselves. He himself succeeded in carrying off one of the ammunition wagons, and on his way back met 'all the different nationalities of our division running pell-mell, making for our camp and lines'.

According to von Riedesel—who does not mention a panic-stricken retreat—Simon Fraser, perceiving the danger in which the centre stood, tried to succour it with the 24th Regiment. At this critical stage of the battle he was seen riding to and fro amongst his men, endeavouring to halt their withdrawal under the deadly fire of Morgan's riflemen who, flushed with victory, came on with savage yells. On the left, the British grenadiers were gone, and in the centre, the Germans were disintegrating. Burgoyne was trying valiantly to form a second line from the mass of fugitives fleeing helter-skelter. Of the British force, the 24th Regiment and the light infantry alone retained some semblance of order. Rallied by Simon Fraser, they could still play a decisive part in the battle, if only to ensure an orderly retreat.

So far the British and Germans had lost 400 officers and men, killed, wounded, or taken prisoner. Six of their ten guns had been taken. Burgoyne's horse had been killed and shots had penetrated both his hat and his waistcoat. It was at this critical moment that General Arnold reached the scene of action.

The eye-witnesses of the battle, as well as modern historians, disagree about the time of Arnold's involvement, and the significance of the part he played in the action. The muffled sounds of the ancient controversy linger still, and they are interpreted according to personal taste. To some people, Arnold was a veritable 'genius of war', the man whose heroic actions won the day. Others call him a madman, a disappointed soldier who, thirsting for glory and intoxicated by the clash of battle, might have jeopardized the victory that had been won before he reached the field. Courageous and brave as he undoubtedly was, Arnold behaved, states Samuel Woodruff (who came from Windsor, Connecticut, and found himself at Arnold's side), 'more like a madman than a cool and discreet officer'.

According to Ebenezer Mattoon, who wrote to General Philip Schuyler after the battle, Arnold, who was accompanied by General Lincoln, rode out from Bemis Heights about one o'clock, on hearing the signal guns that heralded the British advance. They returned after about half an hour to report to Gates. Mattoon continued:

'Gen. Lincoln says, "Gen. Gates, the firing at the river is merely a feint; their object is your left. A strong force of 1500 men are marching circuitously, to plant themselves on yonder height. That point must be defended, or your camp is in danger."

'Gates replied, "I will send Morgan with his riflemen, and Dearborn's infantry."

'Arnold says, "That is nothing, you must send a strong force."

'Gates replied, "Gen. Arnold, I have nothing for you to do, you have no business here."

'Arnold's reply was reproachful and severe.

'Gen. Lincoln says, "You must send a strong force to support Morgan and Dearborn, at least three regiments."

Mattoon adds that Generals Arnold and Lincoln immediately left the camp and proceeded towards the enemy's lines.

Another story, related to Captain Bancroft by Colonel John Brooks (who subsequently became Governor of Massachusetts), states that Arnold was dining with Gates when Brooks and the other officers present heard firing from the advance picket. The firing increased and they all rose from the table. Then General Arnold, addressing Gates, asked 'Shall I go out, and see what is the matter?' General Gates made no reply but, upon being pressed, said, 'I am afraid to trust you, Arnold.'

233

To this Arnold answered, 'Pray, let me go; I will be careful, and, if our advance does not need support, I will promise not to commit you.' Gates told him he might go and see what the firing meant.

The chief point of discussion amongst the officers at dinner, says Brooks, had been 'whether we should commence the attack, or receive General Burgoyne behind our breastwork at the lines, should he attempt to advance. Arnold contended for the former, saying that the assailant had the advantage: for he can always take his own time, and choose the point of attack, and, if repulsed, he has only to retreat behind his own lines and form again. General Gates said, on the contrary, "If undisciplined militia were repulsed in the open field, and the enemy pressed upon them in their retreat, it would be difficult to form them again, even behind their own breastworks; for, if they were under a panic, they would keep on retreating, even after they had passed their own lines." The opinion General Arnold expressed in this discussion was probably the cause why Gates was afraid to trust him to go out when the firing was first heard, lest he should bring on an engagement in the open field, and contrary to his own opinion of its expediency.'

Arnold, says Brooks, lost no time in advancing with his brigade and, finding that the attack was serious, engaged the left of the enemy's right, where, meeting with great obstacles, he ordered Brooks to get a position upon the enemy's right.

Another story relates that, hearing the voice of the cannon, Arnold, unable to stand still, leaped upon a black stallion and 'rode about the camp, betraying great agitation and wrath'. When Gates refused to listen to him, Arnold rode to the troops who were drawn up in ranks, and who asked him for orders. Shouting, 'Victory or Death', he dug his spurs into his horse's flanks and rode to the lovely sounds of battle. Gates sent his aide, Major John Armstrong, to recall Arnold, but he failed to catch up with him. Wilkinson, who omits mention of the dinner at which Arnold was supposedly present, agrees that he rode about the camp, and says that he was observed to drink freely. 'At length he was found on the field of battle, exercising command, but not by order or permission of General Gates.'

Arnold apparently reached the scene of action about 4 p.m., joining Morgan's men who were assaulting the light infantry and the 24th Regiment whom, we recall, Simon Fraser was endeavouring to rally. Spotting the General in his brilliant uniform astride a splendid grey horse, and, as the volunteer Samuel Woodruff described, 'knowing the military character and efficiency' of that officer, Arnold called to Morgan, 'That officer upon a grey horse is of himself a host, and must be disposed of—direct the attention of some of the sharpshooters amongst your riflemen to him.' Morgan, nodding assent, went over to his riflemen, and pointing to Fraser said, 'That gallant officer is General Fraser. I admire him, but it is necessary that he should die, do your duty.'

Tradition has it that an Irishman named Tim Murphy, a famous Indian fighter and a crack shot, climbed a tree and aimed at Simon Fraser. The first rifle bullet cut the crupper of the horse, the next passed through its mane, a little back of the ears. An aide urged the General to retire and not to expose himself longer. Murphy's third bullet penetrated Fraser's abdomen and he fell to the ground mortally wounded.

Lieutenant Digby records that Fraser's fall helped 'to turn the fate of the day', and he was the only wounded man 'we were able to carry off'. Anburey, who had stayed in camp to command the quarter-guard, saw Fraser brought in, supported on his horse by two officers. The scene, he says, was one that 'the imagination must help to paint':

'The officers, all anxious and eagerly enquiring as to his wound—the downcast look and melancholy that was visible to everyone, as to his situation, and all the answer he could make to the many enquiries was a shake of his head, expressive that it was all over with him. So much was he beloved that not only officers and soldiers but all the women flocked round, solicitous for his fate.

'When he had reached his tent and was recovered a little from the faintness occasioned by loss of blood, he told those around him that he saw the man who shot him; he was a rifleman, and up in a tree; the ball entered a little below his breast, and penetrated just below the backbone. After the Surgeon had dressed his wound, he said to him very composedly, "Tell me, Son, to the best of your skill and judgment, if you think my wound is mortal." He replied, "I am sorry, Sir, to inform you that it is, and that you cannot possibly live four and twenty hours." He then called for pen and ink, and after making his will, and distributing a few little tokens of regard to the officers of his suite, desired that he might be removed to the general hospital.'

The dying General was taken to the house of Madame von Riedesel, who had expected him as one of her guests for dinner that day:

'Our dining table, which was already spread, was taken away, and in its place they fixed up a bed for the General. I sat in a corner of the room trembling and quaking. The noises grew continually louder. The thought that they might bring in my husband in the same manner was to me dreadful, and tormented me incessantly. The General said to the surgeon, "Do not conceal anything from me. Must I die?" The ball had gone through his bowels, precisely as in the case of Major Harnage [who had been wounded on September 19th]. Unfortunately, however, the General had eaten a hearty breakfast, by reason of which the intestines were distended, and the ball, so the surgeon said, had not gone, as in the case of Major Harnage, between the intestines, but through them. I heard his often, amidst his groans, exclaim, "Oh, fatal ambition! Poor General Burgoyne! My poor wife!" Prayers were read to him. He then sent a message to General Burgoyne, begging that he would have him buried the following day at six o'clcok in the evening, on the top of a hill, which was a sort of a redoubt. I knew no longer which way to turn. The whole entry and the other rooms were filled with the sick, who were suffering with the camp-sickness, a kind of dysentry.'

Seeing Fraser fall, Burgoyne ordered Phillips and von Riedesel to cover the retreat of the hard-pressed survivors of the ill-fated reconnaissance force, They fell back across the Middle Ravine to the fortified line where, at Freeman's Farm, the Balcarres redoubt had been constructed, and beyond which, and about half a mile from it, stood the Breymann redoubt which protected its rear and prevented access to the Great Ravine, on which rested the whole of the British line. Between the two redoubts, which had been built on little knolls, there stood in a wooded hollow, two little cabins which were defended by the Canadian auxiliaries. Behind the remnants of the British light infantry, the 24th Regiment and the British and German grenadiers, came their pursuers, the regiments of Learned and Poor's brigades, and the Albany Country militiamen, stout Dutchmen, some of whom had fought with Colonel Herkimer. They swarmed up the slope towards the redoubt, which was defended, with two guns, by the Earl of Balcarres. It commanded an open space measuring about 250 yards, and had been constructed of brushwood and logs; and the Americans, with all their numerical superiority, were to find it impregnable.

When he sited Learned's brigade, Arnold galloped across the line. His conduct, says Wilkinson, was 'exceedingly rash and intemperate; he exposed himself with great folly'. Flourishing his sword to encourage the troops, Arnold 'in a state of furious distraction' struck Captain Ball, of Dearborn's infantry, on the head, wounding him. The first impulse of that officer, relates Wilkinson, was to shoot Arnold, for which purpose he raised his musket, but recollecting himself he was about to remonstrate,

237

when the General darted off to another part of the field, galloping again across the line of fire.

Taking command of Learned's men, many of whom were his neighbours from Connecticut, who cheered him on, and who had been baulked by Balcarres's stout defence, Arnold carried them to attack the two stockaded cabins, clearing out the Canadians, an operation which exposed Breymann's redoubt to assault from the wooded hollow. Snatching up some of Morgan's riflemen, Arnold 'raging like a madman', joined Colonel John Brooks, who stood at the head of his Massachusetts Regiment and urged him, according to Mattoon, to assault the Balcarres redoubt. To Brook's reply that 'We can't carry them', Arnold cried, 'Well, then, let us attack the Hessian lines,' meaning the Breymann redoubt. 'With all my heart,' replied Brooks.

Brooks did not recall this conversation in the description of his part in the action which he gave to Captain Bancroft. He nevertheless gave credit to Arnold 'whose energy gave spirit to the whole action', and stated that the Breymann fort, mounting several brass cannon, was 'rather a breastwork, with guns mounted on three sides'. It was built of logs, laid horizontally between perpendicular posts, and it commanded the clearing across which the attackers needed to advance. The breastwork was 200 yards long and had been raised on the little knoll, whence the ground sloped gently to the southwest. It was defended by 200 Germans.

Brooks recalled that, as his regiment deployed from the protecting woods, 'the enemy, surprised at our sudden appearance, fired a volley of musketry at us'. Mattoon, on the other hand, recorded, 'We all wheeled to the right and advanced. No fire was received, except from the cannon, until we got to within about eight rods [about 45 yards] when we received a tremendous fire from the whole line. But few of our men fell.' In Brooks's version of the assault, the Massachusetts infantry took cover at the first discharge, and Arnold, rushing to and fro along the line, snatched up fifteen to twenty riflemen, turned his horse and galloped across the clearing towards the redoubt, 200 yards away.

Arnold is described as 'riding everywhere and commanding everybody', though whether by his 'mad prank', as Wilkinson called it, he won the redoubt which otherwise might have resisted assault, seems doubtful, for the Americans were in overwhelming force, and von Breymann's Germans were in a state bordering upon mutiny. According to Anburey, who necessarily spoke from hearsay, the Germans 'upon the first attack of the enemy were struck with such terror that, instead of gallantly sustaining their lines, they looked on all as lost, and, after firing one volley, hastily abandoned them'. The truth seems to be that the docile German infantrymen turned against the brute who commanded them. Heinrich von Breymann bore an evil and unsavoury reputation as a bully and a tyrant. Seeing that his men were about to flee, he set about them with his sword, striking down those who attempted to leave their posts. This was too much for one man; raising his rifle he shot dead the 'chivalric' von Breymann (as von Riedesel called him).

A wounded German, lying on the ground, seeing an American officer on a horse charging down upon him, raised his rifle and shot the horse at point blank range. The charger rolled over, pinioning Arnold to the ground and breaking his leg, the same one that had been broken previously at Quebec. At this moment Colonel Brooks and his men mounted the works. When a soldier aimed to kill the German, Arnold cried out, 'Don't hurt him, he is a fine fellow! He only did his duty.' Brooks was followed to the redoubt by Major Armstrong, who had so far failed to catch up with Arnold and was carrying Gates's order to Arnold to return to the camp. He was carried back there on a litter.

Arnold, Wilkinson remarked, 'neither rendered service, nor deserved credit on that day'; and the wound he received, 'alone saved him from being overwhelmed by the torrent of

General Gates's good fortune and popularity'. Arnold's bubble of military fame, Wilkinson declared, rested on 'such caprices of fortune.' Burgoyne, on the other hand, attributed the American victory to Arnold's intervention, for the loss of the redoubt exposed the British flank and caused him to withdraw Balcarres's soldiers, and to abandon the redoubt at Freeman's Farm.

A possible evaluation of Arnold's escapade may lie in the words employed seventy-five years later by the French general, Pierre Bosquet, who, observing the charge of the Light Brigade at Balaclava, described it as 'magnificent, but it is not war'. Arnold's heroic intervention contributed nothing to the battle that had already been won by General Gates, to whom alone belongs the distinction of winning the decisive victory that ensured American independence.

By now it was growing dark. The Americans, who had lost about 150 men, were tired. While his men threw themselves down to rest, Learned called his officers together. Learned, whom Brooks calls a 'weak man', advocated the abandonment of the captured redoubt and a retreat to Bemis Heights. At that moment an officer rode up bringing orders from General Gates for the retention of the fort 'at all hazards'. 'There, now, Colonel Brooks,' said Learned, 'I dare say you like that, and, as your regiment had a principal hand in taking the work, I will commit to them the defence of it.'

As night fell, Burgoyne withdrew the depleted ranks of his force to the fortified lines around his headquarters and to the Great Redoubt above the river, where the disgruntled British troops claimed that the loss of the Breymann redoubt, at the vital corner of the defence system, had been due to the cowardice of the Germans, the stain of which had been blotted out only by von Breymann's death. Cut to the quick by these harsh words, Lieutenant-Colonel von Speth, with four officers and fifty men of von Riedesel's regiment, set out to retake the lost redoubt. On his way, the trustful German encountered an alleged American Tory who offered to guide him. The man escaped in the darkness, leaving the betrayed Speth to wander about in the woods. He failed to find the redoubt, which Brooks's men held throughout the night.

The victors returned to Bemis Heights, bearing their spoils, six captured cannon and 240 prisoners of war. That night Ralph Cross noted in his journal that it had been 'a Memorable Day'; and Benjamin Warren, observing that the fire had been very hot on both sides, remarked with apparent inconsequence but possibly in barbed ire against his commander-in-chief that 'the devil took Burgoyne's aide-de-camp', meaning Sir Francis Clerke. Wilkinson, on his return to headquarters found Clerke reposing on Gates's bed, disputing with the general on the merits of the revolution. Clerke's arguments so incensed Gates that he called Wilkinson out of the room, asking if he had ever heard 'so impudent a son of a bitch'. Thus did General Gates spend his hour of triumph.

Burgoyne had lost half the force he had taken out that morning and a number of distinguished and brave officers. Sir Francis Clerke, Colonel Acland, Captain Money, Major Williams, Captain Blomfield, and Lieutenant Howarth had all been wounded and taken prisoner; von Breymann was dead, and Simon Fraser was dying in the house, where Madame von Riedesel sat, surrounded by her three children, anxiously awaiting news of her husband;

'Finally, toward evening, I saw my husband coming, upon which I forgot all my sufferings and thanked God that He had spared him to me. He ate in great haste with me, and his adjutant, behind the house. We had been told that we had gained an advantage over the enemy, but the sorrowful and downcast faces which I beheld, bore witness to the contrary and before my husband again went away, he drew me on one side and told me that everything might go very badly and that I must keep myself in constant readiness for departure, but by no means to give any one the least inkling of what I was doing. I therefore pretended that I wished to move into my new house the next morning, and had everything packed up.'

At the British camp, Anburey watched the return of the troops who were followed by Generals Burgoyne, Phillips, and von Riedesel. He found it impossible to describe the anxiety depicted on the countenance of General Burgoyne, who came up to him enquiring if he was the officer of the quarter-guard. When Anburey said he was, Burgoyne told him, 'You must defend this post to the very last man.' Anburey judged the situation to be very serious.

XVII *Saratoga*

During the night following the battle, Burgoyne withdrew his troops north of the Great Ravine and to the Great Redoubt above the river; and at daybreak the Americans occupied the abandoned lines. During the day the two armies skirmished across the Great Ravine, engaging in desultory firing in which Major-General Lincoln was shot in the leg, a casualty that left Gates without an officer above the rank of brigadier-general. The Americans did not attack, for Gates was content to play a waiting game; Burgoyne was running short of provisions, and Clinton had reached the Highlands and might advance on Albany and attack Gates's rear. Gates sent the Albany County Militia, and ordered Gansevoort from Fort Stanwix, to strengthen the weakly garrisoned town. During October 8th the American army was occupied in revictualling; and the British and Germans were preparing to retreat. Burgoyne had decided to withdraw to Ticonderoga, sixty miles to the north, if that was still possible, as American detachments were gathering in his rear. Prior to the battle on the 7th, Gates had ordered Brigadier-General John Fellows to march his 1300 militiamen up the east bank of the Hudson to Battenkill, and to cross to the west bank at Saratoga. Burgoyne sent Lieutenant-Colonel Nicholas Sutherland, with the 47th and 9th Regiments, to reconnoitre the road to Saratoga.

For Burgoyne one task remained. Simon Fraser, before he died at 8 a.m. had expressed the wish to be buried in the Great Redoubt. Mortally wounded, he had been brought to Madame von Riedesel's house and lain on a bed, at the very spot, she remarks, where he would have sat and partaken of a joyous meal, for she had invited him to dine on the day of the battle. During the evening and night, other wounded men had been brought in and laid in the hall and other corners of the small house, which became so congested that Madame von Riedesel, and her children, were obliged to sleep in the room in which Simon Fraser lay dying. He was never unconscious and he talked with von Riedesel when he came to reassure his wife of his safety. She describes how she spent the night;

'My lady Acland occupied a tent not far from our house. In this she slept, but during the day was in the camp. Suddenly one came to tell her that her husband was mortally wounded, and had been taken prisoner. At this she became very wretched. We comforted her by saying that it was only a slight wound, but as no one could nurse him as well as herself, we counselled her to go at once to him, to do which she could certainly obtain permission. She loved him very much, although he was a plain, rough man, and was almost daily intoxicated; with this exception, however, he was an excellent officer. She was the loveliest of women. I spent the night in this manner—at one time comforting her, and at another looking after my children, whom I had put to bed. As for myself, I could not go to sleep, as I had General Fraser and all the other gentlemen in my room, and was constantly afraid that my children would wake up and cry, and thus disturb the poor dying man, who often sent to beg my pardon for making me so much trouble. About three o'clock in the morning, they told me that he could not last much longer. I had desired to be apprised of the approach of this moment. I, accordingly, wrapped up the children in the bed coverings, and went with them into the entry. Early in the morning, at eight o'clock, he expired. After they had washed the corpse, they wrapped it in a sheet, and laid it on a bedstead. We then again came into the room, and had this sad sight before us the whole day. At every instant, also, wounded officers of my acquaintance arrived, and the cannonade again began. A retreat was spoken of, but there was not the least movement made toward it. About four o'clock in the afternoon, I saw the new house, which had been built for me, in flames: the enemy, therefore, were not far from us. We learned that General Burgoyne intended to fulfil the last wish of General Fraser, and to have him buried at six o'clock in the place designated by him. This occasioned an unnecessary delay, to which a part of the misfortunes of the army was owing'.

Madame von Riedesel, who did not like Burgoyne, criticized him unjustly. The organization of the retreat required many hours of work, and, with the enemy so close, it was preferable to begin it after nightfall.

Although Fraser had requested that his funeral should be attended only by the officers of his personal staff, Burgoyne, Phillips and von Riedesel attended the burial service which was conducted at sunset by the Reverend Edward Brudenell, the chaplain of the Artillery who (says von Riedesel) 'delivered a lengthy sermon'. Discerning a number of men gathering in the Great Redoubt, and suspecting that it foreshadowed a military operation, the American batteries opened up. The shots failed to alarm the officiating chaplain who, as Burgoyne told the House of Commons, read the service for the burial of the dead in unfaltering voice 'though frequently covered with dust which the shots threw up on all sides of him.' Gates said afterwards that, had he known the nature of the gathering, he would not have allowed any firing in that direction. Madame von Riedesel says that many cannon balls flew close to her as she stood outside her house with her eyes fixed upon the hill, knowing her husband was there and that he, also, might find his grave at that very spot. He considered it was a 'real military funeral—one that was unique of its kind'.

After it had grown dark, the pontoon bridge across the river was broken up, and the heavily laden boats were rowed up river, very slowly against the adverse current, and at 10 p.m. the retreat led by von Riedesel began. The wounded, who had been made as comfortable as possible, were left in the hospital tents in the charge of the 'amiable Hibernian', (as Wilkinson calls him), Doctor John Macnamara Hayes, who had elected to remain with his patients. 'Our retreat', states Anburey, 'was made within musket-shot of the enemy, and, though greatly encumbered with baggage, without a single loss. It was near eleven o'clock before the rear-guard marched, and for near an hour we every moment expected to be attacked, for the enemy had formed on the same spot as in the morning: we could discern this by the lanterns that the officers had in their hands, and their riding about in the front of their line, but though the Americans put their army in motion that night, they did not pursue us, in our retreat, till late the next day.'

In order to disguise the movement from the enemy, the soldiers were ordered to march as quietly as possible, and the camp watch-fires were left burning. Madame von Riedesel continues her story;

'The order had gone forth that the army should break up after the burial, and the horses were already harnessed to our calashes. I did not wish to set out before the troops. The wounded Major Harnage, although he was so ill, dragged himself out of bed, that he might not remain in the hospital, which was left behind protected by a flag of truce. As soon as he observed me in the midst of danger, he had my children and maid servants put into the calashes, and intimated to me that I must immediately depart. As I still begged to be allowed to remain, he said to me, 'Well, then your children at least must go, that I may save them from the slightest danger.'' He understood how to take advantage of my weak side. I gave it up, seated myself inside with them, and we drove off at eight o'clock in the evening.

The greatest silence had been enjoined; fires had been kindled in every direction; and many tents left standing, to make the enemy believe that the camp was still there. We travelled continually the whole night. Little Frederika was afraid, and would often begin to cry. I was, therefore, obliged to hold a pocket handkerchief over her mouth, lest our whereabouts should be discovered.

At six o'clock in the morning a halt was made, at which everyone wondered. General Burgoyne had all the cannon ranged and counted, which worried all of us, as a few more good marches would have placed us in security. My husband was completely exhausted, and seated himself during this delay in my calash, where my maid servants were obliged to make room for him; and where he slept nearly three hours with his head upon my shoulder. In the meantime, Captain Willoe brought me his pocket book containing bank bills, and Captain Geismar, his beautiful watch, a ring, and a well filled purse, and begged me to keep all these for them. I promised them to do my utmost. At last, the army again began its march, but scarcely had we proceeded an hour on the way, when a fresh halt was made, in consequence of the enemy being in sight. They were about two hundred men who came to reconnoitre, and who might easily have been taken prisoner by our troops, had not General Burgoyne lost his head.* It rained in torrents.

General von Riedesel also criticized Burgoyne, unfairly it seems, for delaying the retreat; for, he says, the army could have marched the entire night and reached Saratoga at daybreak, where a bridge could have been begun without molestation from the enemy. 'Thus', says von Riedesel, 'the advantage which the army had gained, was completely lost by this hesitation; for the enemy at once availed themselves of this delay to send as many troops as possible behind the English across the river; and thus they not only prevented them from building a bridge, but rallied the nearest townships on the opposite side,

---

* The Editor of Madame Von Riedesel's *Journal* points out in a footnote, that by 'lost his head', she meant that Burgoyne had 'lost his presence of mind', an explanation he evidently thought necessary for her readers.

and effectually opposed the crossing of the army. The gathering of the Americans on the eastern shore could easily be seen; while, at the same time, firing on the patrols and the bateaux became constantly more frequent.' Burgoyne explained later that he ordered a halt until four o'clock in the afternoon, in order to refresh the troops and to give time for the boats, which had not been able to keep pace, to come up with the troops.

Following the disaster on October 7th, von Riedesel became more and more critical of his chief, but he admits that the chief reason for the delay, which is confirmed by Anburey, was the exceedingly bad state of the roads which the incessant rain had churned into a sea of mud. Through it the exhausted and starving teams could not pull the heavily laden wagons and carts, and the cannon to which Burgoyne still clung.

Gates, too, came in for criticism his failure to pursue the retreating enemy, and for leaving Fellows and his small force of militiamen alone to block the road beyond Saratoga. Fellows left his camp so ineffectively guarded that Lieutenant-Colonel Sutherland and his men were able to march round it without being halted. His entreaty to Burgoyne to be allowed to attack Fellows was refused, and the militiamen escaped across the Hudson. Thus, both Gates and Burgoyne missed golden opportunities to catch and to elude each other.

After reaching Dovecot the retreating army spent the whole day in pouring rain. The soaking soldiers consoled themselves, says Anburey, with the thought that, should the enemy attack, 'the fate of the day would have rested solely upon the bayonet', because the heavy rain damped the priming of fire-arms, and overcame the American superiority in that department. The march was resumed at 4 p.m., as Madame von Reidesel relates:

'On the 9th, we spent the whole day in a pouring rain, ready to march at a moment's warning. The savages [the few remaining Indians] had lost their courage, and they were seen in all directions going home. The slightest reverse of fortune discouraged them, especially if there was nothing to plunder. My chambermaid did nothing, cursed her situation, and tore out her hair. I entreated her to compose herself, or else she would be taken for a savage. Upon this she became still more frantic, and asked "whether that would trouble me?" And when I answered, "Yes", she tore her bonnet off her head, letting her hair hang down over her face, and said, "You talk well! You have your husband! But we have nothing to look forward to, except dying miserably on the one hand, or losing all we possess on the other!" Respecting this last complaint, I promised, in order to quiet her, that I would make good all the losses of herself and the other maid. The latter, my good Lena, although also very much frightened, said nothing.

'Toward evening, we at last came to Saratoga, which was only half an hour's march from the place where we had spent the whole day. I was wet through and through by the frequent rains, and was obliged to remain in this condition the entire night, as I had no place whatever where I could change my linen. I, therefore, seated myself before a good fire, and undressed my children; after which, we laid ourselves down together upon some straw. I asked General Phillips who came up to where we were, why we did not continue our retreat while there was yet time, as my husband had pledged himself to cover it, and bring the army through? "Poor woman," answered he, "I am amazed at you!—completely wet through; have you still the courage to wish to go further in this weather? Would that you were only our commanding general! He halts because he is tired and intends to spend the night here and give us a supper." In this latter achievement, especially, General Burgoyne was very fond of indulging. He spent half the nights in singing and drinking, and amusing himself with the wife of a commissary, who was his mistress, and who, as well as he, loved champagne.'

Captain Max von Eelking, the editor of the *German Auxiliaries in America* (1893), sought to improve upon Madame von Riedesel's gibe by adding to her story:

'While the army were suffering from cold and hunger, and everyone was looking forward to the immediate future with apprehension, Schuyler's house was illuminated, and rung with singing, laughter, and the jingling of glasses. There Burgoyne was sitting, with some merry companions, at a dainty supper, while the champagne was flowing. Near him sat the beautiful wife of an English commissary, his mistress. Great as the calamity was, the frivolous general still kept up his orgies. Some were of opinion that he had made that inexcusable stand, merely for the sake of passing a merry night. Riedesel thought it incumbent on him to remind Burgoyne of the danger of the halt, but the latter returned all sorts of evasive answers.'

On reaching Saratoga, Burgoyne had established himself in Schuyler's mansion, and he remained within its warmth and confort, while his army lay on the ground, soaked through and hungry. He roused himself from his alleged indulgence to write a letter to General Gates on behalf of Lady Acland who, taking Madame von Riedesel's advice, had begged permission to leave the camp in order to join her wounded husband. Her request, says Anburey, astonished Burgoyne, as 'it appeared an effort beyond human nature that a woman of such a tender and delicate frame as hers should be capable of such an undertaking as that of delivering herself to the enemy—probably in the night, and uncertain of what hands she might fall into—especially after so long an agitation of the spirits, not only exhausted by want of rest, but absolutely want of food, and drenched in rains for near twelve hours—and this at a time too, when far advanced in a state where every tender care and precaution becomes absolutely requisite! In the harassed and fatigued situation she was in, it was no little chagrin to the

General that he could afford her no assistance to cheer up her spirits for such an undertaking; he had not even a cup of wine to offer her—but from a soldier's wife she obtained a little rum and dirty water! With this poor refreshment she set out in an open boat, which was furnished by the General, with a few lines of recommendation to General Gates, for his protection.'

Lady Acland states Sergeant Lamb, had, joined her husband after he had been wounded at Hubbardton, and had followed him, after his recovery, in 'a two-wheel tumbril, which had been constructed by the artificers of the artillery'.

In the skiff Lady Acland was accompanied by her maid, her husband's valet, who had been wounded on October 7th during his search for his missing master, and by the Reverend Edward Brudenell, who carried a flag of truce. Wilkinson takes up the story;

'Major Henry Dearborn who commanded the guard, was ordered to detain the flag until the morning; the night being exceedingly dark, and the quality of the lady unknown. As this incident has been grossly mis-represented to the injury of the American character, which in arms is that of courage, clemency and humanity; to correct the delusions which have flowed from General Burgoyne's pen, who although the vehicle, could not have been the author, of the calumny—I am authorized by General Dearborn to make the following statement, in which I place entire confidence. His guard occupied a cabin, in which there was a back apartment appropriated to his own accommodation: the party on board the boat attracted the attention of the sentinel, and he had not hailed ten minutes, before she struck the shore; the lady was immediately conveyed into the apartment of the Major, which had been cleared for her reception; her attendants followed with her bedding and necessaries, a fire was made, and her mind was relieved from the horrors which oppressed it, by the assurance of her husband's safety;

she took tea, and was accommodated as comfortably as circumstances would permit, and the next morning when I visited the guard before sunrise, her boat had put off, and was floating down the stream to our camp, where General Gates, whose gallantry will not be denied, stood ready to receive her with all the tenderness and respect to which her rank and condition gave her a claim: indeed the feminine figure, the benign aspect, and polished manners of this charming woman, were alone sufficient to attract the sympathy of the most obdurate; but if another motive could have been wanting to inspire respect, it was furnished by the peculiar circumstances of Lady Harriet, then in that most difficult situation [she was pregnant] which cannot fail to interest the solicitudes of every being possessing the form and feelings of a man: it was therefore the foulest injustice to brand an American officer with the failure of courtesy, where it was so highly merited. Major Acland had set out for Albany, where he was joined by his lady.'

Gates, in his reply to Burgoyne, could not resist the opportunity to compare his own civilized behaviour with the barbarism of his illustrious opponent:

'*Sir*, I have the honour to receive your excellency's letter by Lady Acland. The respect due to her ladyship's rank, and the tenderness due to her person and sex, were alone sufficient securities to entitle her to my protection, if you consider my preceding conduct with respect to those of your army whom the fortune of war has placed in my hands. I am surprised that your excellency should think that I could consider the greatest attention to Lady Acland in the light of an obligation. The cruelties which mark the retreat of your army, in burning gentlemen's and farmers' houses as they pass along, is almost, among civilized nations, without a precedent. They should not endeavour to ruin those they could not conquer. This conduct betrays more of the vindictive malice of a bigot, than the generosity of a soldier. Your friend, Sir Francis Clerke, by the information of the director-general of my hospital, languishes under a dangerous wound. Every sort of tenderness and attention is paid to him as well as to all the wounded who have fallen into my hands, and the hospital, which you were obliged to leave to my mercy.'

Nursed by his wife, Major Acland made a complete recovery. Sir Francis Clerke was not so fortunate. He died on October 13th, attended by the American doctor Townsend, of whom he had inquired the probable issue of the wound in his abdomen. Observing the doctor's reluctance to pronounce his doom, he (in Wilkinson's recollection) remarked, 'Doctor, why do you pause? Do you think I am afraid to die?' The doctor then advised him, as an act of prudence, to arrange his private affairs. 'Thank you, Doctor,' replied he. 'I understand you; as to my private affairs, my father settled them for me, and I have only a few legacies to bequeath.'

Sir Francis Clerke's legacy to the matron of the hospital, who had paid particular attention to him, was discharged by Captain Money, the captured deputy quartermaster-general, who paid it in American continental currency, which was then considerably depreciated. The woman complained later to General Burgoyne who, in order to do justice to the memory of his friend, obliged Money to pay the sum in British coinage.

Gates, on the 10th, decided at last to take the bold course and to pursue his enemy. To that end he sent Learned, Nixon, and Glover with their brigades, and Morgan with his riflemen, with orders to cross the Fishkill Creek, and to attack the British at Saratoga, a movement that was hindered by the early morning fog, which gave Burgoyne time to draw up his army and offer battle on open ground. The Americans retreated, following an unwary advance in the fog which might have been calamitous, to the woods surrounding the village, and Burgoyne withdrew his troops to the heights above. This movement forced him to abandon his comfortable headquarters at Schuyler's mansion, which, together with several other houses, was burned to the ground, 'set on fire', states von Riedesel, by 'wicked hands'. His wife says that Schuyler's beautiful house, and his mills, were burned on Burgoyne's order, to cover his retreat. Charged in Parliament in 1778 with having destroyed the property unnecessarily, Burgoyne denied it, stating that he gave orders to set the buildings on fire because they concealed the ground over which the Americans were advancing from his artillery. The destruction of the mansion caused Burgoyne to re-establish his headquarters in the midst of his troops.

Still believing that he could escape from the American encirclement, Burgoyne sent a detachment of artificers, under a strong escort consisting of Captain Fraser's marksmen and McKay's Tories, and under the command of Lieutenant-Colonel Sutherland, to open a road to Fort Edward and to repair the bridges across the creeks over which the retreat to Ticonderoga would need to be effected. He left this important operation until it was too late, for, by the time Sutherland reached Fort Edward, the place had been strongly garrisoned and fortified by the enemy.

That day, as we learn from her *Journal*, Burgoyne suffered an encounter with the determined and resourceful Madame von Riedesel, who criticized him to his face for failing to provide food for his officers, several of whom came to her for sustenance. This she was able to provide thanks to her cook who, though an 'arrant knave', was fruitful in all expedients, since at night he crossed small rivers in order to steal sheep, poultry, and pigs, for which he charged Madame von Riedesel a high price. Learning of her criticism, Burgoyne came pathetically to thank her for having reminded him of his duty. She begged— his pardon for meddling, saying she had found it impossible to keep silent when she saw brave men in want. Although she believed that he did not forgive her 'lashing', Burgoyne gave express orders that the provisions should be properly distributed. Unfairly, Madame von Riedesel remarks that 'this hindered us anew', for it delayed the retreat. Her hope of escape from the mesh which was closing in around Burgoyne's army had already been dashed, since during the night, the position of the royal army had become, in von Riedesel's opinion, 'very precarious', with the Americans astride the Hudson and circling round the back and sides of the camp.

During the 11th the army was under constant fire the whole day, both front and rear, from the American artillery and from the marksmen who had concealed themselves in the woods surrounding the camp rather than, as Anburey had hoped, 'by giving us battle and running the chance of victory'. Several of the boats by the river bank were taken and retaken and, to secure the provisions they carried, the British were forced to land and drag them up the hill. The outposts were continually engaged and a German picket was (says von Riedesel) 'captured by the enemy', possibly a face-saving explanation, for the expedition's diarists state that these fifty men, the whole picket excluding the officer, sergeant and drummer, 'deserted'. Such behaviour, in the opinion of the 'anonymous diarist' gave no reason 'to place any great confidence in our good Allies, the Germans'. If an attack had been made on the position that had been guarded by these men, he says, the 'consequences might have been fatal'. No one can blame the wretched German 'hirelings', who, by the terms of their contract, were worth more dead than alive to their duke. They bore no loyalty to the cause for which they were compelled to fight, under conditions which are vividly described by the wife of their General:

'The whole army clamoured for a retreat, and my husband promised to make it possible, provided only that no time was lost. But General Burgoyne, to whom an order had been promised if he brought about a junction with the army of General Howe, could not determine upon this course, and lost everything by his loitering. About two o'clock in the afternoon, the

firing of cannon and small arms was again heard, and all was
alarm and confusion. My husband sent me a message telling
me to betake myself forthwith into a house which was not far
from there. I seated myself in the calash with my children,
and had scarcely driven up to the house, when I saw on the
opposite side of the Hudson River, five or six men with guns,
which were aimed at us. Almost involuntarily I threw the
children on the bottom of the calash and myself over them.
At the same instant the churls fired, and shattered the arms of a
poor English soldier behind us, who was already wounded, and
was also on the point of retreating into the house. Immediately
after our arrival a frightful cannonade began, principally
directed against the house in which we had sought shelter,
probably because the enemy believed, from seeing so many
people flocking around it, that all the generals made it their
headquarters. Alas! it harboured none but wounded soldiers
or women! We were finally obliged to take refuge in a cellar,
in which I laid myself down in a corner not far from the door.
My children laid down on the earth with their heads upon my
lap, and in this manner we passed the entire night. A horrible
stench, the cries of the children, and yet more than all this,
my own anguish, prevented me from closing my eyes.'

The stench to which Madame von Riedesel refers came from
the carcases of the dead animals, with which the camp became
strewn as the oxen and horses succumbed to starvation and
exhaustion. 'The stench was very prejudicial,' says Digby, 'in
so small a place.'

That night Burgoyne called Major-Generals Phillips and
von Riedesel and Brigadier-General Hamilton into a council
of war at which he reviewed the situation and proposed five
alternatives;

1. To wait in the present position an attack from the enemy,
or the chance of favourable events.

2. To attack the enemy.
3. To retreat repairing the bridges as the army moves for the artillery, in order to force the passage of the ford.
4. To retreat by night, leaving the artillery and the baggage; and should it be found impracticable to force the passage with musketry, to attempt the upper ford, or the passage round Lake George.
5. In case the enemy, by extending to their left, leave their rear open, to march rapidly for Albany.

The first three and the fifth propositions were ruled out as being impracticable, and it was resolved that the army should attempt to escape by night, abandoning its baggage and cannon—a feat which von Riedesel believed was still possible. His hopes were dashed that night when the scouts reported that the enemy's position on the right was such, and they had so many small parties out, that it would be impossible to move without their march being immediately discovered.

The break-out had been left too late, due to Burgoyne's fatal delay in allowing Colonel Sutherland to attack Fort Edward. Falling back, on Burgoyne's order, he had been abandoned by the Tories, who made their way safely to Ticonderoga.

Burgoyne's diminishing and wasting army was encircled by 16,000 Americans. 'You have brought me to this pass,' Burgoyne complained to Colonel Skene. 'Now tell me how to get out of it.' The resourceful Tory leader had an answer, cynical advice which might have been worth the try. 'Scatter your baggage, stores and everything that can be spared, at proper distances,' he told Burgoyne, 'and the militiamen will be so busy plundering them that you and the troops will get clean off.'

While Burgoyne vainly sought a way out of the difficulty in which he had landed his army, Madame von Riedesel found refuge in the cellar of the house where she lodged, which had become soiled from the women and children being afraid to venture out while the cannonade continued. She had given the cellars, which she says were beautifully arched, a good sweeping and fumigation, when three dangerously wounded officers were brought in, just as a fresh and terrible cannonade began. 'Many persons', she says, 'who had no right to come in, threw themselves against the door'.

'My children were already under the cellar steps, and we would all have been crushed, if God had not given me strength to place myself before the door, and with extended arms prevent all from coming in; otherwise every one of us would have been severely injured. Eleven cannon balls went through the house, and we could plainly hear them rolling over our heads. One poor soldier, whose leg they were about to amputate, having been laid upon a table for this purpose, had the other leg taken off by another cannon ball, in the very middle of the operation. His comrades all ran off, and when they came back again they found him in one corner of the room, where he had rolled in his anguish, scarcely breathing'.

Feeling more dead than alive, she sat with the three other women who had followed the army, the wives of Major Harnage, Lieutenant Reynell, and Commissary Jonathan Clarke, 'bewailing our fate', when someone entered with the news that the Lieutenant had met with a misfortune. His wife was called out and told that a cannon ball had taken off his arm at the shoulder. He was brought into the cellar where he died during the night. Next morning Madame von Riedesel got things better regulated in the cellar, where the other women made a little room in the corner by hanging curtains from the ceiling. There she slept with her three children, next to the three wounded officers who assured her, upon their oaths, that in case of a hasty retreat, each would take one of her children upon his horse. One of these gentlemen, she says, could imitate very naturally the bellowing of a cow and the bleating of a calf, and if her children cried during the night, he mimicked these animals, and they at once became still.

Her great fear was that her husband might be ordered to march away, and at night she reassured herself by creeping from the cellar, returning to sleep when she saw the troops lying around their fires. Although her cook provided good meals, the inhabitants of the cellar were often in want of water, of which there was a great scarcity:

'We at last found a soldier's wife who had the courage to bring water from the river, for no one else would undertake it, as the enemy shot at the head of every man who approached the river. This woman, however, they never molested; and they told us afterward, that they spared her on account of her sex'.

The state of the army, says Anburey, was 'truly calamitous':

'Worn down by a series of incessant toils and stubborn actions; abandoned in our utmost distress by the Indians; weakened by the desertion, and disappointed as to the efficacy of the Canadians and Provincials by their timidity; the regular troops reduced, by the late heavy losses of many of our best men and distinguished officers, to only 3500 effective men, of which number there were not quite 2000 British:—in this state of weakness, no possibility of retreat, our provisions nearly exhausted, and invested by an army of four times our number that almost encircled us, who would not attack us from a knowledge of our situation, and whose works could not be assaulted in any part. In this perilous situation the men lay continually upon their arms, the enemy incessantly cannonading us, and their rifle and cannon shot reaching every part of our camp.'

The troops, says Anburey, still retained their spirits, hoping either that the long expected relief would arrive from New

York, 'which the army implicitly believed', or that the enemy would attack, which would give them the opportunity of dying gallantly or extricating themselves with honour. In this state of distress, another council of war was called.

Following his surrender Burgoyne carefully recorded 'the minutes and proceedings" of this council of war, to which he had summoned all his officers above the rank of captain;

'The Lieutenant-General having explained the situation of affairs, as in the preceding council, with the additional intelligence, that the enemy was entrenched at the fords of Fort Edward, and likewise occupied the strong position on the Pine-plains between Fort George and Fort Edward, expressed his readiness to undertake at their head any enterprise of difficulty or hazard that should appear to them within the compass of their strength or spirit. He added, that he had reason to believe a capitulation had been in the contemplation of some, perhaps of all, who knew the real situation of things; that upon a circumstance of such consequence to national and personal honour, he thought it a duty to his country, and to himself, to extend his council beyond the usual limits; that the assembly present might justly be esteemed a full representation of the army; and that he should think himself unjustifiable in taking any step in so serious a matter, without such a concurrence of sentiments as should make a treaty the act of the army, as well as that of the general.

'The first question therefore he desired them to decide was, Whether an army of 3500 fighting men, and well provided with artillery, were justifiable, upon the principles of national dignity and military honour, in capitulating in any possible situation?'

Von Riedesel states that all the officers agreed that a capitulation would not be disgraceful but, if General Burgoyne saw an opportunity of attacking the enemy, they were ready to offer their lives. If nothing could be gained from such a sacrifice, it would be much better policy to save the King's troops by a thoroughly honourable capitulation.

Upon it being unanimously resolved that 'the present situation justified a capitulation upon honourable terms', the deputy adjutant-general, Major Robert Kingston, was given a message to take to Gates. Under a flag of truce Kingston crossed the Fishkill Creek where he was met by Wilkinson who conducted him, blindfolded, to Gates, who read Burgoyne's letter;

'After having fought you twice, Lieutenant-General Burgoyne has waited some days, in his present position, determined to try a third conflict against any force you could bring to attack him.

'He is apprised of the superiority of your numbers, and the disposition of your troops to impede his supplies, and render his retreat a scene of carnage on both sides. In this situation he is impelled by humanity, and thinks himself justifiable by established principles and precedents of state, and of war, to spare the lives of brave men upon honourable terms. Should Major-General Gates be inclined to trust upon that idea, General Burgoyne would propose a cessation of arms during the time necessary to communicate the preliminary terms by which, in any extremity, he and his army mean to abide.'

To Wilkinson's astonishment, Gates took from his pocket the reply he had already written, in expectation of such an overture. He stated his terms bluntly:

'General Burgoyne's army being exceedingly reduced by repeated defeats, by desertion, sickness, &c. their provisions exhausted, their military horses, tents, and baggage, taken or destroyed, their retreat cut off, and their camp invested, they can only be allowed to surrender prisoners of war'.

Gates, his subsequent behaviour shows, was bluffing; fearing that Clinton might be advancing to attack his rear, he was prepared to offer far more favourable terms. An armistice was agreed until sunset, and Kingston returned to Burgoyne. Another full council of officers unanimously rejected Gates's demand for unconditional surrender. At sunset Kingston returned to Gates, carrying Burgoyne's answer: 'Lieutenant-General Burgoyne's army, however reduced, will never admit that their retreat is cut off while they have arms in their hands.' Burgoyne insisted on surrender with full honours of war. The armistice was extended until 10 a.m. next day, October 15th, to give Gates time to reconsider his terms.

Gates sent his answer early in the morning. He accepted the terms offered by Burgoyne, stipulating that the 'capitulation' should be made at 3 p.m., and that the troops should lay down their arms at 5 p.m. Gates's insistence on the meticulous observance of these times made Burgoyne suspicious. Believing that Gates had received news of Clinton's advance and wished to hurry the surrender, Burgoyne played for time by objecting to the stipulation that his troops 'will be ordered to ground arms' before marching out of their encampment. They must be allowed to march out with full honours of war, before grounding arms, he insisted, and be permitted to return to England on the condition that they did not serve again in North America during the present conflict. Sooner than march disarmed from their camp, his troops, he told Gates, 'will rush on the enemy determined to take no quarter'. To this demand Gates, who had received no news of Clinton, agreed at once, and Lieutenant-Colonel Sutherland and Captain Craig, of the 47th Regiment, crossed the Fishkill to meet Wilkinson, who was accompanied by Brigadier-General Whipple, to draw up the terms of the capitulation, a task that occupied them all that day.

While the plenipotentiaries conferred, Madame von Riedesel endeavoured to divert her mind by busying herself with the wounded, for whom she made tea and coffee. She shared her food with a Canadian officer who was so weak from hunger that he could scarcely stand. But not all of those who came to the cellar deserved her compassion, for some were poltroons who, she observed, were later able to take their places in the ranks. In this horrible situation, Madame von Riedesel and her children remained for six days and, during the cessation of hostilities, her husband was able to lie down on a bed for the first time in a long while.

'About one o'clock in the night, someone came and asked to speak to him. It was with the greatest reluctance that I found myself obliged to awaken him. I observed that the message did not please him, as he immediately sent the man back to headquarters, and laid himself down again considerably out of humour.'

The reason for von Riedesel's ill-humour will become apparent later. Meanwhile, Sergeant Lamb has an incident to describe:

'During the time of the cessation of arms, while the articles of capitulation were preparing, the soldiers of the two armies often saluted, and discoursed with each other from the opposite banks of the river (which at Saratoga was about thirty yards wide, and not very deep), a soldier of the 9th regiment, named Maguire, came down to the bank of the river, with a number of his companions, who engaged in conversation with a party of Americans on the opposite shore. In a short time something was observed very forcibly to strike the mind of Maguire. He suddenly darted like lightning from his companions, and resolutely plunged into the stream. At the very same moment, one of the American soldiers, seized with a similar impulse, resolutely dashed into the water, from the opposite shore. The wondering soldiers on both sides, beheld them eagerly swim towards the middle of the river, where they met; they hung on each others necks and wept; and the loud cries of "My brother!

my dear brother! ! !" which accompanied the transaction, soon cleared up the mystery, to the astonished spectators. They were both brothers, the first had migrated from this country, and the other had entered the army; one was in the British and the other in the American service, totally ignorant until that hour that they were engaged in hostile combat against each other's life.'

By nightfall the representatives had agreed the terms of the capitulation, and Sutherland and Craig returned to Burgoyne, who accepted the treaty with the single exception of the word 'Capitulation', which he said must be changed to the more honourable term 'Convention'. In consequence, at 11 p.m. Craig wrote a letter to Wilkinson, stating Burgoyne's acceptance of the treaty, with that provision, to which Gates immediately agreed. Believing that all was settled, and greatly relieved, for he had heard during the day that Clinton had passed the Highlands, Gates retired to bed.

Next morning Burgoyne refused to be bound by the treaty; during the night he too had learned of Clinton's progress from a Tory, who stated that the British troops had reached Esopus and might already be at Albany. Burgoyne recalled his officers, to whom he put these questions:

1. Whether a treaty which had been definitely settled by fully empowered commissaries—even after the promise of the general to ratify all that the commissaries had agreed upon— could be broken with honour?
2. Whether the intelligence just received was sufficiently reliable to authorize us to break so advantageous an agreement in our present situation?
3. Whether the army had, indeed, a sufficient reliant spirit to defend their present position to the last man?

The Council voted fourteen to eight that Burgoyne could not honourably withdraw from the treaty he had promised to sign, and that, even if the report of Clinton's progress was true, the distance was too great to throw away the advantageous terms. Two-thirds of the officers declared that their troops would not behave well if they were forced to fight on.

Burgoyne refused to accept the council's recommendation. He was not convinced, he said, that there was no hope of relief by Clinton. To gain more time, Burgoyne sent a message to Gates, accusing the Americans of having broken the armistice by despatching troops to Albany, by which move they had reduced the numerical superiority of their army, which had induced him to ask for terms. He 'required' that two of his officers should be allowed to inspect Gates's army. The troops that had been observed leaving the American lines were a contingent of New York militia who, on the expiration of their service, had packed up and marched away without permission.

Burgoyne's delaying tactics infuriated Gates, who feared to precipitate a renewal of hostility, for that morning he had heard of the burning of Esopus. He sent Wilkinson to Burgoyne, with orders to break off negotiations if the treaty was not immediately ratified. There had been no violation of the armistice, Wilkinson told Burgoyne. Still Burgoyne refused to sign the treaty, and Wilkinson started back towards the American lines. He had not gone more than a hundred yards before he was caught up by Kingston who brought Burgoyne's promise to give his answer within two hours. While Wilkinson waited, Burgoyne again conferred with his officers.

Those eight officers, who before had been in favour of breaking the treaty, states von Riedesel, were now of just the contrary opinion. Burgoyne drew von Riedesel and Phillips aside, begging their friendly counsel. Phillips had no advice to offer, and von Riedesel considered that to break the treaty on flimsy intelligence would be hazardous. Brigadier-General Hamilton who joined the group agreed with von Riedesel. Burgoyne still wished to break the Convention, and Sutherland was sent to inform Wilkinson that the truce must end. Wilkinson describes his final meeting with Sutherland which clinched the matter:

'The two hours had elapsed by a quarter, and an aide-de-camp from the General had been with me to know how matters progressed. Soon after I perceived Lieutenant-Colonel Sutherland opposite to me and beckoned him to cross the creek; on approaching me he observed: "Well, our business will be knocked on the head after all." I enquired why. He said, "The officers have got the devil in their heads and could not agree." I replied gaily: "I am sorry for it, as you will not only lose your fusee (which he had owned thirty-five years and had desired me to except from the surrendered arms and save for him as she was a favourite piece) but your whole baggage." He expressed much sorrow, but said he could not help it. At this moment I recollected the letter Captain Craig had written me the night before and taking it from my pocket I read it to the Colonel who declared he had not been privy to it; and added with evident anxiety: "Will you give me that letter?" I answered in the negative and observed: "I should hold it as a testimony of the good faith of a British Commander." He hastily replied: "Spare me that letter, Sir, and I pledge you my honour I will return it in fifteen minutes." I penetrated the motive and willingly handed it to him; he sprang off with it, and directing his course to the British camp, ran as far as I could see him. In the meantime I received a peremptory message from the General to break off the treaty if the Convention was not immediately ratified. I informed him by the messenger that I was doing the best I could for him and would see him in half an hour. Colonel Sutherland was punctual to his promise and returned with Captain Craig, who delivered me the Convention signed by General Burgoyne.'

Realizing that Craig's letter had irrevocably committed him, Burgoyne had signed the Convention. This, states Madame von Riedesel, 'was fortunate for us, as the Americans said to us afterwards that had the capitulation been broken we all would have been massacred; which they could have done the more easily, as we were not over four or five thousand men strong, and had given them time to bring together more than twenty thousand'.

The Convention, now ratified, provided very advantageous terms, for it allowed the British troops to march from their camp with full honours of war and to ground their arms by the river. A free passage to England was granted, on condition of not serving again in North America. The British and German troops would march, under their own officers, to Boston, and the Canadians would be allowed to return home. No defeated general could have hoped for more than that.

XVIII *Cambridge (Mass.)*
— London

The surrender, on the morning of October 17th, was conducted according to eighteenth-century good manners. Burgoyne began the day by calling together his officers, to whom he explained, in Digby's words, 'his manner of acting since he had the honour of commanding the army', but he was too full to speak. Nevertheless, he 'dwelled much on his orders to make the wished-for junction', and as to how his proceedings had turned out, they, he said, must be as good judges as he.

The troops paraded at ten o'clock, and Digby says, 'We marched out, according to treaty, with drums beating and the honours of war, but the drums seemed to have lost their inspiring sound, and though we beat the "Grenadiers' March", which not long before was so animating, yet then it seemed by its last effort, as if almost ashamed to be heard on such an occasion.' He was almost in tears, and if he had been alone, 'I could have burst to give myself vent.'

Burgoyne had already left the camp under the escort of James Wilkinson who conducted him to Gates. They rode to the bank of the river, which Burgoyne surveyed with attention, asking Wilkinson whether it was fordable;

'Certainly, sir, but do you observe the people on the opposite shore?'

'Yes', replied Burgoyne, 'I have seen them too long.'

Accompanied by his adjutant-general, Major Kingston, his aides, Lord Petersham and Lieutenant Wilford, and Major-

Generals Phillips and von Riedesel and their staffs, Burgoyne crossed the Fishkill Creek and, under Wilkinson's guidance, rode across the meadow to the American headquarters:

'General Gates, advised of Burgoyne's approach, met him at the head of his camp, Burgoyne in a rich royal uniform, and Gates in a plain blue frock. When they had approached nearly within sword's length, they reigned up and halted. I then named the gentleman, and General Burgoyne, raising his hat most gracefully, said, "The fortunes of war, General Gates, have made me your prisoner," to which the conqueror returning a courtly salute, promptly replied, "I shall always be ready to bear testimony that it has not been through any fault of your Excellency." Major-General Phillips then advanced, and he and Gates saluted, and shook hands with the familiarity of old acquaintances. (They had known each other when Gates served in the British army.) The Baron Riedesel and the other officers were introduced in their turn.'

Digby, who was present, found the meeting between Burgoyne and Gates well worth watching, for Gates paid almost as much respect as if he was the conqueror; his noble air, tho' prisoner, seemed to command attention and respect from every person'.

Madame von Riedesel, having settled her affairs, also came to the American headquarters:

'Now the good woman, who had brought us water at the risk of her life, received the reward of her services. Everyone threw a whole handful of money into her apron, and she received altogether over twenty guineas. At such a moment, the heart seems to be specially susceptible to feelings of gratitude.

'At last, my husband sent to me a groom with a message that I should come to him with our children. I, therefore, again seated myself in my dear calash; and, in the passage through

the American camp, I observed, with great satisfaction, that
no one cast at us scornful glances. On the contrary, they all
greeted me, even showing compassion on their countenances
at seeing a mother with her little children in such a situation.
I confess that I feared to come into the enemy's camp, as the
thing was so utterly new to me. When I approached the tents,
a noble-looking man came toward me, took the children out
of the wagon, embraced and kissed them, and then with tears
in his eyes helped me also to alight. "You tremble," said he to
me; 'fear nothing." "No," replied I, "for you are so kind, and
have been so tender toward my children, that it has inspired
me with courage." He then led me to the tent of General Gates,
with whom I found Generals Burgoyne and Phillips, who were
upon an extremely friendly footing with him. Burgoyne said
to me, "You may now dismiss all your apprehensions, for your
sufferings are at an end." I answered him, that I should certainly be acting very wrongly to have any more anxiety, when
our chief had none, and especially when I saw him on such a
friendly footing with General Gates. All the generals remained
to dine with General Gates. The man, who had received me so
kindly, came up and said to me, "It may be embarrassing to
you to dine with all these gentlemen; come now with your
children into my tent, where I will give you, it is true, a frugal
meal, but one that will be accompanied by the best of wishes."
"You are certainly," answered I, "a husband and a father,
since you shew me so much kindness. I then learned that he
was the American General Schuyler.'

Philip Schuyler, who had come from Albany despite threats
from the New Englanders that he would be shot if he showed
himself in the camp, gave Madame von Riedesel and her
children a meal of smoked tongue, beefsteaks, potatoes, butter,
and bread, which 'contented' her for 'never have I eaten a
better meal'. She rejoiced most that her husband was out of
danger. Burgoyne dined alone with Gages in his 'hovel', as

Wilkinson calls it, a rude hut, one corner of which was occupied by the General's mattress; the food was abundant and was washed down with hard cider and rum.

Watched only by one of Gates's aides, the British and German troops paraded in the meadow north of the Fishkill Creek, where they laid down their arms. The American army had been kept discreetly out of sight. The disarmed soldiers forded the creek and marched past the headquarters tent where Gates and Burgoyne stood with their staffs. Beyond them Gates's troops were drawn up, standing in silence at his order. As they marched past the American ranks, a band struck up the music of 'Yankee Doodle', the rebel marching song. First came the British soldiers, and then the Germans, many of whom carried or led the pets they had acquired during the campaign: a bear, a deer, several young foxes, and a racoon. Behind straggled the camp followers, the wagon-drivers, the sutlers, and a number of slatternly women, 215 belonging to the British troops and eighty-two to the Germans—rather more than had been listed officially at the start of the campaign. As the soldiers marched away, Burgoyne and Gates turned to face each other; Burgoyne drew his sword, bowed and offered it to Gates, who, equally courteously, bowed and returned it. The 'Convention Army' as it was called, set out on its 200-mile march over the Green Mountains and through the Connecticut valley to Cambridge, Massachusetts, where it arrived on November 6th. Burgoyne was conducted to Albany by an escort of dragoons, which had been provided by Gates due to the threats, by local famers, to tar and feather the captured general, and Gates also provided guards for the handful of Indians and their squaws whom the farmers threatened to massacre. Before the convention was signed, Burgoyne had allowed the remaining Tories to leave the camp and make their way to Canada.

Though deprived of their prey, their neighbours who had embraced the royal cause, the Americans did not gloat at the discomfiture of their enemy. There were no unseemly incidents, and the diarists had little to record. Ralph Cross remarked, 'The Grand Army of Gen Burgoin cappillelated & agreed to be all Prisoners of Warr, a Grand Sight as ever was beheld by Eye of Man in Amerrica.'' Henry Dearborn was equally terse: 'This Day the Great Mister Burgouyn with his whole army, surrendered themselves as Prisoners of War with all their Publick stores,' which he called the 'Greatest Conquest ever known'.

That night Gates wrote to his wife and son:

'The voice of fame, ere this reaches you, will tell how greatly fortunate we have been in this department. Burgoyne and his whole army have laid down their arms and surrendered themselves to me and my Yankees. Thanks to the Giver of all victory for this triumphant success. If Old England is not by this lesson taught humility, then she is an obstinate old slut, bent upon her own ruin. Tell my dear Bob not to be too elated at this great fortune of his father. He and I have seen days adverse as well as prosperous. Let us through this life endeavour to bear both with an equal mind.'

General Washington, when he heard the news on October 18th, said that his happiness had been completed. He called the surrender a 'most important event' which exceeded 'our most sanguine expectations'.

On November 4th, Congress officially thanked Gates, Lincoln and Arnold 'for their brave and succesful efforts in support of the independence of their country'. Arnold learned of the official recognition of the part he had played in the battle while in hospital at Albany, where he abused his doctors as 'a set of ignorant pretenders'.

The Americans had won a prodigious victory, far greater than they realized. The threat to divide the colonies had been defeated. The American Northern Army had taken prisoner seven generals, 300 other officers, 3379 British and 2202 German soldiers, and had captured all the cannon and military stores that remained. During the campaign, the British and Germans had lost 1429 men, killed or wounded. On the day prior to the surrender, the American army numbered, according to the returns made by Gates, 18,624 officers and men, and another 300 stood at Bennington. On November 8th Powell evacuated Ticonderoga and retreated to Canada.

The Americans had gained far more than a local success. The news of Burgoyne's surrender reached Paris on December 5th, and next day King Louis XVI declared his recognition of the United States. On February 6, 1778 he signed the formal Treaty of Alliance, which turned the family quarrel into a world-wide conflict, in which France bankrupted herself in a vain attempt to avenge the defeats of the previous war. By putting his hand to the treaty, Louis had signed his own death-warrant, for the ideas of liberty carried back across the Atlantic by the French soldiers and sailors stimulated the revolution which broke out in 1792.

On his arrival at Albany, Burgoyne was received into his house by Philip Schuyler, who waved aside Burgoyne's regrets for having burnt his fine mansion at Saratoga. Schuyler ordered it to be rebuilt; and, with the assistance of Gates's army, the timber was cut and the house was completed within fifteen days.

Madame von Riedesel and her children were also invited by Schuyler and his wife to share their home:

'I sent and asked my husband what I should do. He sent me word to accept the invitation; and as it was two days journey from where we were, and already five o'clcok in the afternoon, he advised me to set out in advance, and to stay overnight at a place distant about three hours' ride. General Schuyler was so obliging as to send with me a French officer, who was a very agreeable man, and commanded those troops who composed the reconnoitring party of which I have before made mention. As soon as he had escorted me to the house where we were to remain, he went back. I found in this house a French physician, and a mortally wounded Brunswick officer, who was under his care, and who died a few days afterwards. The wounded man extolled highly the good nursing of the doctor, who may have been a very skilful surgeon, but was a young coxcomb. He rejoiced greatly when he heard that I could speak his language, and began to entertain me with all kinds of sweet speeches, and impertinencies; among other things, that he could not believe it possible that I was a general's wife, because a woman of such rank would certainly not follow her husband into the camp. I ought, therefore, to stay with him, for it was better to be with the conquerors than the conquered. I was beside myself with his insolence, but dared not let him see the contempt with which he inspired me, because I had no protector. When night came on he offered to share his room with me; but I answered that I should remain in the apartment of the wounded officers, whereupon he distressed me still more with all kinds of foolish flatteries, until, suddenly, the door opened and my husband and his adjutant entered. "Here, sir, is my husband," said I to him, with a glance meant to annihilate him. Upon this he withdrew looking very sheepish. Yet, afterwards, he was so polite as to give up his room to us. The day after this, we arrived at Albany, where we had so often longed to be. But we came not, as we supposed as should, as victors! We were, nevertheless, received in the most friendly manner by the good General Schuyler, and by his wife and daughters, who showed us the utmost marked courtesy, as, also, General Burgoyne, although he had—without any necessity it was said—caused their magnificently built houses to be burned. But they treated us as people who knew how to forget their own losses in the misfortunes of others. Even General Burgoyne was deeply moved at their magnanimity, and said to General Schuyler, "Is it to *me*, who have done you so much injury, that you show so much kindness!" "That is the fate of war," replied the brave man. "Let us say no more about it." We remained three days with them, and they acted as if they were very reluctant to let us go. Our cook had remained in the city with the camp equipage of my husband, but the second night after our arrival, the whole of it was stolen from us, notwithstanding an American guard of ten or twenty men had been deputed for its protection. Nothing remained to us except the beds of myself and children, and a few trifles that I had kept by me for my own use—and this too, in a land where one could get nothing for money, and at a time when we were in want of many things; consequently, my husband was obliged to board his adjutant, quartermaster, etc., and find them in everything. The English officers—our friends, as I am justified in calling them, for during the whole of my sojourn in America they always acted as such—each one gave us something. One gave a pair of spoons, another some plates, all of which we were obliged to use for a long time, as it was not until three years afterwards, in New York, that we found an opportunity, although at great cost, to replace a few of the things we had lost.'

Having written certain letters to Germain and his friends in England, Burgoyne left Albany and travelled to Boston, *en route* to Cambridge, as did Madame von Riedesel:

'Fortunately, I had kept by me my little carriage, which carried my baggage. As it was already very late in the season, and the weather raw, I had my calash covered with coarse linen, which in turn was varnished over with oil; and in this manner we set out on our journey to Boston, which was very tedious, besides being attended with considerable hardship.

'I know not whether it was my carriage that attracted the curiosity of the people to it—for it certainly had the appearance of a wagon in which they carry around rare animals—but often I was obliged to halt, because the people insisted upon seeing the wife of the German general with her children. For fear that they would tear off the linen coverings from the wagon in their eagerness to see me, I very often alighted, and by this means got away more quickly. However, I must say that the people were very friendly, and were particularly delighted at my being able to speak English, which was the language of their country.

'In the midst of all my trials, however, God so supported me, that I lost neither my frolicsomeness, nor my spirits; but my poor husband, who was gnawed by grief on account of all that had happened, and on account also of his captivity, became by these constant stoppages peevish in the highest degree, and could scarcely endure them. His health had suffered very greatly, especially by the many damp nights that he had spent in the open air; and he was, therefore, often obliged to take medicine. One day, when he was very sick from the effects of an emetic, he could not sleep on account of the noise that our American guard made, who never left us, but were continually drinking and carousing before our very door; and when he sent them a message begging them to keep quiet, they redoubled their noise. I resolved to go out myself; and I said to them that my husband was sick, and begged that they would be less noisy. They at once desisted from their merriment and all became still. A proof that this nation, also, have respect for our sex.

'Some of their generals who accompanied us were shoemakers; and upon our halting-days they made boots for our officers, and, also, mended nicely the shoes of our soldiers. They set a great value upon our money coinage; which with them was scarce. One of our officers had worn his boots entirely into shreds. He saw that an American general had on a good pair, and said to him jestingly, "I will gladly give you a guinea for them." Immediately the general alighted from his horse, took the guinea, gave up his boots, and put on the badly worn ones of the officer, and again mounted his horse.'

Hannah Winthrop, a resident of Cambridge, watched the captives come into the town:

'Last Thursday, which was a very stormy day, a large number of British troops came softly through the town via Watertown to Prospect Hill. On Friday we heard the Hessians were to make a procession in the same route. We thought we should have nothing to do with them, but view them as they passed. To be sure, the sight was truly astonishing. I never had the least idea that the Creation produced such a sordid set of creatures in human figure—poor, dirty, emaciated men, great numbers of women, who seemed to be the beasts of burden, having a bushel-basket on their back, by which they were bent double; the contents seemed to be pots and kettles, various sorts of furniture, children peeping through grid-irons and other utensils, some very young infants who were born on the road, the women bare-feet, clothed in dirty rags; such effluvia filled the air while they were passing, had not they been smoking all the time, I should have been apprehensive of being contaminated by them.

'After a noble-looking advance guard, General Johnny Burgoyne headed this terrible group on horseback. The other generals, also clothed in blue coats, Hessians, Anspachers, Brunswickers, etc., etc., etc., followed on. The Hessian General gave us a polite bow as they passed. Not so the British. Their baggage wagons were drawn by poor, half-starved horses. But to bring up the rear, another fine, noble-looking guard of American brawny, victorious yeomanry, who assisted in bringing these sons of slavery to terms. Some of our wagons drawn by fat oxen, driven by joyous-looking Yankees closed the cavalcade.

'The generals and other officers went to Bradish, where they quarter at present. The privates trudged through thick and thin to the hills, where we thought they were to be confined, but what was our surprise when in the morning we beheld an inundation of those disgraceful objects filling our streets. How

277

mortifying is it? They in a manner demanding our houses and colleges (it had been intended to use the buildings of Harvard College to house the prisoners, but the idea was abandoned), for their genteel accommodation. Did the brave General Gates ever mean this? Did our legislature ever intend the military should prevail above the civil? Is there not a degree of unkindness in loading poor Cambridge, almost ruined before this great army seemed to be let loose upon us, and what will be the consequence time will discover.

'Some polite ones say, we ought not to look on them as prisoners. They are persons of distinguished rank. Perhaps, too, we must not view them in the light of enemies. I fear this distinction will be soon lost. Surprising that our General or any of our Colonels should insist on the first university in America being disbanded for their more genteel accommodation, and we poor, oppressed people seek an asylum in the woods against a piercing winter.

'General Burgoyne dined a Saturday in Boston with General Heath. He rode through the town, properly attended down Court Street and through the Main Street, and on his return walked on foot to Charlestown Ferry, followed by a great number of spectators as ever attended a pope and generously observed to an officer with him the decent and modest behaviour of the inhabitants as he passed, saying if he had been conducting prisoners through the city of London, not all the guards of Majesty could have prevented insults. He likewise acknowledges Lincoln and Arnold to be great generals.

'It is said we shall have not less than seven thousand persons to feed in Cambridge and its environs, more than its inhabitants. Two hundred and fifty cord of wood will not serve them a week. Think then how we must be distressed. Wood is risen to £5.10. per cord, and but little to be purchased. I never thought I could lie down to sleep surrounded by these enemies. But we strangely became inured to those things which appear difficult when distant.'

At Cambridge, the British troops were quartered on Prospect Hill, and the Germans on Winter Hill, both armies in rough barracks. The officers, who had been given parole by the terms of the Convention (other than three belonging to each regiment who stayed in barracks) were provided with or found for themselves quarters in and around the town. Seven or eight, Burgoyne complained to Gates, were crowded together in rooms ten feet square, and he and Phillips were forced to share a bed in a small, dirty tavern, while their staff slept on the floor. General Glover told Washington that the residents were averse to accommodating the officers, because they could not forget the burning of Charlestown by the British earlier in the war.

Madame von Riedesel was little better accommodated;

'We were billeted at the house of a countryman, where we had only one room under the roof. My women servants slept on the floor, and our men servants in the entry. Some straw, which I placed under our beds, served us for a long time, as I had with me nothing more than my own field bed. Our host allowed us to eat in his room, where the whole family together eat and slept. The man was kind, but the woman, in order to revenge herself for the trouble we brought upon her, cut up the prank, every time we sat down to table, of taking that time to comb out her children's heads, which were full of vermin— which very often entirely took away our appetites. And if we begged her to do this outside, or select another time for this operation, she would answer us, "It is my room, and I like to comb my children's hair at this time!" We were obliged, therefore, to be silent lest she should thrust us out of the house.'

The wretched conditions in which the prisoners were housed, the lack of provisions, the local scarcity of fuel, their inactivity and disappointment at not being immediately sent home, led to trouble, brawls with guards, and "many irregularities", as

Burgoyne admitted, when the soldiers flocked into the town where they were allowed to go between 8 a.m. and 3 p.m. In his letter to General Heath, the commanding officer in Massachusetts, dated January 10th, Burgoyne acknowledged complaints of the 'most enormous abuses', including the misconduct of a number of officers at Bradish's tavern on the night of December 25th, prisoners being removed from guards, sentries abused and insulted, passes counterfeited or filled up in the 'most affrontive manner', and several highway robberies. He agreed there had been levities, indiscretions, faults of omission and neglect, and of liquor, which he had spared no effort to correct by punishment. The fault was not on one side only, for the American Colonel Henley stabbed a British soldier, when provoked, his defenders claimed, by 'haughtiness'. At his court martial Burgoyne alleged that wanton barbarities had been committed and a general massacre of his troops threatened.

Annoyed by the condition of his soldiers, for the cost of whose accommodation and provisions he had been forced to advance £20,000 of his own money, about a quarter of a million dollars (or £100,000) by present day reckoning, which placed him for some time in 'a very distressed condition', Burgoyne inadvertently committed an indiscretion which was seized upon by members of Congress, anxious to repudiate the Convention to which Gates had tamely agreed. In his justification, which Wilkinson carried to Congress, Gates had claimed that 'Lt. General Burgoyne at the Time he Capitulated, was strongly intrenched on a Formidable Post, with 12 Days' Provisions. That the Reduction of Fort Montgomery and the Enemies consequent Progress up the North River endangered our Arsenal at Albany; a Reflection which left him no Time to Contest the Capitulation with Lieut. General Burgoyne, but induced the Necessity of immediately closing with him.'

Invalid as were his reasons, Gates was fully empowered to make the treaty which, by stipulating that Burgoyne's troops would be returned to England, on the condition that they did not serve again in America, had sacrificed the benefits of the hard-earned and sorely needed victory; for the return home of these troops would release an equivalent number to serve in America, and they themselves could be employed in campaigns in Europe, against France, the United States' new ally.

The temptation to repudiate the treaty was very great. As a pretext for doing so, Congress seized upon the remark made by Burgoyne in his letter to Gates, written on November 14th, in which, in respect to the deplorable condition of his troops, he stated, 'The public faith is broke.' This expression of irritation was taken by Congress to mean that, as the Americans had broken faith, there was no need for the British to keep faith with the rebels. Henry Laurens, the President of Congress, claimed that Burgoyne's remark had been prompted by more than exasperation. The British intended, he believed, once their troops had been embarked, to sail the transports, not across the Atlantic, but to New York where the captive soldiers would join Howe's army. Laurens based his belief in British duplicity on the inadequate tonnage of transports available, and the scarcity of provisions for a voyage to Europe.

'Had Laurens', says Jane Clarke (*American Historical Review* XXXVII, Vol. 4, July 1932), 'had definite proof against the British, it might have saved the Americans much devious reasoning and kept from this page of our history a faint brown stain.'

The 'proof', claims Jane Clarke, came to light in 1932, in a letter written by Howe to Burgoyne on November 16th. It was marked 'Secret', and it directed Burgoyne, after the troops had been embarked upon the transports, to give his 'secret directions' to the officer commanding the convoy, who had been instructed to follow his orders, to carry the British troops to New York, where they would be exchanged for an equal number of rebel prisoners, the return of whom 'has been pointedly refused under the most frivolour Pretences'. The foreign troops were to proceed to England.

At first glance, Howe's intention does not seem to have constituted proof of British duplicity other than by the secretiveness involved in the whole transaction. Howe proposed to exchange the British troops for an equal number of Americans, as provided for by Article Three of the Convention, in order 'to repair an injury in which Mr Washington so obstinately persists'. In the previous April, an exchange of prisoners had been arranged. Those sent by Howe 'were in such a debilitated condition that many of them had died before reaching their homes', complained Washington, who refused to send the healthy British prisoners in return. To rectify the balance, Howe proposed to keep the 2202 British 'Convention' soldiers in New York and add them to his own army.

Concluding his letter, Howe enjoined Burgoyne 'to use every possible Precaution to keep the Enemy Ignorant of my Intentions, as on the least Suspicion the Troops will be infallibly stopt'.

In ignorance of Howe's intentions, Congress justified its repudiation of the Convention on various minor alleged infringements; that Burgoyne had refused to provide descriptive lists of his troops, for the discovery of any who returned to America; and that, contrary to the treaty, the British had failed to surrender certain 'public stores', to wit a number of cartouche boxes. While these ammunition boxes had certainly been lost or had been stolen before or after the Convention had been signed, both the British and the Germans had concealed their regimental colours, which von Riedesel admitted, and his wife disclosed by her statement that, on the transfer of the army to Virginia, she concealed them in a mattress. The British regimental colours had been secreted in Burgoyne's own baggage and were taken to England by Lieutenant-Colonel Hill of the 9th Regiment in 1781, and he presented them to the King.

On January 3, 1778, Congress resolved to detain the

Convention Army until the Convention was explicitly ratified by the British Government, which the Americans well knew it would never do, for it would thereby have accorded official recognition to the United States.

Whatever were the rights and wrongs of these minor contentions and arguments, the 'stain' on American reputation was faint indeed. The stain on the record of the British was darker. They had refused to treat as prisoners of war captured American seamen, and forced them to serve in the Royal Navy against their own countrymen. And Burgoyne, we recall, wished to repudiate the treaty, to which he had given his verbal consent.

From these protracted negotiations, however, it seems that Gates emerged in a dubious light, for it is disclosed by Karl van Doren (*Secret History of the American Revolution*, 1941) that he was offered, and accepted the promise of a bribe, from General Phillips, to assist in the release of the prisoners for a ransom to be paid by the British Government. To Burgoyne himself, Congress granted parole, so that he could return to England to defend himself from 'aspirations after an intricate and unsuccessful campaign', and he was allowed to sail to Britain on March 3rd, but only after he had paid in coin all the bills owing by his army.

Foreseeing that the angry public would demand a scapegoat for the Saratoga disaster, the Colonial Secretary and the generals began at once to erect their defences, in order to shift the blame for the failure of the expedition, the first news of which reached London on December 3rd, in a message from Carleton, who had heard from deserters of Burgoyne's surrender. Burgoyne's dispatch, which was carried by Lord Petersham, arrived on December 15th. Knowing his man, Burgoyne took the precaution of sending copies of his private letter to his nephew, the Earl of Derby, to prevent Germain from censoring the section which criticized his orders for the campaign.

The opinion of the defeated army was expressed by Anburey and Digby. Anburey wrote, 'It was universally understood throughout the army, that the object of our expedition was to effect a junction with that under General Howe. You can easily conceive the astonishment it occasioned, when we were informed that General Howe's army had gone to Philadelphia.' It was evident, he declared, that 'some great error has been committed, either unintentional or designed', but 'where to fix it is impossible to say'. He thought that 'Time, that great discloser of secrets, will no doubt reveal this'.

The disappointed Digby, said, 'Thus was Burgoyne's army sacrificed to either the absurd opinions of a blundering ministerial power, the stupid inaction of a general [Howe], who, from his lethargic disposition, neglected every step he might have taken to assist their operations, or lastly, perhaps, his own misconduct in penetrating so far as to be unable to return, and tho I must own my partiality to him is great, yet if he or the army under his command are guilty, let them suffer the utmost extent, and by an unlimited punishment in part blot out and erase, if possible, the crime charged to their account.'

Time has partially cleared the veil that obscured the truth from eighteenth-century Englishmen. They were left in doubt whether or not some great error had been committed, for by his adroit political management, Germain succeeded in keeping from the public his correspondence with the generals, and in muzzling Burgoyne, who was denied both a military and a parliamentary inquiry. Although he spoke in the House of Commons on his return to England, his motion calling for 'Papers' was defeated by the Government's majority. He printed his version of the afiair, and Howe also had his say in the House of Commons. Burgoyne criticized Germain for having given too precise orders, and Howe criticized him for not giving positive orders. Of the two generals, Burgoyne came off best with his popularity with the army and public unimpaired. Some stigma attached to Howe who, it was believed, had left Burgoyne in the lurch; he had either disobeyed orders or, more probably, Germain had muddled the plans for the campaign, or had, at least, in Carleton's opinion, pretended 'to direct operations of war three thousand miles distant'. All three men survived the blow to their reputation. Germain distorted the truth by telling partial truths; Burgoyne insisted that his orders had been inflexible 'to force his way to Albany', and that he had been given no latitude—a claim Germain easily refuted by drawing attention to Burgoyne's instructions which stated that, until he received orders from Howe, he should act as exigencies required, and by pointing out that 'every man of common understanding must see that orders given at such a distance presuppose a discretionary power'. Howe's candour shocked rather than appeased those who believed that he had shown lack of military judgment.

The unpalatable facts remained unexplained, for they were obscured by the three men concerned, all of whom were in some degree at fault. Burgoyne had failed to reach Albany, and Howe had failed to come to his rescue. The vaunted Grand Strategy had collapsed. In truth, it was not put into execution for, as Washington believed, it was beyond British capability; though he may not have understood that the British suffered from a dangerous overconfidence in their ability to overcome any obstacle, and that Burgoyne was dangerously ambitious.

'The whole plan was suggested by General Burgoyne,' Germain told the House of Commons in November 1777. He spoke partial truth, for the plan to invade New York State from the north had been proposed in 1776, but too late in the season for Carleton to execute it. Meanwhile Howe had first advocated and then abandoned the plan for a junction of armies on the Hudson. His letter, stating his intention to go to Philadelphia, reached Germain on February 23rd. Five days later, Burgoyne's over-confident claim that he could reach Albany unaided and maintain himself there while he waited for Howe dispelled the doubts that Howe had created. Both plans could be accomplished; Howe would capture Philadelphia, return to New York, and move up the Hudson, where he would find Burgoyne entrenched at Albany. Germain did not, as is supposed, approve two opposing plans, for he believed that the two plans, Howe's and Burgoyne's, were complementary. He misunderstood the timing of the operations, and ignored their difficulties, and he failed to make abundantly clear to Howe the part he was expected to play. Although he had promised to inform Howe of his part in the campaign 'by the first packet', Germain forgot to write and he allowed his secretary merely to send Howe a copy of Burgoyne's instructions, without further explanation.

Burgoyne did not desire the junction of armies, for that would diminish his glory. When he said it would be 'the sole purpose of the Canadian army to effect a junction with General Howe', he intended to achieve a junction 'after co-operating so far as to get possession of Albany, and open up communication with New York, to remain upon the Hudson, and thereby enable General Howe to act with his whole force to the southward'. Burgoyne believed he could reach Albany and remain there on his own, and thereby enable Howe, when he had finished in Pennsylvania, to advance up river from New York. He did not expect to find Howe awaiting him at Albany. He did not insist, in his *Thoughts*, on aid from the south, and he clamoured for it only after things had begun to go wrong. He made no suggestion that the success of his expedition depended upon Howe's co-operation, and he intended that Howe should complete the span after he had built the arch. He had no doubt of his ability to control the upper Hudson, and he hoped, once he was established, to invade New England. He overestimated his power to crush resistance, and he underestimated American vigour and will to fight.

After his capture of Ticonderoga, Burgoyne was in high spirits. He lamented only his lack of discretion to make a real effort against New England, which indicates that he had no doubt of his ability to accomplish the much lighter task of reaching Albany. After the reverse at Bennington, Burgoyne's doubts grew; only then did he request aid from the south, implying that it was part of the bargain. After he surrendered, he claimed that his orders had been peremptory—to force his way to Albany—and he created the entirely new and unjustified defence that his army had been intended to be sacrificed 'to employ forces that otherwise would have joined General Washington'.

Germain also felt guilt for the disaster, for why, otherwise, did he go to such lengths to suppress the correspondence which might prove, by its ambiguity, difficult to explain? By stating that he would write to Howe, he gave Burgoyne the impression that Howe would be ordered to postpone his attack on Philadelphia, if that move conflicted with his advance up the Hudson later on in the year, or that Howe would leave in New York a force strong enough to assist if Burgoyne needed help. This was thought to be an unlikely contingency, for Howe, it was believed, would draw Washington's army away from the Hudson and leave the coast clear for Burgoyne. No one thought that the Americans could muster another army strong enough to bar Burgoyne's passage.

That was the unpredictable factor, the possibility of which the British ignored. Burgoyne's disaster came about, not because anyone in particular blundered, but rather because thousands of American farmers and shop keepers rallied to repel the invasion which they believed threatened their independence.

Howe's conduct was technically impeccable. He did not wilfully disobey a command to co-operate with Burgoyne, whom he believed was strong enough to reach Albany unaided, for his plan had been approved by the King. He had, he claimed, postponed his advance on Philadelphia until Burgoyne's optimistic letter of July 11th satisfied him that the

Northern Army stood in no danger, and he had left Clinton at New York in case Burgoyne needed help. He believed that Burgoyne was strong enough to crush local resistance and he would be imperilled only if Washington moved north, in which case, as he told Germain, he would be hard on his heels. Howe was genuinely surprised when he learned from Burgoyne's letter to Clinton, which was carried by Captain Campbell, that 'he would not have given up his communication with Ticonderoga had he not expected a co-operating army at Albany'. Howe wrote at once to Burgoyne to remind him that he had warned Carleton that 'no direct assistance could be given by the southern army'.

Howe's defence was only partly true. He showed a certain lack of enthusiasm and indifference for the fate of the northern expedition, a charge he sought to counter in his defence in the House of Commons, where it was claimed that he should have advanced up the Hudson:

'What would have been the consequences of such an expedition? Before the object of it would have been attained, the forts in the Highlands must have been carried, which would probably have cost a considerable number of men, defended, as they would have been, by Washington's whole force. But those forts being carried, how would the enemy have acted? In one of these two ways; He would either have put himself between me and New York, or between me and the northern army. In either case I am of opinion that the success of our efforts upon Hudson's River, could not, from the many difficulties in penetrating so strong a country, have been accomplished in time to have taken possession of Philadelphia that campaign. But admitting I had at length reached Albany, what would I have gained, after having expended a campaign upon that object alone, that I had not a right to expect by drawing off General Washington, with the principal American army, from my operations on that side?

'Had I adopted the plan of going up Hudson's River, it would have been alleged that I had wasted the campaign . . . merely to ensure the progress of the northern army, which could have taken care of itself, provided I had made a diversion in its favour by drawing off to the southward the main army under General Washington. Would not my enemies have gone farther, and insinuated that, alarmed at the rapid success which the honourable General had a right to expect when Ticonderoga fell, I had enviously grasped a share of the merit . . .? Would not ministers have told you, as they truly might, that I had acted without any orders or instructions from them; that General Burgoyne was instructed to force his own way to Albany, and that they had put under his command troops sufficient for the march? Would they not have referred you to the original and settled plan of that expedition . . . to prove that no assistance from me was suggested? And would they not have readily impressed this House with the conclusion, that, if any doubt could have risen in their minds of the success of such a well digested plan, they should, from the beginning, have made me a party to it, and have given me explicit instructions to act accordingly?'

Germain had no effective answer to disprove Howe's statement. Burgoyne did not challenge it, and the two generals remained friends.

Possibly, Howe had the right idea. By drawing Washington from the Hudson, he would clear effective opposition from Burgoyne's path; that would be better than advancing himself up the Hudson, for then Washington would have placed himself between the two British armies, and might have been difficult and costly to dislodge.

No one at the time seems to have considered that the British objective, the severing of the colonies, might have been achieved quite simply by a single advance from New York on Albany, the American supply base for Ticonderoga, the loss of which would have forced the evacuation of the fort, which in turn would have forced Washington to fight a decisive battle which, if he had lost, would have decided the war.

No one criticized Clinton. With the small force at his command, he had done his best to make a diversion in Burgoyne's favour, and by his intervention he had helped him to secure very favourable terms. He had advocated the necessity for a co-operation with Burgoyne, and had urged it on Germain in March and on Howe. As late as July 6th, he had written, 'My God, these people cannot mean what they give out; they must intend to go up the Hudson and deceive us.' Even so, Clinton feared for the safety of the Northern Army only if Washington moved against it, and like Howe, Clinton did not expect Burgoyne to fail. That Clinton considered it necessary to protest against Howe's intention to go to Philadelphia denies the suggestion that Howe ignored the wishes of the government, which had approved his plan.

Clinton became Commander-in-Chief when, in 1778, Howe resigned and returned to England, to defend himself against his critics. The Government, as part of its scheme to silence Burgoyne, ordered him to return to captivity in America, which he refused to do, pleading ill health. The Americans did not ask him to relinquish his parole and, on February 2, 1782 he was exchanged for 1047 enlisted men and minor officers, which Edmund Burke called 'taking a quantity of silver in exchange for gold'.

His officers, British and German, were paroled and allowed to return to their homes. The soldiers were not so fortunate. In November 1778 they were marched, during the depths of winter, from Massachusetts to Virginia and few, if any, reached Europe. They disappeared, becoming merged into the population.

Sergeant Lamb escaped *en route* and rejoined the British army with which he campaigned until he was captured again at Yorktown. He was exchanged and returned home to Dublin.

after an absence of twelve years, to find that his aged mother and two sisters had given him up for dead.

The Riedesels accompanied the troops to Virginia; when Madame von Riedesel prepared to leave Cambridge she discovered that her very fine cook had absconded, leaving the bills unpaid. He joined General Gates who found him too expensive to employ. The Riedesels returned to Canada, where their fourth daughter was born and appropriately named America; and in 1783 they went home to Brunswick, where the general died in 1800.

Of the diarists, Anburey disappeared into private life, and Digby retired from the army on half-pay in 1786. Hadden rose to the rank of major-general. Major Acland died in 1778, from a heart attack it is said, following a duel which resulted from his over-enthusiastic defence of American independence. His widow did not, as has been reported, marry the Reverend Edward Brudenell. Alexander Lindsay, the sixth Earl of Balcarres, rose to the rank of full general and died in 1825. William Phillips, following his exchange, died in Virginia in 1789. Sir William Howe became a full general and died in 1814. Burgoyne resigned all his official appointments, wrote a comedy, begat four children by a popular singer whom he did not marry, died in 1792, and was buried in Westminster Abbey. His son rose to the rank of field-marshal in the British army. Germain was the only beneficiary of the war, retiring from office at its conclusion with a peerage (his previous title had been an honorary one). He died in 1788, 'happy and content' with his life.

Of the American heroes, both John Stark and Daniel Morgan retired into private life at the end of the war, Stark dying in 1822 and Morgan in 1802. Henry Dearborn witnessed Cornwallis's surrender at Yorktown, and served two terms in Congress and as Secretary of War to President Jefferson. He became a major-general and served in the 1812 war against Britain, dying in 1829. Philip Schuyler was elected a United

States senator and died in 1804. James Wilkinson fell out with Gates and retired from the army, which he rejoind in 1791, becoming Commander-in-Chief and serving with distinction in the war of 1812. He died in 1825.

Gates's success at Saratoga emboldened him to intrigue against Washington, whose post he coveted. The cabal he formed failed to oust the Commander-in-Chief, and Gates was forced to content himself with command of the army in the south, where, in 1780, his blunders lost the battle of Camden. He galloped 200 miles, ostensibly to bring help, but more probably in panic. He retired to this estate and lived until 1806, performing a generous act before he died, when he freed his slaves and provided for their future.

Bendict Arnold, disgruntled by the failure of Congress to recognize his merits, and encouraged perhaps by his Tory wife, changed sides in 1780. His attempt to betray the fort at West Point, where he commanded, was foiled, and he joined the British army, in which he was given the rank of major-general. He campaigned in the south against his former friends, and at the end of the war retired to England. He died in 1801 and was buried, at his request, in the uniform of the nation whose independence he had helped to achieve.

The Revolutionary War ended in 1782 following the British surrender in the previous year at Yorktown, which has been called the 'Child of Saratoga'. Of the consequences of Burgoyne's surrender, Sir Edward Creasy (*The Fifteen Decisive Battles of the World*, 1858) still retains the last word:

'Nor can any military event be said to have exercised more important influence on the future fortunes of mankind, than the complete defeat of Burgoyne's expedition in 1777; a defeat which rescued the revolted colonists from certain subjection; and which, by inducing the courts of France and Spain to attack England in their behalf, ensured the independence of the United States, and the formation of that Transatlantic power which, not only America, but both Europe and Asia, now see and feel.'

Whether Burgoyne's defeat rescued the colonists from 'certain subjection' is doubtful, for history proves that indigenous people in revolt usually achieve their freedom. Nor is it certain that Burgoyne failed owing to lack of transport or because he was unsupported. His attempt to reach Albany was defeated by the vigour and enthusiasm of his enemy. After his surrender, he told Germain that the American Continentals had proved themselves a disciplined force. 'I do not hazard the term', he said, 'but apply it to the great fundamental points of military resolution, sobriety, regularity and courage.' Though inferior in method and movement, the militia were 'not less serviceable in woods'. The 'panic' of the American troops, he said, was 'confined and of short duration', their enthusiasm was extensive and permanent. He confessed that he had been wrong about the American soldiers after Ticonderoga.

At Bennington, Freeman's Farm, and Bemis Heights, a makeshift army, composed of amateur soldiers, defeated 5000 disciplined veterans, commanded by experienced soldiers. The Americans won these battles because they fought for a principle, for freedom to run their own lives. Burgoyne's campaign was an honourable attempt to achieve the impossible.

Bibliography

PRIMARY SOURCES

BURGOYNE CAMPAIGN
Papers Public Record Office (London), C.O.5. Class 42, Vols. 36, 37.

CLINTON SIR H.
Clinton Papers, Ann Arbor, William L. Clements Library, Michigan.
Historical Detail of Seven Years Campaign in North America from 1775 to 1782, William L. Clements Library, Ann Arbor, Michigan.

GATES, HORATIO
Gates Papers, Library of Congress, Washington, D.C.
Gates Papers, New York Historical Society (N.Y. Public Library).

GERMAIN, LORD G.
Germain Papers, William L. Clements Library, Ann Arbor, Michigan.

SCHUYLER, P.
Schuyler Papers, New York Public Library; New York State Library.

STOPFORD-SACKVILLE
Manuscripts II, Great Britain Historical Manuscripts Commission, 1904–10.

VARICK R.
Varick Papers, New York Public Library.

BOOKS PERIODICALS AND HISTORICAL COLLECTIONS

ADAMS, R., *The Papers of Lord George Germain*, William L. Clements Library, Ann Arbor, Michigan, Bulletin 18, 1928.

ANBUREY, T., *Travels Through Interior Parts of America*, 2 vols., Boston and New York, 1923.

ANDERSON, T. S., *Command of the Howe Brothers during the American Revolution*, London, 1936.

ARNOLD, J., *Life of Benedict Arnold*, Chicago, 1880.

——, *The Annual Register, 1777*, London, 1778.

BALDWIN, COL. J., *Revolutionary Journal*, Bangor, Maine, 1906.

BATCHELDER, G. E., *Burgoyne and his Officers in Cambridge*, [Mass.], London, 1926.

BENEDICT, G. G., 'Vermonters at Bennington', *New York State Historical Association*, Vol. V, 1906.

BRANDOW, J. H., 'Morgan's Part in Burgoyne's Campaign', *New York State Historical Association*, Vol. XII, 1912.

——, 'Guide to Saratoga Battlefield and Revolution Sites at Schuylerville', *New York State Historical Association*, Vol. XII, 1912.

BURGOYNE, LT.-GEN., SIR JOHN, *Letter to Constituents*, London, 1779.

——, *Orderly Book*, Albany, 1860.

——, *State of Expedition*, London, 1780.

——, 'Proclamation', *Massachusetts Historical Society Proceedings XII*.

BREYMANN, H. VON, 'Relation of Bennington, *Gentleman's Magazine* Vol. XLVIII, 1778, and *Vermont Historical Society Collections*, I.

BROWN, G. S., *The American Secretary: Colonial Policy of Lord George Germain*, Ann Arbor, 1963.

CLARK, J., 'Responsibility for Failure of Burgoyne's Campaign', *American Historical Review*, Vol. 35, 1930.

——, 'The Convention Troops and Perfidy of Sir W. Howe', *American Historical Review*, Vol. 37, 1932.

CLINTON, GEORGE, *Public Papers*, (ed. H. Hastings), Albany, 1904.

CLINTON, LT-GEN. SIR HENRY, *The American Rebellion* (Narrative of his Campaigns 1775–1782 with appendix of original documents; ed. W. B. Willcox). New Haven, Yale University Press, 1954.

COLMAN, D., 'Eye Witness to Burgoyne's Surrender', *Magazine of American History*, Vol. 29, 1883.

CROSS, R., 'Journal', *Historical Magazine* (N.Y.), Vol. 7, 1870.

CURTIS, E. E., *Organisation of the British Army in the American Revolution*, London, 1926.

DABNEY, W. H., *After Saratoga: Story of the Convention Army*, Albuquerque, 1954.

DEARBORN, MAJ-GEN. H., 'Journal', *Massachusetts Historical Society*, Vol. III, 2nd Series, 1886–7.

DECKER, M., *Benedict Arnold*, Tarrytown, N.Y., 1932.

DEERING, J. A., 'How an Irishman Turned the Tide at Saratoga', *American Irish Historical Association*, Vol. 10, 1911.

DE FONBLANQUE, E. B., *Political and Military Episodes in the latter Half of the Eighteenth Century (derived from the life and correspondence of the Rt. Hon. John Burgoyne, General, Statesman, Dramatist)*, London, 1876.

DIGBY, LT. W., *The British Invasion of North America* (ed. J. P. Baxter), Albany, 1887.

DILLIN, J. G. W., *The Kentucky Rifle*, National Rifle Association, Washington, D.C., 1924.

DUPUY, R. E., *Battle of Hubbardton*, Vermont Board of Historic Sites, 1960.

DWIGHT, T., *Travels in New England and New York* (re. John Horst Schuyler), 4 vols, New Haven, 1821–2.

EELKING, CAPT. MAX VON, *Memoirs, Including Letters and Journals of Maj.-Gen. Riedesel* (trans. William Stone), 2 Vols., Albany, 1868.

——, *The German Allied Troops in War of Independence 1776–1783*, Albany, 1893.

EGGERTON, H. E., 'Howe and Burgoyne Letters', *English Historical Review*, Vol. 25, Oct. 1910.

FITZPATRICK, J. C., *The Writings of George Washington, 1745–1799*, 39 vols, Washington, 1931–44.

FLETCHER, E., *Narrative* [Wounded and taken prisoner at Hubbardton], New Ipswich, New Hampshire, 1827.

FLEXNER, J. T., *The Benedict Arnold Case*, New York, 1962.

FOLSOM, W. R., 'Battle of Hubbardton', *Vermont Quarterly*, 1952.

FOSTER, H. B., AND STREATER, T. W., 'Stark's Independent Command at Bennington', *New York State Historical Association*, Vol. V, 1905.

——, 'Calendar of Bennington Documents', *New York Historical Association*, Vol. V, 1905.

GLICH, 'Account of the Battle of Bennington', [not employed in this book due to highly suspect nature], *Vermont Historical Society Collections*, I, 1870.

GRAHAM, J., *Life of Daniel Morgan*, New York, 1859.

GREENE, G. W., 'The Convention of Saratoga', *Magazine of American History*, Vol. III, 1879.

GUILD, R. A., *Chaplain Smith and the Baptists*, American Baptist Pub. Soc., 1885.

GUTTERIDGE, G. H., 'Lord George Germain in office', *American Historical Review*, October, 1927.

HADDEN, J. M., *Journal and Orderly Book* (ed. H. Rogers), Albany, 1884.

HANSON, J. H., and, FREY, S. L., *Minute Book of the Committee of Public Safety of Tyron County*, New York, 1905.

HEADLEY, J. T. *Washington and His Generals.* 1: Arnold–Gates, 2: Schuyler, New York, 1847.

HOLDEN, J. A., Jane McCrea, *New York State Historical Association*, Vol. XII, 1912.

HOWE, SIR W., *Narrative of Sir William Howe*, Lonbon, 1780.

HUGHES, J. M., 'Aide to Gates', *Massachusetts Historical Sociey*, Vol. III, 1858.

JOHNSON, SIR J., *Orderly Book During the Oriskany Crmpaign*, Albany, 1882.

JONES, W., 'A Scrap of Unwritten History' [Lieut. Jones and Jane McCrea], *Catholic World*, Vol. XXXVI, 1882.

LAMB, R., *Journal of Occurrences During the late American War*, Dublin, 1809.

LAW, R. R., 'General John Stark', *New York State Historical Association*, Vol. V, 1905.

LINGLEY, C. B., 'Treatment of Burgoyne's Troops', *Political Science Quarterly*, Vol. 22, Sept. 1907.

LOSSING, B. J., *Pictorial Field Book of the Revolution*, New York, 1851–2.

——, *Life of Philip Schuyler*, 2 vols, New York, 1860–73.

LUZADER, J. F., *Documentary Research Report on the Saratoga Campaign*, National Park Service (Saratoga). 1960.

——, 'Arnold–Gates Controversy', *West Virginia Historical Association*, Vol. 27, No. 2, Jan. 1966.

LYTTLE, E. W., 'Nicholas Herkimer', *New York State Historical Association*, Vol. V, 1905.

MILLS, B. H., 'Troop Units at Saratoga', *New York Historical Association*, Vol. IX, Ap. 1928 (Prov. Vol. 26).

NEILSON, C., *The Original, Compiled and Corrected Account of the Burgoyne Campaign and the Memorable Battle of Bemis Heights*, Albany, 1844.

NICKERSON, H., *The Turning Point of the Revolution*, Boston and New York, 1928.

O'BRIEN, M. J., 'Morgan's Riflemen at Saratoga', *American Irish Historical Association*, Vol. 26, 1927.

PARKER-LYON, G., *Memoirs and Official Correspondence of General John Stark*, Concord, 1860.

PARKINSON, CYRIL H., *Edward Pellew, Viscount Exmouth*, London, 1934.

PARTICIPANTS, 'Saratoga Campaign', *Massachusetts Historical Society Proceedings*, Vol. III, 2nd Series.

PAUSCH, GEORGE, *Journal 1776–1777*, (trans. W. L. Stone), Albany, 1886.

PELL, J., 'Diary of Joshua Pell, Officer of British Army in America, 1776–1777', *Magazine of American History*, Vol. 2, 1878.

PEYSTER, J. W. DE, *Major-General Philip Schuyler and Burgoyne Camp 1777*, New York, 1877.

REID, W. M., *Story of Old Fort Johnson*, New York, 1906.

RIEDESEL, BARONESS FREDERIKA VON, *Letters and Journals* (trans. W. L. Stone), Albany, 1867.

RICHARDS, SAMUEL, *Diary*, Philadelphia, 1909.

ROBY, L., *Life and Military Adventures of Major General John Stark*, Concord, 1831.

SHERWIN, O., *Benedict Arnold, Patriot and Traitor*, New York, 1931.

SMITH, W. H., *The St Clair Papers*, 2 vols, Cincinnati, 1882.

SNELL, C. W., *Report on Strength of British Army Under Burgoyne*, National Park Service (Saratoga), 1951.

SPARKS, J., *Correspondence of the American Revolution*, 4 vols, Boston, 1853.

SQUIRE, E., 'Journal', *Magazine of American History* (N.Y.), Vol. II, 1878.

STANLEY, G. F. C., *For Want of a Horse: Journal of a Campaign. 1776–1777* (The Anonymous Diarist), Sackville, New Brunswick, 1961.

STILLMAN, W. O., 'The Memorable Battle Fought on 16th Day of August at Walloomsac', *New York State History Association*, Vol. V, 1905.

STONE, W., *The Camp of Lt. Gen. John Burgoyne and the Expedition of Col. Barry St. Leger*, Albany, 1877.

STONE, W., 'Correspondence of George Clinton,' *Magazine of American History*, Vol. III, 1879.

SYLVESTER, N. B., *History of Saratoga County* Philadelphia, 1878.

THACHER, J., *A Military Journal During the American Revolutionary War*, Boston, 1827.

TODD, C. B., *The Real Benedict Arnold*, New York, 1903.

TRUMBULL, COLONEL J., *Reminiscencies of His Own Times from 1756–1841*, New York, 1841, 1884.

TUCKERMAN, B., *Life of Philip Schuyler*, New York, 1903.

VALENTINE, A., *Lord George Germain*, London, 1962.

VAN DOREN C., *Secret History of the American Revolution*, New York, 1941.

WARREN, CAPTAIN B., 'Diary', *Journal of American History*, Vol. 3, 1909.

WASHINGTON, G., *Writings* (ed. W. C. Ford), New York, 1890.

WILKINSON, J., *Memoirs of My Own Times*, 3 Vols, Philadelphia, 1816.

WILLET, M., *Narrative of Military Actions*, New York, 1831.

Index

Abercrombie, Gen., 42, 57
Acland, Maj. John Dyke, 41, 78–81, 157, 158, 223, 227–9, 241, 252, 253, 291; Lady Harriet, 41, 139, 157, 158, 188, 244, 250–3, 291
Albany (New York) 19, 23–5, 27–33, 35, 44, 51, 52, 58, 59, 74, 87, 89–94, 100-2, 104, 105, 107, 112, 113, 116, 119, 133–5, 146, 148, 152–4 159, 161, 191, –200, 213, 216, 218, 219, 243, 257, 264, 265, 270–5, 280, 285–9, 293
Allen, Ethan, 15, 55; Ira, 115; Thomas, 124, 127, 129
Amherst, Gen., 42
Amsbury, William, 59
Anburey, Capt. (Lt) Thomas, 42, 47, 49, 50, 62, 66, 67, 80, 83, 96, 99, 141, 157, 159, 175–7, 186, 187, 194, 207, 222, 235, 242, 246, 250, 255, 259, 284, 291
Anne, Fort, 68–72, 96
Anstruther, Col., 139, 177
Arnold, Gen. Benedict, 15, 18, 50, 55, 58, 105, 112, 113, 120, 147–9, 152, 159, 160, 167–71, 175, 182, 183, 198–206, 226, 230, 232–5, 237–40, 272, 278, 292

Balcarres, Earl of, 40, 41, 78–83, 176, 197, 223, 229, 231, 237, 238, 291
Baldwin, Col. Jeduthan, 58, 169
Bancroft, Capt. Edward, 168, 233, 238
Barner, Maj., 123
Barnes, Capt., 128
Battenkill, 120, 154, 211, 243; river, 121, 123
Baum, (Lt-)Col. Frederick, 117–25, 127–9, 131, 136, 209
Bellows, Col., 82, 83
Bemis Heights, 159, 161, 164, 166, 167, 171, 191, 198, 212, 222, 223, 226, 233, 240, 241, 293; map of battle, 225
Bennington, 84, 114–119, 121, 122, 124, 132, 133, 135, 136, 139, 140, 145, 148, 149, 151–3, 161, 197, 273, 287, 293
Blomfield, Capt., 241
Bloomfield, Maj., 183
Boquet river, 47, 48

Boston (Mass.), 14, 15, 21, 23, 25, 118, 134, 149–51, 192, 267, 275,
Braddock, ——, 36, 149
Brant, Joseph, 106, 108; Molly, 108
Broeck, Col. Ten, 182, 226, 229
Brooks, Col. John, 226, 230, 233, 234, 238–41
Brown, Col. John, 197, 198, 214, 218
Brudenell, Rev. Edward, 41, 245, 251, 291
Brunswick, 46, 291; Duke of, 22, 44, 45, 117
Bunker Hill, 14, 21, 22, 115
Burgoyne, Lt-Gen. Sir John ('Gentleman Johnny'), 13, 15, 18, 20–3, 26–46, 48–51, 58, 59, 61–75, 86–106, 113, 114, 116–22, 133–6, 139, 140, 143–5, 147–60, 163, 164, 167, 171, 172, 174, 180, 181, 183–7, 189, 191–9, 202, 206, 207, 209–16, 218–24, 229, 232, 236, 237, 240–3, 245, 247–57, 260–2, 264–6, 268–75, 277–81, 283–93
Burich, Sergeant, 137
Burke, Edmund, 49, 290
Butler, Col. John, 106, 108; Lt-Col. Richard, 148, 173
Byng, Admiral, 22

Cambridge (Mass.), 85, 117, 120, 123, 129, 131, 268, 271, 275, 277–9, 291
Campbell, Capt. Alexander, 129, 196, 212, 216, 221, 288; Lt-Col., 217, 218
Canada, 13, 15, 23, 25, 27, 29, 30, 33–5, 37, 39, 42, 43, 46, 48, 49, 51, 52, 55, 58, 59, 61, 89, 92, 95, 98, 99, 101, 126, 136, 139, 143, 144, 148, 152–4, 156, 196-8, 207, 211, 271, 273, 291
Carleton. Sir Guy. 18, 20, 22, 30, 32–8, 41, 44, 49, 95, 101, 153, 207, 283, 285, 288
Castleton, 63, 74, 76, 77, 79, 81–3, 94, 117, 119
Chamby, 46, 47
Champlain, Lake, 15, 18–20, 54, 59, 63, 67, 73, 76, 87, 134. 139, 170, 203
Chatham. Lord, 26
Cilley, Col. Joseph, 176, 182, 226, 228
Clerke, Sir Francis, 122, 229, 241, 253

Index

Hamilton, Alexander, 89; Brig.-Gen., 164, 181, 223, 256, 265; James, 40
'Hampshire Grants' (Vermont), 56, 86, 94, 114, 115, 117, 147, 160
Hardin, Lt, 195, 207
Harnage, Maj., 177, 188, 236, 246; Mrs, 188, 189, 258
Harrington, Earl of (Viscount Petersham), 41, 156, 179, 283
Harvard College, 278
Harvey, Lord, 36, 102, 213
Herkimer, Nicholas, 58, 107–12, 145, 237
Herrick, Col., 125
Hervey, Lt, 177
Highlands, The, 212, 213, 215, 216, 218–20, 243, 264, 288
Hill, Col. John, 70, 71
Hope, Mount, 54, 62, 63
Hopkinson, Francis, 48
Hothan, Commodore, 215, 218
Howe, Admiral Lord, 15, 20; Gen. Sir William, 13–18, 20–32, 36–9, 51, 52, 58, 59, 90, 91, 100–5, 114, 133–5, 140, 145, 153, 209, 213, 214, 220, 281, 282, 284–91
Hubbard, Col., 125
Hubbardton, 63, 67, 73, 74, 76, 82, 84, 85, 96, 114, 117, 198, 226, 251
Hudson, river, 19, 20, 23, 25–9, 34, 36, 38, 51, 52, 58, 73, 78, 84, 90, 92, 94, 96, 97, 100, 101, 103–5, 112, 114, 119, 133, 134, 151, 153–6, 160, 209, 211-15, 220, 243, 248, 255, 256, 285-90; valley, 28
Hutchins, Col., 116

Independence, Declaration of, 17, 48
Independence, Mount, 54, 55, 60, 62, 63, 66, 73, 74, 76, 198
Inflexible (ship), 47, 48, 62, 69

Jefferson, Thomas, 41, 117, 291
Jessup, brothers, 42; Ebenezer, 35, 78, 125
Johnson, Capt., 64; Col. Guy, 108, 110, 197, 198, 230; Sir John, 48, 106, 108, 111; Sir William, 106, 108
Jones, Capt., 181; David, 42, 97–9

Kingston, Maj. Robert, 41, 144, 187, 261, 262, 268
Kingston (formerly Esopus), 217, 219, 221, 264, 265
Knox, William, 31, 32
Kosciuszko, Col. Thaddeus, 59, 151, 159, 162

Lamb, Col., 218; Sergeant Roger, 42, 70, 72, 98, 178, 251, 263, 290
Langdon, John, 115
Latimer, Col., 182
Learned, Brig., 112, 169, 182, 183, 204; Col. Ebenezer, 160, 226, 227, 229, 237, 238, 240, 253
Ligonier, Col. Viscount, 42
Lincoln, (Maj.-)Gen., 105, 115–17, 149–51, 197, 198, 204, 233, 243, 272, 278
Lincoln, Earl of, 101
Livingston, Col. Henry Brockholst, 82, 84, 182, 199, 200, 202–4, 226; Col. James, 160, 168, 182, 226
Logan, Maj., 217, 218
London (England), 13, 17, 22, 23, 26, 32, 90, 268, 278, 283; Tower of London, 49; Westminster Abbey, 219; Westminster School, 28
Loring, Mrs, 16
Louis XVI, 273
Louisburg, 40, 106, 126

McCrea, Jane, 42, 97–9, 150; John, 97
MacKay, Capt., 35, 254
McNeil, Mrs, 97–9
Manchester (Conn.), 83, 84, 116, 118, 119, 121
Marshall, —, 168, 182
Massachusetts, 29, 57, 71, 106, 280, 290; Governor, 59, 233
Mattoon, Ebenezer, 229, 233, 238
Miller, Fort, 119, 144
Minden, battle of, 22, 41, 42, 45
Mohawk, river, 29, 30, 51, 59, 108, 134, 151; valley, 52, 58, 105, 106, 107, 112
Money, Capt. John, 40, 241
Monin, Capt., 35
Montgomery, Capt., 71, 72; Gen., 15; Fort, 52, 195, 196, 215, 217, 218, 280

Index

Schuyler, Kitty, 156; Gen. Philip, 51, 52, 55, 56, 58–60, 84, 87–90, 92, 94, 96, 97, 105, 106, 112, 114–17, 119, 120, 145–8, 156, 168, 191, 199, 200, 202, 203, 233, 250, 254, 270, 273, 274, 291
Schuylerville, *see* Saratoga
Scott, Capt. Thomas, 196, 216
Sellick cabin, 76–8, 81, 84
Seven Years War, 14, 22, 41
Shelburne, Lord, 13, 32
Shrimpton, Capt., 85
Skene, Col. Philip, 35, 42, 69, 94, 117, 118, 124, 125, 129, 130, 257
Skenesborough, 42, 66–74, 78, 86, 90, 92–6, 99, 143, 198
Specht, Brig., 184, 223
Springster, Brom, 217
Squire, Ephraim, 193
Standish, Miles, 97
Stanwix, Fort (now Fort Schuyler), 87, 95, 105–8, 113, 116, 120, 133, 145, 243
Stark, Gen. John, 115–17, 121, 122, 124, 125, 127, 128, 131, 145, 147, 151, 160, 161, 297, 291; Molly, 125
'Stars and Stripes' (flag), 72
Stedman, Edmund, 168
Stillwater, 105, 114–16, 120, 151, 201, 205
Sucker Brook, 77, 78
Swords Farm, 153, 158

Taylor, Sergeant Daniel, 196, 221
Thacher, Dr James, 65, 68–71, 88, 89, 168, 221
Ticonderoga, Fort, 15, 18, 22, 29, 30, 33, 35, 37, 42, 44, 48–52, 55–62, 64–7, 73, 74, 78, 86–90, 92–6, 100, 115, 135, 139, 143, 145, 152, 154, 197, 198, 207, 214, 243, 254, 257, 273, 286, 288, 289, 293
Trenton, 18, 33, 114
Trumbull, Col. John, 54, 55, 88
Twiss, Lt, 40, 47, 64

Valcour Island, 18, 47, 170
Van Courtland, Col. Philip, 182, 226
Van Rensselaer, Col., 70
Van Swearingham, Capt., 175
Varick, Col. Richard, 168, 171, 199, 200, 202, 204
Vaughan, Gen., 217, 219, 220

Vermont, 54, 56, 58, 114, 115, 125, 149, 151
Virginia, 41, 149, 282, 290, 291
von Breymann, Lt-Col. Heinrich, 82, 86, 122–4, 128–31, 133, 154, 164, 184, 186, 197, 223, 239–41
von Riedesel, Frederika, 45, 136, 140, 144, 155, 188, 222, 236, 241, 243–6, 248, 250, 254–8, 262, 263, 267, 269, 270, 273, 275, 279, 291; Gen. Friedrich Adolf, 42, 45, 48, 63, 65, 66, 73–5, 78, 79, 82, 83, 86, 94, 116–20, 122, 136, 140, 148, 154, 158, 164, 166, 167, 172, 181, 183–6, 189, 208–11, 223, 224, 227, 229, 230, 232, 237, 239, 242, 245, 247, 248, 250, 254–7, 260, 263, 265, 282, 291

Wakefield, Capt. E., 168, 169
Walpole, Horace, 22, 49, 90, 147
Warner, Col. Seth, 76–83, 114–16, 121, 122, 124, 128, 130–2, 152
Warner, Col. Benjamin, 160, 193, 194, 206, 241
Washington, Gen. George, 14, 15, 18, 26, 28, 29, 33, 36, 38, 51, 52, 55, 58, 59, 87–91, 95, 101–6, 114, 117, 134, 145, 149, 201, 205, 206, 209, 214, 216, 272, 279, 282, 285, 287–90, 292
Wayne, Maj.-Gen. Anthony, 55–58
Webster, Daniel, 127; Ebenezer, 127
Whitcomb, Col. Asa, 57; Maj. Benjamin, 58
Wilkinson, Col. James, 60, 63–5, 82, 146, 147, 150–2, 159, 160, 162, 168, 169, 171, 172, 174, 176, 179, 182, 191–5, 199, 203, 206, 224, 227–9, 234, 237, 239–41, 246, 251, 253, 261, 262, 264, 265, 268, 271, 280, 292
Willett, Lt-Col. Marinus, 107, 110, 112
Williams, Maj. Griffith, 174, 181, 223, 227, 229, 241
Willoe, Capt., 137–9, 183, 184, 247
Wolfe, James, 16, 28, 40, 128
Wood, Dr, 149, 150
Wood Creek, 68–70, 93, 106, 107

Yale University, 42
Yost, Hon, 112, 113

Zion Hill (Mount Zion), 77, 79, 80